D1105895

The Archaeology of Place and Space in the West

The Archaeology of Space and Place in the West

edited by

EMILY DALE *and* CAROLYN L. WHITE

THE UNIVERSITY OF UTAH PRESS
Salt Lake City

The Defiance House Man colophon is a registered trademark of The University of Utah Press. It is based on a four-foot-tall Ancient Puebloan pictograph (late PIII) near Glen Canyon, Utah.

LIBRARY OF CONGRESS CATALOGING-IN-PUBLICATION DATA

Names: Dale, Emily, 1985- editor. | White, Carolyn L., 1969- editor.
Title: The archaeology of space and place in the West / edited by Emily Dale and Carolyn L. White.
Description: Salt Lake City : The University of Utah Press, [2021] | Includes bibliographical references and index.
Identifiers: LCCN 2020051848 (print) | LCCN 2020051849 (ebook) | ISBN 9781647690472 (cloth) | ISBN 9781647690489 (ebook)
Subjects: LCSH: Landscape archaeology—West (U.S.) | Landscapes—West (U.S.) | Place (Philosophy) | Space. | Archaeology and history—West (U.S.) | West (U.S.)—Antiquities.
Classification: LCC F591 .A73 2021 (print) | LCC F591 (ebook) | DDC 978/.01—dc23
LC record available at https://lccn.loc.gov/2020051848
LC ebook record available at https://lccn.loc.gov/2020051849

Errata and further information on this and other titles available online at UofUpress.com

Printed and bound in the United States of America.

Contents

List of Figures vii

List of Tables ix

1. The Push and Pull of the Place of the West 1
   EMILY DALE *and* CAROLYN L. WHITE
2. Western Mythology and the Historical Archaeology of the Upper Missouri River Basin 8
   LOTTE GOVAERTS
3. Inside the Fence and Out: Placemaking along the El Paso and Northeastern Railroad in New Mexico 17
   RACHEL FEIT
4. In Defense of the Fence 28
   MELONIE SHIER
5. Axes and Agency: Chinese Choices at Mineral County, Nevada, Woodcutting Camps, 1880–1920 37
   EMILY DALE
6. Persistence and Place among the Northern Paiute in Aurora, Nevada 46
   LAUREN WALKLING
7. Sisneros and Cisneros: Place-Based Community Development among Hispanic Homesteaders in Northeast New Mexico 55
   ERIN HEGBERG
8. Writing on the Trees: Observing the Marks Left by Hispano Sheepherders in New Mexico 67
   S. JOEY LAVALLEY
9. Gathering Places: Alsatian Migration and Placemaking on the Texas Frontier 79
   PATRICIA MARKERT
10. The Ordeal and Redemption of Betsy Brown, Christina Geisel, and Mary Harris: Historical Memory, Placemaking, and the Archaeology of Oregon's Rogue River War 91
    MARK TVESKOV *and* CHELSEA ROSE
11. "The Battlefields Are the Only Thing We Have": Archaeology, Race, and Thanatourism in the Trans-Mississippi South 101
    CARL G. DREXLER

12. Terminal Narratives and Indigenous Autonomy: Fragmented Historicity in the Santa Ana Mountains of Orange County, California 110
NATHAN ACEBO

13. From the Land: An Indigenous Perspective of Landscape and Place on the Northern Plains 119
AARON B. BRIEN *and* KELLY J. DIXON

14. Epilogue: Widening the Western Lens 129
MARK WARNER

Bibliography 133

Index 157

Figures

2.1. The locations of the five main-stem dams on the Upper Missouri. 9
2.2. Scenes from Khao Yai Cowboy Festival in Thailand. 12
2.3. A selection of Western-themed comic books for sale in Antwerp, Belgium. 14
3.1. The El Paso and Northeastern Railroad in Eastern New Mexico extended from El Paso to Tucumcari and Dawson. 18
3.2. Buildings depicted on a 1942 aerial photograph and detail from a 1948 topographical map. 22
3.3. Chase storm anchors. 23
3.4. A 1921 map of Escondida Siding. 24
3.5. A perforated sardine can likely used as a sieve. 26
4.1. Fence post typography. 32
4.2. The road leading into Headquarters in San Emigdio Canyon of the Wind Wolves Preserve. 35
5.1. Map of Aurora, Nevada; Bodie, California; and nine rural Chinese woodcutting camps north of the urban centers. 38
5.2. Dugout cabin at one of the Chinese woodcutting camps. 41
5.3. Artifacts of recreation and entertainment from various woodcutting camps. 43
5.4. Chinese brownware ceramics used for storing and shipping food found at various woodcutting camps. 44
6.1. Overview of sites. 49
6.2. Advertisement for Paiute War Dance at "Boone & Wrights' Corral." 51
7.1. Hispanic settlement patterns surrounding the project area. 57
7.2. Homesteads in the survey parcel and surrounding area. 58
7.3. LA 185318 Feature 1, Works Progress Administration schoolhouse. 61
7.4. Masonry styles. 63
7.5. LA 185276 Feature 1, west wall exterior with doorway blocked by masonry. 64
8.1. Typical aspen grove encountered in the Sangre de Cristo Mountains. 68
8.2. Dendroglyphs by Patrocinio Valencia. 74
8.3. Partial view of dendroglyphs. 74
8.4. Partial view of dendroglyphs. 75
8.5. Partial view of dendroglyphs made by Patrocinio Valencia. 76
8.6. Art motifs. 76
9.1. The location of Castroville and D'Hanis, Texas, in relation to San Antonio. 80
9.2. D'Hanis, Texas in July 2016. 81
9.3. D'Hanis, Texas in August 2017. 81
9.4. The Steinbach House, a seventeenth-century Alsatian townhouse reconstructed in Castroville, Texas. 83
9.5. An example of the stone cottages that are characteristic of early Castroville architecture. 88
10.1. A sample of the domestic artifacts recovered from the Geisel homestead excavations. 95

10.2. A plan view of the Harris Cabin excavations. 96
10.3. A sample of the ammunition recovered from the Miners' Fort excavations. 97
10.4. A plan view of the Miners' Fort. 98
11.1. Location of the major Civil War engagements discussed in the text. 104
12.1. Map of Los Angeles Basin and the Black Star Canyon Village location. 112
12.2. Sample of Late Prehistoric projectile points. 114
12.3. Reimagined publication of the Black Star Canyon Massacre. 115
12.4. *OC Weekly* title page. 117
13.1. Map showing areas mentioned in this chapter. 120
13.2. Much was learned about this *Bilisshíissaannuua Alaxape* (fasting bed) in the Pryor Mountains. 123
13.3. Image showing the Pryor Mountain landscape. 125
13.4. *Bilisshíissaannuua Alaxape* (fasting bed) in the Pryor Mountains. 126

Tables

3.1. Summary of Investigations at Four Sites along the El Paso and Northeastern Railroad. 22
4.1. Percent of Each Kind of Fence. 33
5.1. Location and Number of Chinese in the Woodcutting Industry, 1870–1910. 42
6.1. Historic Artifact Count, Total, and Types of Sites AN-CC-1 through AN-CC-6. 50
6.2. Lithic Artifact Count, Total, and Types from Sites AN-CC-1 through AN-CC-6. 50
6.3. Ecofact Count, Total, and Types from Sites AN-CC-1 through AN-CC-6. 50
7.1. Homestead Sites and Features. 60
8.1. Summary of Names, Dates, Places, and Presence of Art. 70
8.2. Martinez Family Details as Reported in the 1940 US Census. 73

1

The Push and Pull of the Place of the West

EMILY DALE *and* CAROLYN L. WHITE

When historical archaeologists study the American West, they confront its multipronged mystique, hoping to reveal the realities of its diversity. The push and pull between beguiling stereotype and mundane reality undergirds an understanding of what the American West was, what it is, and how we comprehend its past in the present. Using the concept of place as a lens through which to see the West, the authors in this volume simultaneously embrace and reject the West's allure and deep mythology as they parse its unifying elements as well as those that are distinctive about the site, town, city, or region.

We chose the concept of place—a term so broad as to mimic the vastness of the West itself—to organize this volume. We selected such a broad organizational prompt for the purpose of inclusivity as well as to allow the many ways that archaeologists define "the West" to surface within the volume. Many of the contributors focus on ideas of landscape and placemaking; historical archaeology offers manifold opportunities to develop new perspectives here. The contributions also attest to the problem of trying to define what "the West" is. Is it a geographically bounded place? Is it defined by its master narrative? Is it demarcated by its legacy of pain and ruination of people, plants, and animals? What is the role of myth and nostalgia in such definitions? The push and pull of the ideas that delineate the West physically and metaphorically are found in these pages.

What is the American West?

This volume seeks to answer a question that seems simple but is, of course, highly complex: "What is the American West?" In looking for answers, one of the first tasks is to circumscribe the West—and as we choose a boundary, some of the tensions between what puts something inside or outside the American West come into relief. The possible boundaries are multiple and simultaneously enacted, and all are problematic. Physically, we can look to geography and environment, relying on features like the Mississippi River, Pacific Ocean, or Rocky Mountains for the former and reduced precipitation and unique species of plants and animals for the latter. Cultural boundaries can be traced using language, immigration, labor, as well as ethnicity, religion, and other forms of identity. Historical confines delineated through statehood, culture contact, treaties, and colonial intrusions offer additional modalities for determining what is inside and what is outside our boundaries. All these factors create a sense of the West that is both united and disparate and still made up of smaller components such as the Pacific Northwest, Great Basin, Plains, and Southwest.

Temporal scales further complicate matters. On the one hand, the Prehistoric West can be seen as vastly different from the Historic West—they are separated by time, after all. Shifting perspective slightly, the prehistoric/historic boundary is a false one based on western ethnocentrism and fails to consider the geographic dimensions of the American West. Within temporal scales things get murkier still; commonly used time divisions create an idea of cultural consistency that is not the reality. For example, the Spanish Colonial Periods of California and Arizona were contemporaneous, but were vastly different culturally and even more distinct from the mining booms of the 1800s in those same states. Moreover, the ways in which the West was "settled" creates a false sense of time in the history of the West. The boundaries of the West shifted further and further west as exploration, colonialism, and immigration opened up more and more of the continent to historic settlers, and the area that was "seen" as the western frontier changed through time. How can we understand the slipperiness of the concept for those who lived in the place?

We are not the first people to tread the path of defining the West. The scholars in historical archaeology whose tracks we follow walked a trail broken by two waves of historians of the American West. The first, of course, was that defined by Frederick Jackson Turner, and his "frontier thesis," which characterized the American West as a place where nationalism, democracy, individualism, and American intellect was shaped (Turner 1999 [1893]). Turner's frontier was a moving line that shifted further and further westward along a fall line that lay on the margins of what he called "free land." The end of that open space marked the close of the frontier, creating a break between two Wests—the West before and after the frontier "closed" in 1890.

The "New Western History" upended Turner's thesis and marked a new line of scholarship about the West in the late twentieth century. Scholars like William Cronon (1983, 1991), Patricia Limerick (1987, 2000), Richard White (1991), and Donald Worster (1985) moved away from the West as a process and as a place where essentialist American traits were defined and towards an idea of the West as a geographical locale that can allow scholars to see social and cultural patterns as well as power dynamics and environmental impacts and reactions. Further, that scholarship blurred the boundaries between the two Wests defined by Turner, arguing for continuity and change. Historical archaeologists are indebted to the New Western History for, first, deepening and widening the path defined by historians, and then blazing new and innovative trails.

Several key works define common patterns of research, outline fundamental theoretical perspectives useful for understanding the region, and determine future directions for research. Three of these merit consideration here. Hardesty began to build the field of the historical archaeology of the West, and his foundational publications emphasized the importance of the American West in the development of historical archaeology as a unique field of study (1991a:29). Nearly two decades later, he viewed Nevada as a "microcosm of the western mining experience" (2010:xiii) and used his case studies as a means of understanding the landscape changes that resulted from the architectural, technological, and social implications of Nevada's mining past. In discussing technological, economic, social, and political processes, Hardesty's analysis encapsulated a broad spectrum of realms for the archaeologist or historian to explore. Many of those processes identified remain relevant today and appear in this volume. For example, the legacy of conquest (Hardesty 1991a:31–32) and frontier urbanism (Hardesty 1991a:32–33; Hardesty 2010:109–177) are discussed by Walkling (Chapter 6), Tveskov and Rose (Chapter 10), Acebo (Chapter 12), and Brien and Dixon (Chapter 13).

Dixon's (2014) comprehensive review of historical archaeology in the West defined the place as the land west of the ninety-eight meridian. Settling on a purely physical boundary, she moved to identify the work that happens within the West as operating through four themes: colonialism and postcolonialism; landscape transformation; migration and diaspora; and industrial capitalism. Most relevant to this volume is that of landscape transformation, addressed by Govaerts (Chapter 2), Feit (Chapter 3), and Shier (Chapter 4), though we hope that the contributions here demonstrate the interconnectedness of the other aspects identified by Dixon with the role of landscape.

Most recently, Warner and Purser's (2017) volume confronted the impacts of economics, racialization, and the role of the "mythic" West on our modern understandings of the region. Within that volume, the role of popular literature is highlighted as defining a critical role in understanding the relationship between myth and reality in modern times (Purser 2017). Authors like Wallace Stegner, John Muir, and Jack Kerouac have left a deep mark on the American psyche and its conception of the West.

The chapters in this book deftly navigate the complexities of dealing with an area that is simultaneously colonial, territorial, state, and federal; Indigenous, immigrant, and American; and mythic/past and real/present. The contributions by Dale (Chapter 5), Hegberg (Chapter 7), and LaValley (Chapter 8) highlight the importance of ethnicity and its connection to place and to the built environment, echoing the role of colonial relationships and cultural context in making the American West.

Drawing on the legacies of these previous works, this volume pivots on the centrality of landscape. All the contributors situate the role of landscape at the center of their contributions and, in doing so, offer insights into how the role of the landscape moves in multiple directions. Architecture, technology, and culture are both changed by and change the landscape simultaneously. Rooting the volume in the concept of place allows for wide-ranging perspectives and flexibility in application. By exploring place in the American West, the authors confront the ways people have adapted to the landscape, creating new ones in the process. Our volume emphasizes the unreliability of the boundaries of the American West, underscored by the inclusion of two pieces that press against the edges of what is typically considered to be "the West": Arkansas (Drexler, Chapter 11) and Texas (Markert, Chapter 9), though it is important to note that they are not considered to be outside the West in many historiographies.

Landscape Archaeology and Placemaking

Before addressing scholarship on landscape and placemaking, it is important to make the distinction between place and space. Place is cultural, space is geographical (we elucidate this point more in this section). Both are necessary to understand placemaking—people apply meanings to geographic features and landscapes, and, rather than emphasize the difference between these concepts, we underscore that the two are bound together. In encountering new spaces, people build places through names, structures, changing the land, and those new places then accumulate cultural meanings (Thomas 2008:302).

Many scholars use landscape and placemaking to understand the past in a way that informs our use of these terms and approaches. These scholars work in both the prehistoric and historic contexts in North America. As noted in Johnson's overview of landscape archaeology, archaeology provides myriad approaches to study and address the concept of landscapes, though it was "one of the most theoretically dormant areas" (M. Johnson 2007:1) of study in the discipline. He traces the history of approaches to landscape, most notably from its beginnings in the 1950s in England to the role of the New Archaeology and processualism to the impact of a phenomenological approach. Another thread of Johnson's analysis relates to the consideration of historical boundaries through an examination of landscapes of nationalism, areas defined by political ideologies and borders (M. Johnson 2007:162–192). This field of inquiry especially grew in the postwar and Cold War periods, when nostalgic impulses coupled with nationalistic pride spurred many countries to embrace the landscapes of the past. At nearly the same time, David and Thomas (2008) provided a wide range of landscape archaeology case studies to understand place and placemaking from a diverse global and methodological perspective in prehistory and history.

One of the early approaches to landscape in the historic period in North America was Yamin and Metheny's *Landscape Archaeology* (1996).

Contributors to the volume took a literal approach to understanding the landscape, focusing on gardens, farms, architecture, and other physical changes to the environment. Within this framework, the role of class, religion, politics, and other elements of culture and ideology were examined in relation to the physical features of the landscape. The volume broke important ground for bringing landscape studies to the historic period.

As landscape archaeology has become more ingrained in historical archaeology, scholars have increasingly interpreted landscape in relation to social angles, including labor, industrialization, immigration, indigeneity, multivocality, and myriad cultural factors. We are especially interested in how landscape archaeology has been used to address questions of labor, politics, and subjectivities—all realms intrinsic to the study of the American West.

Labor has received considerable attention through the lens of landscape and placemaking. Archaeologists examining labor sites often use landscape archaeology to understand the industrial and social impacts of labor on the ground. Cassell and Stachiw (2005:1) argued that landscape archaeology should be combined with labor studies:

> Landscapes begin and end as the result of human social activity. Their configurations are predicated upon the active social construction and manipulation and consumption of material elements and attributes by human actors. They are comprised of consciously and unconsciously placed things and altered environments and arranged spaces. They are archaeological sites writ large.

In conjunction with labor and subjectivities, scholars invoke landscape studies to examine industrialization, settlement patterns, and site organization and distribution in relation to gender, ethnicity, and race, evidence of resistance and dominance, and culture contact (e.g., Cassell, ed. 2005; Mayne and Murray, eds. 2001; Shackel 2004a; Spencer-Wood 2010; Van Bueren, ed. 2002). Understanding the ways the American West's industries centered around mining, railroads, ranching, and related businesses requires an examination of how those industries impacted the landscape, as well as how the landscape impacted people's abilities to succeed in those industries.

Another perspective on landscape is offered in Rockman and Steele's (2003) volume, which investigates how people begin to know and learn their landscapes upon immigrating to or colonizing new areas. Their volume mainly grapples with prehistoric peoples encountering empty landscapes, but their perspective resonates with similar issues encountered by historic settlers and immigrants arriving in unfamiliar places who needed to navigate new resources, topography, and relationships with Indigenous peoples or national governments, as demonstrated by Hardesty's contribution on nineteenth-century mining landscapes (2003) and Blanton's study of the colony of Jamestown (2003).

Archaeologists also emphasize the need for Indigenous and other diverse, emic perspectives on landscape. As noted, landscape studies largely grew out of Western, especially British, worldviews, which all too often neglect to account for other cultures' connections and perceptions of the environmental and geological landscapes (David and Thomas 2008:35–36). Feld and Basso's ethnographic volume, *Senses of Place* (1996), embraces the fact that people in the same landscape have different ideas of place. By introducing various Native American and Melanesian groups' connections to places, the volume "emphasize[s] places and populations whose geographical closeness and presumed familiarity made them, ironically, more, not less, "other" and remote" (Feld and Basso 1996:7), rather than monolithic in their views of place. In the pages of this volume, the authors demonstrate the potential for multivocality and multiple meanings when place is centered in archaeological study.

The contributions in Rubertone's (2008) edited volume, *Archaeologies of Placemaking*, focus on Native North America and emphasize the role of placemaking in both the past, as people encountered new landscapes and continued to make meaning out of them, and in the present, as those places are reinterpreted for new audiences—in effect a second phase of placemaking. Rubertone defined places as "specific portions of landscapes entwined with personal experiences and historical narratives," highlighting the connection between the natural and geographic with the cultural and human (2008:13). Many of the chapters make such overt connections between the natural world and the cultural world.

Similarly, in another edited volume, Casey argues that Western approaches to landscape have neglected to consider place for far too long (2008:46–48). He emphasizes the difference between space and place noting the role of a place as "a basic unit of lived experience" (44) rather than a mere location. Landscape archaeology is a necessary approach to study the way placemaking occurred in the American West.

Our volume reflects ideas eloquently framed by Yentsch: "Landscapes were multivocal and carried meaning, within American society, at each different social level. The historical landscape served different constituencies simultaneously" (1996:xxv). The movement of new peoples into the West from abroad or elsewhere in the country created new places and new views of the American West. Of course, the frontier was already occupied by Indigenous peoples with their own connections to the land, and the contact between these groups is still an intrinsic element to the cultural milieu of the American West. The vastness of the American West and its cultural and physical diversity offers many circumstances to see the distinctive role(s) and influences of the landscape on people and people on the landscape.

Volume Overview

This volume is divided into three sections, and each explores three aspects of placemaking in the American West: The West as Space; The West as Community; and The West Today. Within each section, we group contributions that investigate distinctive elements of the construction of space, the use of landscapes, and the creation of western identities in the past and present. All the contributions share common ground in that they examine the ways that people come to places, build places, and create places—they are all stories of placemaking.

The West as Space

The first section, The West as Space, deals with issues of geographic conceptions of space. Questions considered include: How do historical archaeologists define the West in time and space? How did people make space on the landscape through physical and cultural features? And how did geographical, topological, and man-made features create meaningful boundaries?

Govaerts discusses the role of the Turner Thesis in shaping the frontier in South Dakota as well as the ongoing redefinition of the South Dakota frontier into the 1940s with the construction of dams along the Upper Missouri River (Chapter 2). Feit explores the construction of the El Paso and Northeastern Railroad in New Mexico, and their role in moving the resources necessary for the economic and social creation of New Mexico as a state (Chapter 3). Taking an archaeological feature as the center of her chapter, Shier emphasizes the importance of fences as archaeological features (Chapter 4). She investigates the roles of fences in defining ranching and farming lands as ways of both keeping the wanted in and the unwanted out.

The West as Community

While the American West was defined through geography, space was defined by the people who inhabited it. All of the authors in this section explore issues of community and identity through lenses of ethnicity, race, labor, gender, or nationality and through the permutations of those identities on and in the landscape.

Two authors examine the city of Aurora, Nevada, from contrasting perspectives. Dale compares the archaeology at urban and rural Chinese sites in and around Aurora to explore different expressions of labor, economics, and identity in turn-of-the-century woodcutting camps (Chapter 5). Walkling discusses the importance of persistence strategies for Indigenous Paiute populations in the aftermath of the establishment of the town (Chapter 6). Such strategies are visible in the historic Paiute camps outside of the mining town.

Moving further south, two authors observe space within the state of New Mexico. Hegberg explores the creation of Hispanic community through homesteading, railroads, households, and a school (Chapter 7). She compares two smaller communities and their connections to the larger towns in the area and changes in the region from the early 1900s to the 1930s. LaValley analyzes dendroglyphs purposefully left behind by Hispano sheepherders (Chapter 8). He identifies patterns in tree carvings to follow a single family over time and across their grazing lands.

Pushing the boundaries of the West, Markert explores the construction of Alsatian identity in two neighboring towns in Texas (Chapter 9). Castroville and D'Hanis displayed different approaches to celebrating or showcasing their Alsatian heritage through architecture after immigrating to Texas.

The West Today

As evident from the first two sections, the American West and frontier were established and re-established, defined and redefined across the decades. The process of creating the American West is a continuing one that is explored in the final section of this volume. As Rubertone (2008:16) noted, "past and present are inextricably intertwined on the contemporary landscape." The landscapes of the American West are no exception. Here the authors address questions such as: How do past groups' constructions of the West impact people today? And how do past ideologies influence modern conceptions of the American West? Whose past and whose places are we examining and saving? Although these questions are raised throughout the volume, the authors in this section address them head-on.

The authors take a more overtly political perspective as they engage in the legacy of the past as it is remade in the present. For example, Tveskov and Rose confront the role of settler narratives in Oregon in creating a false history of interactions between colonists and Native Americans (Chapter 10). They examine how the creation of memorials in the present day perpetuate false narratives created in the past. Drexler places Civil War–era Arkansas on the edges of the American West frontier (Chapter 11). He argues that thanatourism (tourism of death and dying) at Civil War battlefields must invite a more diverse set of voices that includes African American perspectives. In a related vein, Acebo examines the role of political historicity in the construction of a mythical narrative of the Black Star village massacre in California (Chapter 12). Through a series of interviews with visitors to the site, Acebo assesses dispersals of misinformation of the history and archaeology of the site today. In the final contribution, Brien and Dixon advocate a multivocal approach to landscape studies in their assessment of Apsáalooke place-based narratives (Chapter 13). They stress the importance of including Apsáalooke stories, names, histories, and voices through ethnographic work and collaboration with Indigenous peoples in Great Plains historical archaeology.

The Making and Unmaking of the West

As this volume illustrates, placemaking in the West takes many different forms. As we close, we turn toward an important parallel narrative that accompanies the actions of creating and defining the West. Alongside the chronicles of making places, there are stories of unmaking places, of leaving places, of place destruction. The actions of making places is also one of displacement and of undoing. We are reminded by Acebo that colonization and preservation efforts can simultaneously unmake one place as they make another (Chapter 12). Tveskov and Rose similarly engage with historical memory and captivity narrative in Oregon, facing the problematic ways that these stories are retold at the expense of Native American heritage—making one narrative occur at the expense of another (Chapter 10). Walkling describes making places at the margins of a European-American colonial settlement that pressed former inhabitants to the edges of the space, which is yet another way that one set of placemakers is pushed out by another

(Chapter 6). And the collaborative archaeology endeavors of Brien and Dixon underscore the relationship between place names and the roles that colonization have played in removing Native American presence from those places, particularly in connection to spiritual landscapes. Their contribution offers numerous examples of the way that an undoing of placemaking can be rehabilitated through active efforts to address displacement and to remake places.

The contributions in the pages that follow capture the tensions present in the study of the West today. As a new generation of scholars comes forward, they rework the narratives about the ways that the West is and was made, unmade, and remade. Threads of the past that have been overlooked, forgotten, and intentionally pushed away are pulled through and rewoven into the fabric of history. The contributors in this volume embrace the push and the pull of the ideas of the West, ranging from our responsibilities as archaeologists to create narratives and counter-narratives, to understanding the multiplicity of voices that can contribute to understanding both individual sites and the larger West, and to the role of capitalism and economics and their reverberations in the place of the West. Like so many stories of the West, these contributions are pieces of a much longer and ever-evolving story.

2

Western Mythology and the Historical Archaeology of the Upper Missouri River Basin

Lotte Govaerts

This chapter examines how mid-twentieth-century archaeological collections from nineteenth-century sites reflect the interaction between American West scholarship and American West mythology in popular culture, and how this interaction changes over time. Specifically, the chapter investigates how collections from sites along the Missouri River in North Dakota and South Dakota were shaped by now-outdated theories that defined the West in space and time, which influenced decisions on what aspects of Western history should be studied. These biases indirectly shape the twenty-first-century study of these places. Additionally, the chapter examines how American West mythology directly affected me as a foreigner studying the nineteenth-century northern Plains. Finally, the chapter expands on how these biases do not preclude use of twentieth-century collections to answer twenty-first-century research questions but can in fact allow for a better contextualization of the material when closely examined.

The River Basin Surveys

The United States experienced a dam-building boom in the twentieth century, particularly between the 1930s and the 1960s. One of these dam projects was the Pick-Sloan Plan for the Upper Missouri. It included the construction of five large dams on the main stem of the Missouri in the Dakotas (Figure 2.1). The reservoirs in those two states inundated over 81% of their 1,217 km river kilometers (756 miles; Banks and Czaplicki 2014:13).

The threat to archaeological sites posed by massive dam-building projects across the United States led to the foundation of the Interagency Archeological Salvage Program (IASP) in 1945 (the program's official name was "Interagency Archaeological and Paleontological Salvage Program," but the name is usually shortened). The program was administered by the National Park Service (NPS). The Smithsonian created the River Basin Surveys (RBS) unit to undertake archaeological field and lab work for the IASP, which they conducted along with various educational institutions, museums, and historical societies. The Missouri Basin was by far the largest of the RBS project areas. The RBS operated in the region between 1945 and 1969 (Thiessen et al. 2014).

Much has been written about the enormous impact a survey project of this unprecedented magnitude had on the field of archaeology in the United States (Banks and Czaplicki 2014; Jennings 1985; Thiessen and Roberts 2009; Wedel 1967). Historical archaeology was just beginning to establish itself as a separate field during the RBS (Lees 2014; Scott 1998). Since then, there have been discussions on what constitutes historical archaeology, where the separation between "prehistoric" and "historic" lies, and what the distinctions mean for the field of archaeology in the United States (Gilchrist 2005; Lightfoot 1995). I

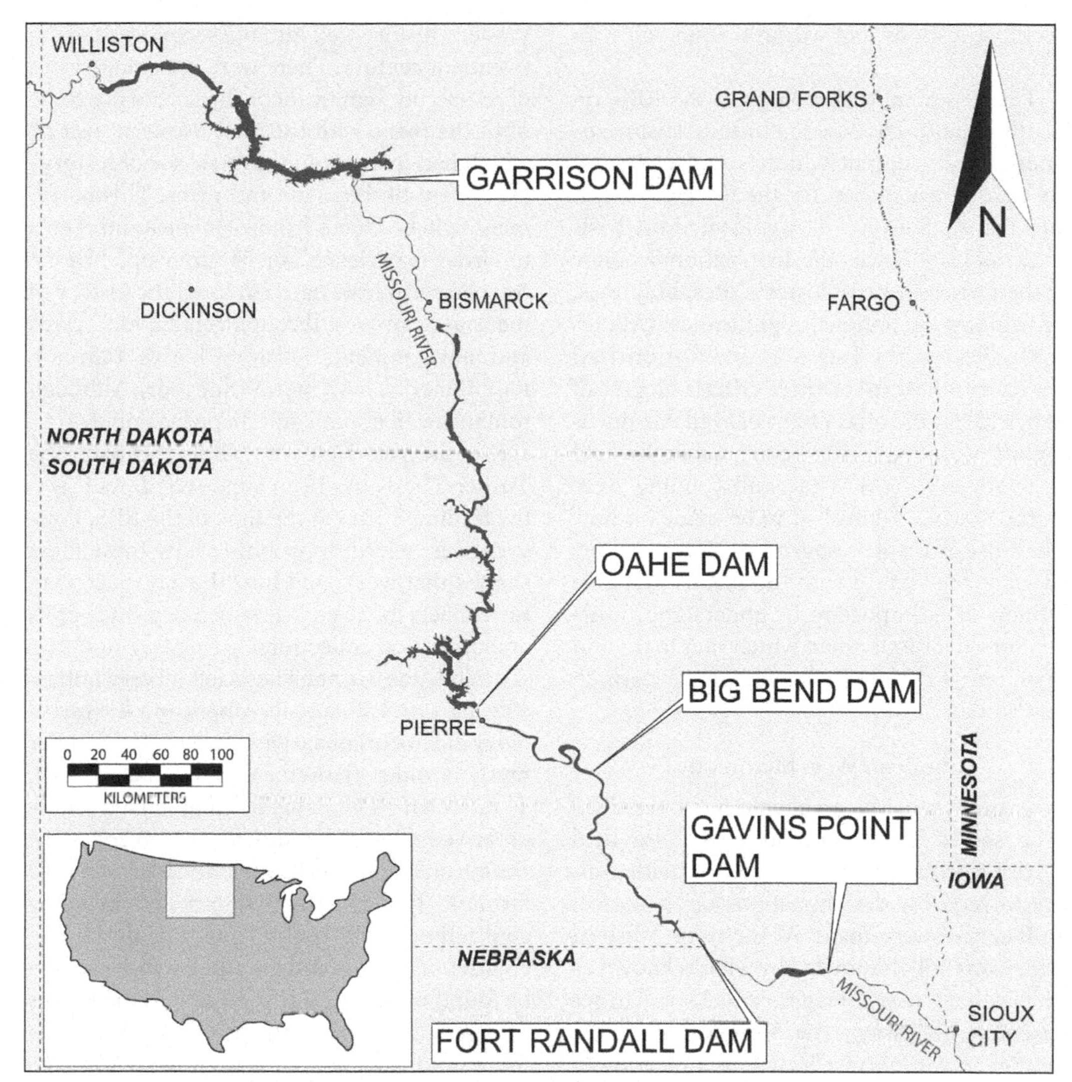

FIGURE 2.1. The locations of the five main-stem dams on the Upper Missouri. Based on data from Google Maps.

will not delve into these discussions here, except to explain how RBS researchers categorized sites.

During the RBS, "historic sites archaeology" was separated from "archaeology." The "historic sites" definition did not include historic period Native American sites, but solely sites associated with the American (and European) presence in the area. RBS reports frequently use the words "of White origin" to describe these sites. That description excludes quite a few inhabitants of some places and obfuscates some of the decision-making power in the selection of locations for trade posts. The investigation of these "historic sites" was a new development on the Great Plains. Prior to the RBS, archaeological investigation of historic period sites on the Great Plains was largely limited to Native American sites (G. Hubert Smith's work at Fort Laramie in the 1930s is a notable exception [Smith 1939]). Archaeologists used the "direct historical approach" to investigate these sites, working backwards from documented periods to learn more about prehistoric Native American sites (Steward 1942). The method was employed to answer specific questions and was anthropological in nature.

The historical archaeology of the RBS, on the other hand, was based in history. Historians conducted document searches and compiled lists of "historic places" for the reservoir areas. The Historic Sites Act of 1935 formed the basis for these lists. It was the first national policy for the preservation of historic sites, buildings, and objects of national significance (Mattes 1947). Sites on the lists were then prioritized for excavation based on three criteria: degree of historical significance, extent of available documentation, and ability to be located in the field (Lees 2014:153–156). Time and funding were limited, and decisions had to be made on how to best use available resources. RBS researchers did what they could with the means available to them. It is important to understand, however, how decisions about which sites to list and which ones to prioritize shaped future research possibilities.

American West Mythology

Since the historical archaeology of the RBS was based in history, one can look to the field of Western history in the mid-twentieth century to see how determinations of "historical significance" were made. At the time, Western history was still dominated by what is known as the "Turner Thesis." Frederick Jackson Turner presented his essay "The Significance of the Frontier in American History," at a meeting of the American Historical Association in 1893 (Turner 1921). In the essay, Turner proposed the theory that the frontier shaped the character of the nation and its inhabitants. It was prompted by the fact that the United States Census Bureau declared the frontier "closed" in 1890, meaning all land was claimed and there was no longer a frontier. Turner wondered what this meant for the future development of American culture. He called the American West "the meeting point between savagery and civilization" (Turner 1921:3). The frontier was where heroic white men conquered the wild and built America, more a process than an actual place, as it moved over time.

Turner's views on the frontier dominated Western history well into the second half of the twentieth century. There were opposing views, of course, but significant pushback did not come until the 1970s with the New Western history, which had its roots in the "new social history" movement of the 1960s and 1970s. This movement switched focus from big names and events to "lived experience," or "bottom up" history. New Western historians explored the history of the American West through gender, race, class, and environmental history lenses (Cronon 1991; Limerick 1987, 1991; White 1991). Although romanticized notions still shape the popular images of the American West, among scholars, the Turner Thesis has been superseded. As it was the leading theory at the time of the RBS, however, it is helpful to examine how these ideas shaped that work, and how this perspective in turn affects the twenty-first-century study of its archaeological collections.

While the Turner Thesis left its very noticeable mark on scholarship, American West mythology did not originate with Turner. The frontier myth is older than the United States itself. Thomas Jefferson, in his writings, talked fondly of the yeoman farmer ideal (Jefferson 2010:135). European colonizers brought the idea of heroic farmers "taming" the "wilderness," bringing civilization (while at the same time disdaining civilization, or at least urban life), which can also be found in Roman writings such as the poems of Tibullus (Putnam 1987:37, 156–157). Some more unique American aspects were added to the agrarian myth over time to make it the myth of the American West. Turner was presumably as influenced by the frontier myth as he influenced it in turn.

Because reverence of the West as a frontier location predated the "arrival" of said frontier on the Great Plains, events taking place there during the "frontier era" were already part of the mythology as they occurred. Pioneer settlers and conflict with Native peoples were a staple of the frontier narrative, and, as the frontier moved, different types of characters like cowboys and fur traders became local Western heroes.

John Filson's description of Daniel Boone was the first in a long tradition of Western adventures (Filson 1784). James Fenimore Cooper added to the genre with his historical romances in the 1820s. Even more popular were mass-produced Western dime novels, starting in the 1840s (Brown 1997). These novels were full of white male heroes, conflict with Native Americans, and idealization of rugged individuality. In the twentieth century, Western movies served as a vehicle to affirm, canonize, and spread Western mythology. Starting with *The Great Train Robbery* in 1903, Westerns made up at least a third of movies produced in the United States for some 60 years (Faragher 2012).

By the 1970s, Westerns were no longer a staple, though they continue to be made. Along with the new social history movement came Westerns that presented different perspectives. To be sure, these later movies are still full of stereotypes such as "noble and ignoble savages" (Lindberg 2013), and they largely continue to center the stories of white male heroes. They also tend to show somewhat more nuanced perspectives on conflict (e.g., *Dances with Wolves* [Costner 1990]; *The Revenant* [Iñárritu 2015]).

How Ideas About the West Influenced the RBS

Archaeologists use data to interpret and illuminate real pasts, but they are not immune to the influence of prevailing ideas in mainstream culture. Much like Turner in his time, archaeologists are immersed in and influenced by mainstream culture, even as they influence it in turn. The historical archaeology of the RBS certainly both influenced and was influenced by ideas about the West.

Merrill Mattes (1960:12), in the first RBS paper on historic sites, explains that RBS selection criteria for "historic site archaeology" resulted in the investigation of three site categories: trade posts, military posts, and Indian Agencies, all places he considered "representative of significant frontier eras." He adds that "[s]teamboat landings, villages, missions, and other communities of fairly recent origin" were not investigated because "[they] might bear such similarity to still-existent communities that archaeological findings might not be rewarding." In the same paper, he also describes the Missouri Basin as "the heartland of the traditional frontier American West," further adding that it was

> the last major region in the United States to settle down to a peaceful domestic routine. Long after territories east of the Mississippi had been well populated and methodically "civilized," the wild empire of the buffalo, the Sioux Indian, and the bighorn sheep attracted only the more rugged citizens—traders, trappers, soldiers, freighters, prospectors, missionaries, and Indian fighters—typical frontiersmen all [Mattes 1960:7].

Indeed, with the exception of two domestic sites excavated during attempts to locate fur trade posts (Smith 1968:33–43, 47–54), all "historic sites" investigated by RBS archaeologists fall into the three categories mentioned by Mattes. There is a hierarchy to be observed among these categories as well. Many sites were visited briefly by RBS researchers, while others were extensively excavated. Among the six "historic sites" that received the most attention in terms of both fieldwork and publication, five were associated with the fur trade (32ML2 [Fort Berthold/Like-A-Fishhook Village], 32MN1 [Fort Floyd, which RBS researchers called "Kipp's Post"], 39CO5 [Fort Manuel], 39ML57 [unidentified trade post and other occupations], and 39ST217 [Fort Pierre II]). The remaining site (32ML1) was a military fort by the name of Fort Stevenson, later used as an Indian school. (More complete lists of historic sites investigated during the RBS and their associated publications can be found online [Govaerts 2014, 2015]).

It is clear from RBS reports that there was some pushback against the investigation of places that fall under the "historic sites" definition. Funds for excavations were not secured until 1950 (Mattes 1960:13). A fairly significant portion of the text in RBS publications on historic sites is devoted to explaining exactly why these sites were investigated at all (Mattes 1960:6–7; Smith 1960:87–90, 1968:1–2). It seems likely that in such an environment, the excavation of places associated with popular stories would be

FIGURE 2.2. Scenes from Khao Yai Cowboy Festival in Thailand, December 2016. Photographs by Lotte Govaerts.

easier to defend than the excavation of a different type of historic site.

The general public's views on how the excavations fit with their ideas of The West can be gleaned from newspaper reports. For example, the Billings County Pioneer (1953:2) reported on the RBS excavations in an article titled "Time running out for archeologists at Garrison." The article is accompanied by a photo titled "Where Once Embattled Pioneers Stood." The photo caption reads: "Pictured above is a blockhouse similar to those which were constructed on opposite corners of the Ft. Berthold stockade. It is from one of these that Pierre Garreau made some of his spectacular moves on the Indians." The short article provides some information on the RBS project, some background on Fort Berthold and Fort Stevenson, and a story about Pierre Garreau, "a daring and picturesque man of mixed French and Cree blood" who "knew the ways of and had great influence among the Indians" and apparently heroically fought off a raiding party. This story sits right next to a half-page "Lone Ranger" comic episode.

Into the Twenty-First Century: A Transnational Perspective

Since the RBS historical archaeology focused mostly on fur trade sites, these sites have the largest associated collections and the best documentation. As I evaluated the available material and its potential for studying aspects of the United States colonization of the Upper Missouri Basin in the nineteenth century, I decided to focus on the fur trade as well. Thus, decisions made by researchers 70 years ago directly influenced my own research topic.

In addition to the secondhand influence of mid-twentieth-century thinking through the collections, Western mythology also influences me directly. Since the time of the RBS, half a century has passed, and Western mythos has further established itself. The West by its very name reveals itself to be an eastern construct. Not only do I live on the East Coast, I grew up several thousand kilometers away on a different continent, where a local version of American West mythology exists, and few people have directly experienced the American West. This distance has added several more layers of investigation between the material and me.

The United States has exported its cultural identity as consumable products since at least the late nineteenth century. In the twentieth century, Hollywood made iconic Western imagery ubiquitous all around the world (Figures 2.2 and 2.3). While these messages are interpreted in various ways on the receiving end, certain ideas about American identity are inextricably linked to Western imagery everywhere. The landscapes of the West are seen as the realm of freedom (Kroes 1999:468). I grew up in Europe, where these ideas have been around at least since Buffalo Bill's Wild West show toured there. As a child in the late twentieth century, I watched *Bonanza* reruns, played with a toy Fort Randall set (modeled after the nineteenth-century military fort studied in the RBS [Mills 1960]), and read a large volume of European Western novels and comics, many undoubtedly created by people who never set foot on United States soil, but whose work is nonetheless indistinguishable from that of their American counterparts (Figure 2.3). All of these experiences shaped my view of the United States and the West (essentially one and the same to an outsider).

Building Perspective

I came to the United States as an adult with all these unexamined ideas about The West as a place and had to reevaluate them over time as I visited the actual West and started studying its past. I learned the American West can still be defined both as a specific place, or geographical area (with a somewhat nebulous eastern boundary), and as a historical space or setting of "frontier" history, but that "frontier" is interpreted rather differently than it was in the past. Instead of the site of white man's victory over the wild, it is now studied as a site of colonization, colonialism, landscape transformation, migration, industrial capitalism, and other processes (see Dixon 2014).

While twentieth-century collections were shaped by twentieth-century theories, this process does not mean these collections cannot

FIGURE 2.3. A selection of Western-themed comic books for sale in a bookstore in Antwerp, Belgium, July 2018. Photographs by Lotte Govaerts.

answer twenty-first-century research questions. In his overview of RBS historic sites archaeology, Merrill Mattes defined the purpose of these investigations as follows:

> Archaeological excavation of a historic site is justified primarily to fill important gaps in documentary or archival research.... A second and oftentimes quite important justification for this type of project is the collection of historical objects that help to throw light on the living conditions of the period and place, or that may illuminate specific problems [Mattes 1960:6–7].

From a twenty-first-century perspective, the first part of that statement seems outdated (However, most archaeological work undertaken in the United States at present falls into the cultural management category [McManamon 2018:560–561]. This type of work uses criteria for determining historical/archaeological significance or eligibility to the National Register of Historic Places—authorized by the National Historic Preservation Act of 1966, which includes somewhat similar language in places [Andrus and Shrimpton 2002]). The second part, however, is still relevant. Many collections from Native American sites excavated by RBS crews have been used to investigate various questions. One example is Craig Johnson's (2007) Plains Village chronology research. The "historic site" collections have not been used as much, although Raymond Wood co-published new insights based on the material he uncovered decades ago (Wood and Casler 2015). Going beyond the RBS "historic site" definition, collections associated with historic period Native American sites can also be used to investigate change brought about by cultural contact (Rogers 1990).

Several sites that are similar to or associated with the flooded historic sites have been investigated in the area since the RBS. The many publications on sites like Fort Union (Midwest Archaeological Center 2008) and Fort Clark (Wood et al. 2011) show a range of possibilities for new interpretations of existing collections and data.

My dissertation research (forthcoming) examines collections from six trade posts along the Missouri between northern North Dakota and central South Dakota, all established by American companies and operated for various lengths of time between 1812 and circa 1863. Colonization of this area started with these trade posts, followed by military forts, railroads, telegraph lines, and settlements. Over the course of the nineteenth century, this colonization caused significant changes to the environment and demographics of the region, to the cultures and economies of local Native peoples, the expanding United States, and to some extent, the rest of the world. The comparison between collections from different trade posts, delineates spatiotemporal differences in the assemblages which I interpret within this historical context.

Closely examining the twentieth-century origins of the collections allows a better understanding of how they relate to the nineteenth-century sites in question (i.e., what was or was not collected? How did artifact assemblages represent what was actually present at the sites?). This analysis also revealed continuity among the many, sometimes rapid and drastic, demographic and environmental changes across the region. Accounting for these factors permits for an understanding of the nineteenth-century events in a wider context.

For example, the influx of outside capital to extract finite resources during the fur trade can be compared to the recent Bakken boom (the rapid expansion of oil extraction from the Bakken formation in North Dakota that started after the discovery of Parshall Oil Field in 2006), and similar extraction booms in the recent past (Becker 2016). Booms in general provide temporary benefit to local people (e.g., access to jobs or trade goods), but in the end they mostly benefit outside capitalists and damage local ecosystems and communities (Braun 2016). The Missouri River fur trade was a different kind of boom, in that resource extraction took place largely through trade, but nonetheless both can be seen as part of the same process that continues to transform the region.

Similarly, comparisons can be made when studying Native American reservations. Reservations were created for the various tribes living in this area in the mid-nineteenth century. Over the next half century, different acts greatly reduced their territories. The building of the Pick Sloan dams essentially continued this process. Research has shown that the dam sites were deliberately chosen to avoid certain towns, and impact Native American reservations instead (Schneiders 1997). The impacted tribes fought a long legal battle over the effects of the dams, which eventually ended in some compensation for their losses (Lawson 2009). It is clear from the oil pipeline protests recently in the news that the situation is not much different in the late 2010s. These particular conflicts are about water rights rather than land as such, but the underlying dynamics are much the same.

Conclusion

In contemporary archaeological investigations, the West can be defined as a space shaped by processes such as colonialism, landscape transformation, migration, and industrial capitalism. Nonetheless, popular narratives on Western history endure and continue to influence perceptions of the West. These narratives can influence archaeologists and historians both directly and indirectly. In my ongoing dissertation research, I examine multiple layers of bias including twentieth-century researchers' views on the American West—influenced by ideas of the American West as a mythical place and imagined past—and the ways they in turn propagated these ideas and physically manifested them onto the landscape of the Missouri basin through their excavations and into the resulting collections. I also examine my own views of the American West, based on exported American mythologies and their foreign interpretation and reconstruction. Doing this allows me to better understand the collections, and to see the sites I investigate in a wider context, as part of ongoing processes transforming the region. Additionally, this examination also illuminates the role of archaeology in these ongoing processes and the ways in which the field has changed since the time of the RBS, and the ways in which it has not. Regulations have been put in place intended to protect both archaeological sites and the rights and sovereignty of tribal nations. These regulations, however, frequently prove inadequate (see Rowe et al. 2018; Marincic 2018). My ongoing research demonstrates how critical examination of twentieth-century collections allows the researcher to answer twenty-first-century questions and build alternative narratives of the West.

3

Inside the Fence and Out

Placemaking along the El Paso and Northeastern Railroad in New Mexico

Rachel Feit

This chapter explores a phenomenology of place along the El Paso and Northeastern Railroad (EP & NE) system through archaeological remains at four section camps in the Tularosa Basin in New Mexico: Newman Camp, LA 97713; Desert Siding, LA 97690; Turquoise Station, LA 37044; and Escondida Siding, LA 101183 (Figure 3.1). Specifically, it attempts to unpack the contingent spaces formed at the intersection of corporate planning, landscape, and lived experience that shaped daily life among section workers and their families.

The EP & NE Railroad system encompassed four different railroads and a multitude of subsidiary ventures that supported the entire system. The railway operated under the EP & NE name until 1905, when it was sold to the El Paso & Southwestern (EP & SW). In 1924, the EP & SW sold the railroad to Southern Pacific. During changes in ownership, all lines and subsidiary ventures conveyed as a single entity intact, and one of its founding partners remained involved. While the EP & NE was technically only in existence until 1905, for simplicity in discussing the historical arc and impact of the road on Southeastern New Mexico, I refer to it by its original name, the EP & NE.

The line served as a key artery during the golden age of railroads (1896–1918), opening up vast timber and mineral resources in the mountains of eastern New Mexico to development, fostering new towns, and transporting people and goods across the country. Its development and geopolitical impact left a lasting historical and archaeological legacy throughout eastern New Mexico.

The spatial organization of the railroad's built environment reflects its programmatic planning and placemaking. Meanwhile, archaeological remains from four section camps in the Tularosa Basin offer more intimate glimpses of the lived experience of the section workers in the early twentieth century. This lived experience was mediated through ethnicity, class, and a network of power relations between the corporate architecture of the railroad and the mostly Mexican American workers who populated its company space. The various ways these actors negotiated spaces along the EP & NE Railroad could be seen as a framework of strategies and tactics (de Certeau 1984), wherein strategies were employed by the architects of the EP & NE as a means of controlling place, while tactics were the unrehearsed acts of everyday life that situated those spaces culturally and historically. The dialectic between the places programmed by the railroad and the lived experience of them is what gave these locales "placeness" (Relph

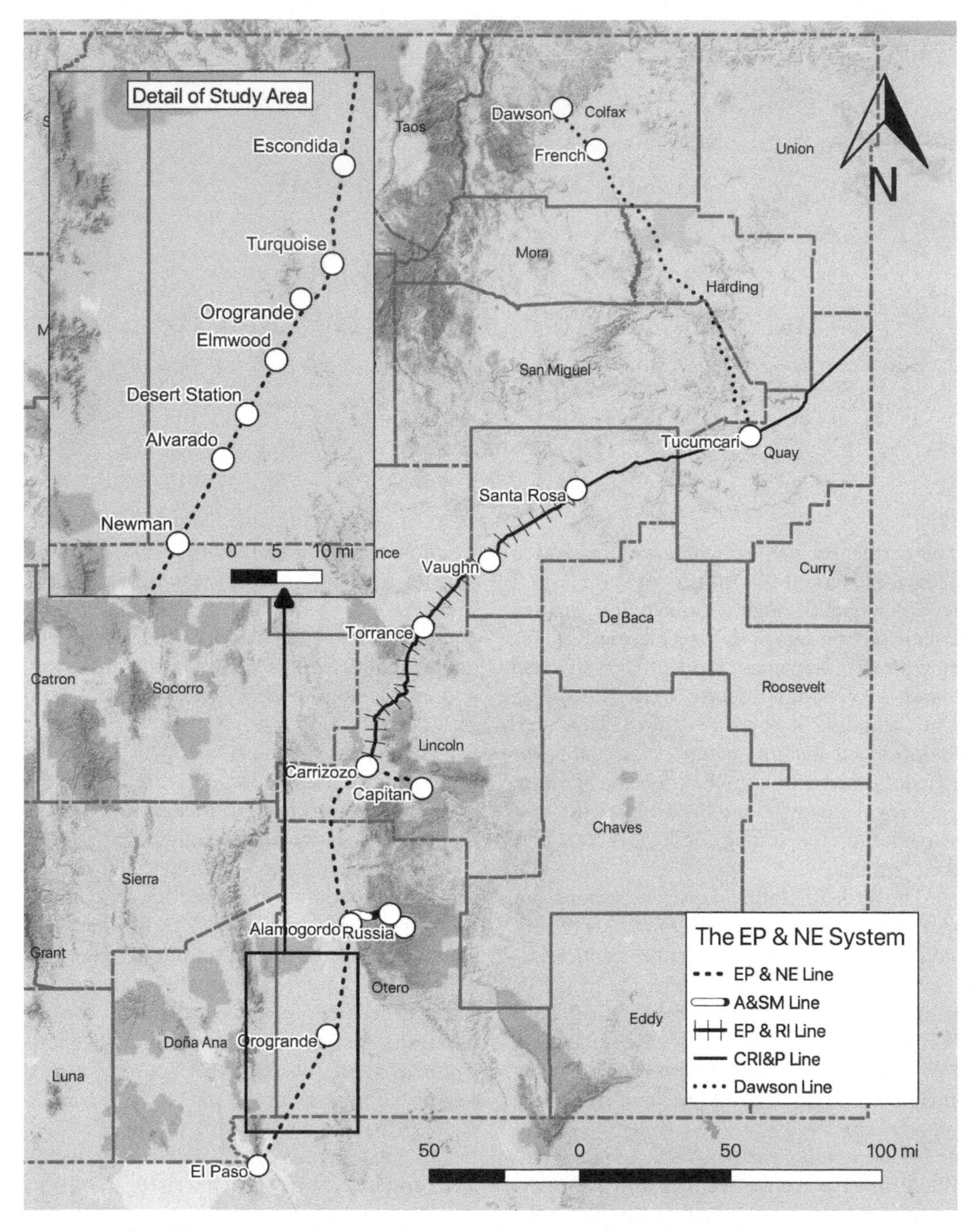

FIGURE 3.1. The El Paso and Northeastern System in Eastern New Mexico extended from El Paso to Tucumcari and Dawson. The inset shows railroad sites on Fort Bliss discussed in this chapter. Map by Rachel Feit.

2017), or what some would call a "sense of place" (viz. Feld and Basso 1996; Hayden 1995).

Place, as a concept, is a "plenary presence permeated with culturally constituted institutions and practices" (Casey 1996:46). Places are not static entities, but are received, made, and remade by a series of interactions that are situated historically, culturally, and politically in time and space (Appadurai 1996; Harvey 1996). In a phenomenology of place, placeness is created when space and culture operate dialectically. Quite simply, "the meaning of a place is produced through the interactions and activities that occur there" (Voss 2008:148).

This chapter attempts to demonstrate how archaeological remains of EP & NE Railroad section camps in the Tularosa Basin reflect a placeness that was characterized by a tension between the programmed, physically enclosed spaces constructed by the EP & NE, and the informal, unplanned spaces fashioned by the rail workers and their families. I call this duality the inside-the-fence/outside-the-fence dynamic. This duality was not necessarily absolute, but rather created contingent spaces where the EP & NE and individuals acted upon each other to forge new cultural landscapes in the Tularosa Basin.

Imagining the Road

The story of the EP & NE Railroad is straight out of the pages of a Frank Norris novel in which cartoonish industry bosses conjure up ambitious construction plans, all supposedly for the greater good, even as they remorselessly bend laborers and landowners into submission. The full story exceeds the space allotted here. Suffice to say that well into the twentieth century, the very fabric of domestic, social, and economic life in eastern New Mexico was dominated by the EP & NE railroad (Seligman 1958). The railroad owned the stores where people shopped, the utility companies that supplied water, and even dictated where alcohol could be sold and consumed in the towns where it stopped.

Like many rail lines, the idea for the EP & NE began in imagination long before a mile of track was ever laid. In 1879, gold was found at White Oaks in the Sacramento Mountains and coal in the Capitan Mountains. The discovery brought prospectors and mining companies to the region, racing to extract mineral wealth from land that, to American speculators, seemed virtually depopulated (the Native American presence was conveniently overlooked and is another chapter of New Mexico history altogether). At the time, it took more than two weeks for wagons to travel by oxcart from White Oaks through the dusty Tularosa Basin to El Paso and back to deliver the ore. A better mode of transportation into the White Oaks district was needed. Political and business leaders were already keenly aware that the key to unlocking the territory's rich resources was rail transportation. When New Mexico's first rail line, to Santa Fe, was completed in 1880, for instance, the New Mexico territorial legislature eulogized that the event was the "most important in the history of the territory," and that railroads would at last connect the remote corners of New Mexico to the rest of the nation (Anderson 1907:896).

The El Paso and White Oaks Railroad was incorporated in 1882, though nothing ever came of this venture. Over the next 15 years, several other false starts were made under various names. Inevitably, funding, land acquisition, or simply lack of will hobbled the rail enterprise (Myrick 1970). Finally, in 1896, Charles and John Eddy, in partnership with a whip-smart lawyer named William Hawkins, secured rights to a line going from El Paso to the Sacramento Mountains (Reed 1981). Two days later, the partners gained an important concession for a 100 ft right-of-way from the Fort Bliss Reservation, which was at that time without rail access (SPRGDA, Box LCT2, Folder 1). Building a railway through Fort Bliss had obvious benefits for both parties. It guaranteed traffic and freight to the EP & NE line while connecting the new military post to goods, people, and supplies from other parts of the nation (Feit and Silberberg 2015). The partners' next move was to organize a group of Pennsylvania coal investors to come out to the Sacramentos and see the coal resources for themselves. The coal men were sufficiently intrigued to invest in the EP & NE railroad, and with these funds, as well as other capital from East Coast investors, they began construction (Faunce 1997, 2005; Myrick 1970).

By June 15, 1898, about 85 miles of track were completed from El Paso to the Oliver Lee Ranch in New Mexico. There, Charles Eddy had planned to build a new town site, which would serve as the railroad headquarters. He named the town Alamogordo (Faunce 1997, 2005; Myrick 1970). The trip from El Paso to the Sacramento Mountains was shortened from a week to just six hours. This track became the core of the EP & NE. By 1902, track reached deep into the Sacramento and Capitan Mountains and north of Carrizozo where, under the name El Paso and Rock Island (EP & RI), owned by the same consortium, it would eventually connect to the existing Chicago, Rock Island & Pacific Railroad (CRI & P), thus linking El Paso to Chicago by rail (Myrick 1970).

Chartering the Alamogordo and Sacramento Mountain Railway in 1898, the Eddy brothers built a line from the Lee Ranch deep into the Sacramento Mountains where good timber could be harvested (Glover 1984). The Eddy brothers had a second interest in the region: they planned to develop a private mountain resort town, Cloudcroft, reached only by rail line. Called an "engineering marvel," the line to Cloudcroft and beyond climbed more than 4,700 feet in under 30 miles through a series of switchbacks, its trestles crossing deep gorges and making sharp S-turns (Jensen 1966). Once the Eddy brothers and their associates had finally completed construction of the entire EP & NE system in 1903 they controlled more than 600 miles of rail lines through New Mexico, in addition to ownership in town sites and leases on timberlands and mines across the state (Faunce 1997; Myrick 1970; SPRGDA, Box LTA21, Folder 2).

The owners of the EP & NE recognized that railroad operation was risky business. Successful rail lines operated at marginal profits for years before significant investment returns were realized (White 2011). When the EP & NE partners began promoting their idea for a railroad into the Sacramento Mountains, they knew that real profits did not come from operating the railroad, but from related business investments in developable land, mines, and other resources. In chartering the EP & NE, the partners simultaneously incorporated a number of other business interests along the route. Over the next five years, Charles Eddy, his brother John Eddy, and William Hawkins acquired interests, together or separately, in nearly a dozen companies, as well as ownership or leases in timberlands and mines throughout the areas surrounding the railroad (Feit and Silberberg 2015). The owners of the EP & NE Railroad owned the Nannie Baird Mine near Orogrande where gold and copper deposits had been found, coal mining lands near Capitan and at Dawson, and thousands of acres in the Sacramento Mountains where they harvested timber for ties and buildings. Under various corporation names (owned by the same individuals), the holding company spawned mining and timber camps, mills, smelters and coke ovens, small company towns, and, in the case of Cloudcroft, a popular resort town. To support the system, run entirely on steam power, the railroad drilled wells, built dams, and constructed pipelines to supply water to the trains (Feit and Silberberg 2015).

The partners' influence spread far and wide, directing not just business interests, but also seeping into politics and law. The enterprising William Hawkins was a member of the Territorial Council, and through his influence, the territorial legislature successfully passed an unprecedented law limiting the liability of railroads and mines in personal accident and death cases both within and outside of the territory (Keleher 2008). Hawkins used his influence many times to pass legislation favoring his railroad and mine interests. Hawkins and the Eddy brothers were so powerful that, in 1904, territorial Governor Miguel Otero asked Charles to provide a list of his railroad employees to help secure the Republican nomination in the next election (SPRGDA, Box LCR3, Vol. 18). Through their vast holdings and political patronage, they leveraged considerable power over the people within its shadow.

The EP & NE Landscape: Marking Space and Making Place

Writing about the Southern Pacific, the novelist Frank Norris compared the railroad to a giant octopus, whose groping interests crept into every corner of society (Norris 1901:551). The EP & NE applied the same strategies toward empire building in southeastern New Mexico. The railroad dictated the physical and social development of towns and infrastructure at the various stops, with the built environment oriented to the tracks and sidings along a rectilinear plan. For example, the town of Alamogordo was planned and largely owned by the EP & NE, which intentionally oriented the streets towards the tracks. Industrial buildings and warehouses were built on the west side of the tracks, where spur lines and sidings were also built. Commercial development occurred east of the tracks. Residences were built east of the commercial streets. The city's park and institutions extended in linear fashion adjacent to the tracks north of the commercial center. The railroad designated a section outside of town for Mexican workers (Harwell 1998). Finally, all properties—except for one-half of one block—contained deed restrictions prohibiting the production and sale of alcohol. These same restrictions appeared in every deed for every town and settlement the EP & NE served (Eddy 1998; Keleher 2008).

Stops were built every 10 to 13 km for water and access to and from surrounding ranches. Between El Paso and Alamogordo there were at least 14 stops that were built in the sparsely populated desert. In fact, very few of the stops along the EP & NE and its subsidiary roads were named places or towns before the railroad came through. Alamogordo, Tularosa, and Carrizozo became important commercial centers, company towns, and key operational points for the railroad. Meanwhile, other stops served as shipping points for cattle and agricultural goods, or to house section workers. Very few of them could have existed without the railroad (Feit and Silberberg 2015). The railroad owned every one of them, and it applied the same built-environment formula to each at varying scales.

The story of the EP & NE, like the railroad itself, is a sprawling one that seeped deep into the very crevices of everyday life, molding the cultural landscape. Today, however, the infrastructure, industries, and many of the places built by the road are little more than archaeological remains (Kovacik et al. 2000). Its once hopeful towns are now desolate and remote. The cultural landscape surrounding it today is more a site of memory than lived experience. While the core of the EP & NE line is still active, now owned by the Union Pacific, all of the stops, the subsidiary lines, the mills, and the mines are abandoned. First the mines played out, then the timber market crashed. Automobiles superseded rail transportation, ranches failed, and the dieselization of rail transportation in the 1940s and 1950s completely changed the need for the infrastructure the EP & NE built to support itself. In the end, the United States Department of Defense and the National Park Service purchased much of the land formerly controlled by the railroad (Feit and Silberberg 2015).

In the Tularosa Basin, the Sacramento Mountains, and beyond, one can still see the railroad's imprint in abandoned rail lines, former mills, mines, towns, reservoirs, and pipelines. Unlike a few of the towns along the EP & NE that eventually grew organically (such as Alamogordo or Carrizozo), the archaeological sites in the Tularosa Basin were intrinsically tied to the railroad. Infrastructure, building, and all residential activities relied almost entirely on rail operations to sustain them. They existed only to take on water, for maintenance of the engines, and for repair of the road itself, the maintenance of which was particularly heavy in the Tularosa Basin (Feit and Silberberg 2015). In the early twentieth century, the stops were remote, wild spaces, despite local ranchers' investments in stock corrals, businesses, and post offices. Ultimately, the construction and organization of these camps were first and foremost determined by rail needs.

TABLE 3.1. Summary of Investigations at Four Sites along the El Paso and Northeastern Railroad.

Site Name/No.	Archaeological Effort	Features
Newman Camp, LA 97713	TRU[a] survey, mapping	18 features including five trash pits/scatters, two dugout ice houses, possible cesspit, depression, concrete pads for structures and platforms, water tank pad, upright pipes and posts, and piled wood.
Desert Siding, LA 97690	TRU survey, mapping, two test units	11 disturbed features including seven structure foundations, three trash pits, and concrete water tank.
Turquoise Station, LA 37044	TRU survey, mapping, one test unit	Seven features: two structure foundation, rail ties, pit feature, large can scatter, and two concrete stock water tank pads.
Escondida Siding, LA 101183	TRU survey, mapping, six test units	21 features including structure remains for section housing, tool house, bath house, pump house, garage, commissary, cesspits, jacal, chicken coop, multiple trash scatters, and buried trash pit.

[a] Fort Bliss Transect Recording Unit.

Fieldwork

In 2014, archaeologists from AmaTerra Environmental, Inc. investigated four EP & NE section camps as part of a larger effort on Fort Bliss in the Tularosa Basin between El Paso and Alamogordo. The sites include Newman Camp, LA 97713; Desert Siding, LA 97690; Turquoise Station, LA 37044; and Escondida Siding, LA 101183 (Figure 3.1). Archaeological investigations at the four stops involved survey and mapping at each location following Fort Bliss's standardized Transect Recording Methodology (TRU, Miller et al. 2009). Due to the desert environment of the Tularosa Basin, most artifacts and features were visible on the surface. Archaeological testing through 1 × 1 m units was undertaken at three of the sites with potential buried deposits, producing more than 10,000 artifacts in total (Table 3.1). Investigations found that the material culture of these places offers a keen illustration of the interplay between the railroad's absentee programmatic planning and the pragmatic tactics of everyday life.

Programmatic Planning Inside the Fence

The railroad employed a variety of strategies to maintain and control each of these places, including the governance of physical space. Photographs and plat maps show that buildings were unfailingly oriented towards the railroad and clustered in one or two rows (Figure 3.2).

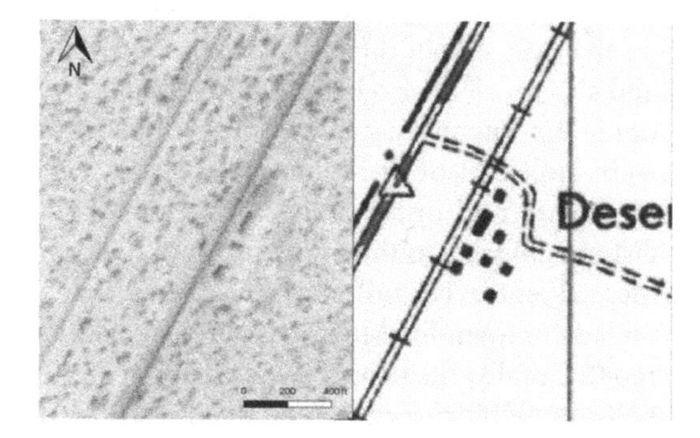

FIGURE 3.2. Buildings depicted on (*left*) a 1942 aerial photograph and (*right*) detail from a 1948 topographical map (United States Geological Survey 1942, 1948). Note the visible fence line in the aerial photograph. Map by Rachel Feit.

In all cases, a fence surrounded planned spaces. The fence was largely symbolic, given the surrounding region's vast emptiness, but no doubt sent a powerful message about corporate control and ownership. Platforms, tool buildings, and section housing were all inside the fence. The spaces within were ordered, arranged, while the buildings and use-areas outside the fence exposed the cracks in corporate planning: outhouses, chicken coops, and, as we shall later see, informal structures. In fact, I argue that the fence formed a crucial axis for

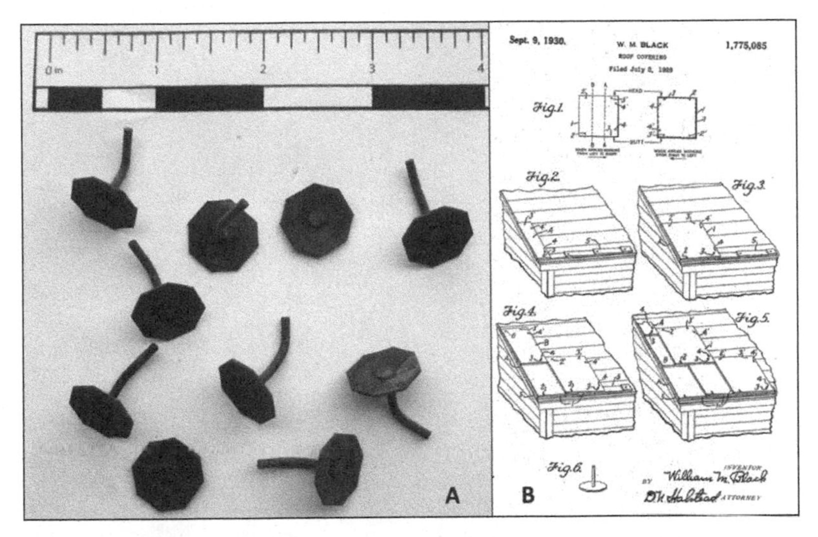

FIGURE 3.3. Chase storm anchors: (*a*) used anchors found in test units inside the fence at Escondida Siding (photograph by Amy Silberberg, 2015); (*b*) patent image for Chase storm anchors (Black 1930).

placemaking along the road. It symbolized an important duality that was replicated many times over and reflected the imperfect alignment of the railroad's programmatic planning with the everyday experience of the residents who lived in those places along the railroad.

EP & NE section housing inside the fence followed a common formula. Section foremen's houses were 20 by 32 ft frame dwellings that housed a single employee and his family. These individuals would have been in direct contact with the railroad's management, and United States Census Bureau records (1910a, 1920a, 1930a, 1940a) indicate that they were invariably white. Section worker housing was often built using a 16 by 57 ft four-room plan to house four separate laborers and their families. One-room section housing was also built at some stations and these buildings were generally 12 by 14 ft frame dwellings. All of the section workers who lived in these dormitory style dwellings were Mexican or Mexican-American.

To capture the wastewater and human waste generated at these various stops, the railroad built cesspits at the outer edges of the sites often along the fence line, and sometimes outside them, using 8 ft long railroad ties to frame the pit opening at about ground level. Additional rail ties were placed upright at corners. Plat maps suggest that the pit dimensions were originally 8 by 8 ft (erosion has made them larger over time), and investigations confirmed that size was largely standardized. Metal water pipes protruding into the pits indicate that water flowed into them, supported by evidence from plat maps. Cesspits of this sort were documented at Newman Camp, Turquoise Station, and Escondida Siding.

One artifact type found at Escondida Siding embodies not only the EP & NE's system-wide calibration, but also the national networks on which the system relied. Investigations recovered more than 50 bronze roofing shingle storm anchors embossed with the word "Chase" from two excavation units around housing inside the fence at Escondida Siding (Figure 3.3). Chase storm anchors were used to hold fire-resistant asbestos roof shingles in place in the windy conditions that prevailed in the Tularosa Basin. They became part of a roofing system used by the Johns Manville Corporation in 1929 (Black 1930). This company produced fire-resistant roofing tiles, beginning in 1858, and eventually became a leading supplier for the U.S. military (Johns Manville 2021). Railroad correspondence indicates that the EP & NE used Johns Manville roofs at a number of stations in the 1930s (SPRGDA, Box LTA20, Folder 2).

FIGURE 3.4. A 1921 plat map of Escondida Siding shows its layout, buildings, features, and perimeter fence (SPRGDA, Box DE-25, File 1). Reprinted by permission of Special Collections Department, University of Texas at El Paso Library.

Snapshot Demographics of the EP & NE

Census records (1910a, 1920a, 1930a, 1940a) offer a fairly clear picture of the demographic make-up of the section camps. A comparison of these with plat maps and aerial photographs of the stations is telling. At Escondida Siding in 1920 (United States Census Bureau 1920a), 15 Mexican railroad workers were all listed as laborers living there. Some lived with wives and small children, although one household composed entirely of single men suggests those individuals lived in a single dormitory. The siding also had one section foreman, Clyde McLopin, who was white and lived with his wife and two small children in the section house. In total, up to 25 people (21 Mexican and four white) lived at Escondida Siding in 1920 (United States Census Bureau 1920a). A short-lived soapworks camp located near the siding hosted an additional 75 Mexican laborers. A plat map for 1921 shows the station with a section house and two long multi-room dormitories, one of brick and one more informal made of rail ties (placed at the fence edge, no less) where Mexican workers and their families lived (Figure 3.4).

However, even if each structure contained four small rooms, those would not have been adequate shelter for 21 people. The enumeration of households and industries in the census suggests that living arrangements must have spilled outside the fenced limits proscribed by the railroad. By 1930 the soapworks camp was gone from the Escondida Siding area, and two section foremen, both white, were living with their families in single family residences (United States Census Bureau 1930a). The remaining 25–30 laborers were Mexican American, most born in either Texas or New Mexico, living dormitory-style in small family units. Although later plat maps and photographs show that the station was remodeled around 1926, worker housing almost certainly remained inadequate to accommodate the number of people stationed there.

Outside the Fence: Making-Do along the EP & NE

As much as the railroad attempted to systematize the places in its domain, the spaces both inside and outside the fence reflect the messiness of daily life that must have contributed to their evolving placeness. The outside-the-fence spaces, in particular, offer vivid examples of the tactics that the mostly Mexican American section workers employed as they negotiated everyday life in what could at times be a desolate wilderness. An informal one-room structure, interpreted as a jacal built from rail ties and scrap lumber, was found at Escondida Siding (Feit and Silberberg 2015:8–90). This ruin, found northeast and outside of the section camp fence, may be one makeshift response to the overcrowding of the railroad-designed space. Although daily negotiations of proscribed versus practical space almost certainly took place inside the fence as well, the jacal's location outside the fence throws the disparity between corporate design and lived experience into glaring relief.

Along these same lines, one of the more interesting patterns to emerge from the investigations of these sites relates to refuse disposal. The archaeological investigations show that the residents of these railroad stops relied heavily on bottled, canned, and refrigerated goods supplied by the railroad. The EP & NE's records indicate that at Desert Station even water had to be supplied (Feit and Silberberg 2015). Consequently, residents generated a large amount of nonperishable refuse. There is no documentary evidence to suggest that the EP & NE organized refuse disposal. Yet, at each residential site, disposal patterns were largely similar. Since the railroad neglected to provide organized trash disposal, section workers created their own system of throwing trash in piles near their camps but outside the fence. Large refuse middens were recorded at Newman, Desert Station, Turquoise Station, and Escondida Siding east of the main camps, outside the fence. In some cases, trash was simply dumped on the surface. In others it was burned, buried, or both. At Escondida Siding, a burned and buried trash scatter, which probably represents a single disposal event that occurred sometime around 1920, was documented in one excavation unit (Feit and Silberberg 2015:8–94).

The material vestiges of the mainly Mexican section workers also reflect a make-do approach to daily life that diverged from the proscriptive nature of the EP & NE's corporate architecture. As previously noted, the railroad supplied many canned foodstuffs. Canned milk, canned fish, and potted meat were among the items carried by railway to the section camps, and remains of those containers were evident on all four sites discussed here. Another foodstuff shipped over the rail line was lard. During investigations, lard buckets were found in abundance at every site. In fact, one feature at Turquoise Station was a large can pile comprising more than 50 lard buckets and other metal containers. Lard combined with nixtamalized corn and water are the key ingredients for masa, used to make the tamales and tortillas that are the foundation of Mexican cookery. A basalt mano and metate found outside the fence at Escondida Siding also suggest that tortillas and tamales were an important part of local diets. Unlike the generic canned goods and other products that were shipped far and wide over the rail line, the mano and metate reflect a more specific identity. Hand-grinding corn on a metate was common in Mexican American households along the borderlands until well into the twentieth century, and it is reasonable to infer that section camp workers or their wives made tamales and tortillas from lard shipped by rail mixed with corn they ground by hand.

The remoteness of stations such as Turquoise or Escondida Siding meant that some resources not brought by train were scarce. Making-do was almost surely part of everyday life. At Turquoise Station, this practice was exemplified by an intentionally perforated sardine tin likely reused as a sieve (Figure 3.5). For access to fresh eggs and meat, section workers raised chickens. A plat map from Escondida Siding shows that residents had their own chicken coop, outside the fence incidentally. Eggshells uncovered in test units at both Escondida Siding and at Desert

FIGURE 3.5. A perforated sardine can likely used as a sieve, from a refuse pile at Turquoise Station. Photograph by Rachel Feit (2014).

Station probably came from chickens that residents raised themselves. Meanwhile, battery cores seemed to be particularly prevalent at one site: Desert Station. Investigators noted more than 30 battery cores through surface survey and unit excavation. These finds imply that reliable electricity was rare at this stop, and that residents had to depend heavily on battery-powered machines and tools rather than utility-supplied energy, which the railroad was apparently not able, or too cheap, to supply.

Conclusion

Places are, to borrow a metaphor from Delores Hayden, like overstuffed suitcases, resonant with meaning (Hayden 1995:15). Importantly, places embody a set of power relations that layer them with multivalent significance. For the spaces built by the EP & NE in the Tularosa Basin, these power relations manifested materially through a misalignment between the planned, corporate architecture of the camps and the pragmatic solutions resorted to by the mostly Mexican American workers who inhabited these places.

For 40 years, the EP & NE railroad promised new wealth, commercial growth, and industry to its supporters in this remote corner of the continent. It defined the built environment through its command over commerce, infrastructure, and even local politics. Its strategic planning was exemplified by an organization of space that boldly signaled its jurisdiction, even in the remote Tularosa Basin where jurisdiction was, by the turn of the century, virtually uncontested. While its section camps, emblemized by the fenced enclosure, were highly programmatic in design, material remains suggest that make-do tactics were a defining aspect of the lived experience of the workers along the EP & NE. This spirit of making-do also had ethnic and class dimensions, since the majority of the inhabitants of the camps were Mexican or Mexican American, who neither exercised control nor had direct contact with the railroad's decision-makers and planners. Yet they both adapted within and altered the framework given to them by the railroad to create unique communities of practice. Their lived experience of making-do—of finding solutions to food, shelter, waste disposal, and even electrical supply—circumscribed daily life and conferred placeness to the railroad stops of the Tularosa Basin.

4

In Defense of the Fence

Melonie Shier

In comparison to other placemaking themes of the American West, homestead sites of farming and ranching as place have been underrepresented in archaeological research. John Wilson (1990) and Mark Groover (2008) both observed that although there are "thousands of them," many archaeologists tend to ignore the research potential of homestead sites. Homesteads are "frequently determined either eligible for the National Register simply because they 'may contain data on nineteenth-century lifeways' or ineligible because they are 'typical of thousands of nineteenth-century farm sites'" (Wilson 1990:23). Agricultural properties, of which homesteads are generally a type, are incredibly important to understanding past lifeways. One in three Americans lived and worked on an agricultural property, even as late as the 1920s (Groover 2008; Hardesty and Little 2009:146).

Frequently, the only part of an agricultural property that is recorded is the domestic locale (Adams 1990). While the domestic site is important, it is of equal research value to determine the full extent and boundary of a homestead through present and extinct fence lines (Adams 1990; Wilson 1990):

> A site is more than just the house, yard, and outbuildings. Thus, a 640 acres farm comprises a site. It must be studied in its entirety, not in pieces. Such a site included affected and unaffected environments. All areas used by a farm family to produce a crop or to produce energy would be included whether the land was owned or leased [Adams 1990:93].

Fence lines were commonly used to delineate boundaries in Euro-American domestic and agricultural sites. Fence lines not only created a functional boundary between locales but a spatial boundary from which place was made as spaces were defined and assigned meaning.

Placemaking occurred through the appropriation of space beyond the domestic sphere. Of vital importance to this placemaking practice in agriculture is the building, maintaining, altering, and/or neglect of fence lines. As a linear feature, with both a strong physical presence and the propensity for extended usage, fence lines can provide insight into the ideological placemaking habits of people in the past. Placemaking was undertaken through fence construction as a part of outward expressions of gentility, reflecting personal and family wealth, status, and notoriety (Bourcier 1984:547). In particular, the quality and overall aesthetics of the fence was equated to the competency of the farmer (Bourcier 1984; Danhof 1944:169). A competent farmer had a well-defined space and place.

Folklorist Henry Glassie (1968) argued that various regions of the United States could be identified strictly by looking at the shape, form, and construction of the fences people made in that area. In other words, the performativity of placemaking is identifiable through fence lines. Performativity is not performance in the manner of actors on a stage, but the "stylized repetition of acts" (quoting Butler 1990 in Fortier 1999:48) in a particular social context. Performative acts go beyond the individual in that they are binding to the larger community (Fortier 1999:43).

Due to their connection to the larger community, an understanding of the performative nature of fence line choice and construction can lead to a better understanding of the view that agricultural communities hold toward placemaking. Construction of fence-lines was not only driven by utilitarian usage but by the performative ideology of homesteaders. An international comparison between the Western United States and Australia demonstrates this point. Barbwire fence lines are deeply ingrained in American West mythologies and have become paramount in the visual landscape as a methodology of space delineation (Bennett and Abbot 2014; Hayter 1939). Comparatively, although wire technology is common in Australia, the post and rail is the most dominant fencing form in Australia (Pickard 2005). The post and rail fence has come to represent the rurality of Australia and, as such, is an iconography that is used in popular media to represent an intentional performativity there (Pickard 2005:44–45). Thus, the ways in which Australian and American West agriculturalists utilize fence lines in placemaking is rooted in historical performative ideologies.

Introduction to Area of Study

This chapter seeks to not only understand how fence types defined placemaking practices, but also the performative nature of fence lines. The Wind Wolves Preserve provides an excellent study area as an example of how placemaking through fence construction occurred in a large landscape. The 93,000 acre preserve spreads across the San Emigdio Hills west of Highway 5 in Southwest Kern County, California (Shier 2016).

The San Emigdio Hills has a rich history that includes a 1840s Mexican-era land grant and over 200 American homesteads. Eventually, the various individual properties were amalgamated into the Kern County Land Company (Morgan 1914). Over the next 65 years, the San Emigdio Hills served as an important cattle husbandry locale in a greater network of agricultural and manufacturing ventures across the globe operated by the Kern County Land Company (Robbins 1994). With the purchase of the San Emigdio Hills by the Wildlands Conservancy in 1995, the Hills were set aside as the Wind Wolves Preserve, a nature preserve dedicated to educating youth on the outdoors (Shier 2016).

The Wind Wolves Preserve continues to utilize many of the fence lines put into place by historical figures (Kern County Land Company 1969; Shier 2016). During work undertaken for my doctoral thesis, I recorded a number of sites throughout the San Emigdio Hills which include historic fence lines. The primary site discussed in this paper is the administrative center or "Headquarters" of the San Emigdio Hills complex and is located, both historically and contemporarily, at the mouth of San Emigdio Canyon. With this brief introduction to the area of study, the work of understanding the historic background and importance of fence lines can begin.

Fence Line Features and Dating Strategies

Much of the available cross-discipline research on fence lines occurred in the mid-1900s (e.g., Danhof 1944; Hayter 1939, 1945; Larsen and Kalm 1947; Mather and Hart 1954; McFadden 1978; Raup 1947). Only very recently have researchers started to refocus their attention on these historically significant linear features (see Bennett and Abbott 2014; Pickard 2005; Shier 2016). The bulk of the scholarly work focuses on the costs of particular fence typographies (such as Hayter 1939; McFadden 1978; Pickard 2005), or on the patent and monopoly of fencing strategies (Bennett and Abbott 2014:568; McFadden 1978).

The cumulative sum of the available literature provides clues to the ideology behind the construction, even when focused on the functionalism. While fence lines are strong linear features, they are composed of various parts, many of which can be used to date and understand the construction and alterations of the fence line.

The California Department of Transportation released a series of thematic studies of California archaeology "to assist with evaluating the information potential of [archaeological] properties in California, that is, for their eligibility for the National Register of Historic Places" (California Department of Transportation 2007:i). These works are primarily for proposing research designs and an evaluation framework for researchers in California (California Department of Transportation 2007:i).

Fences are included in the thematic guide for agricultural properties. The guide suggests looking at "posts for machine-cut vs wire nails, and other types of hardware" (California Department of Transportation 2007:107), including wire segments, for possible clues to understanding when the fence was constructed. Of the wire fence lines, barbwire can be dated, if recorded accurately with a guide to its identification in mind.

Perhaps the best guide to identify and date different types of barbwire is the Harold Hagemeier (2010) guide, originally printed in 1998, with several updated additions. The guide primarily provides patent numbers which can then be correlated back to the online patent registry through the United States Patent and Trademark Office or through Google Patents. To best use the Hagemeier guide, I strongly suggest taking a picture of an example barb on the line to compare with the guide's illustrations of several hundred samples, instead of just a description. Barbs can be placed over one or both strands of the wire; additionally, the angle and style of the twist of the barb is what differentiates one kind from another (Hagemeier 2010; Shier 2016).

At historical sites, it is very common for only the posts of extinct fence lines to remain. Regardless of the material of the fence post, they can provide some insight into the life biography of the general fence line as related to the performative ideologies of the past. Unfortunately, the California Department of Transportation framework does not recognize the dating and informational potential of the fence posts individually. The posts are datable, such as through dendrochronology, morphology, or seriation studies of the types of fencing methods used. Further research into fence posts needs to be undertaken to create timelines of usage, as well as to highlight regional variation of materials.

For the first half of the twentieth century, the preferred post type was the wooden fence of local wood sources (Mather and Hart 1954:212). In California, John S. Hittell suggested the use of "5 ft board fences, with redwood posts spaced 8 ft apart and five spruce rails 6 in wide" (Raup 1947:2). An 1888 manual remarks that "the best timber for posts, in the order of its durability, is red cedar, yellow locust, black walnut, white oak, and chestnut" (Adams 1990:94). The Sears Roebuck Catalog (1955:1202) primarily includes white cedar and chemically treated pine poles. These primary historical documents suggest that seriation studies are possible.

The biggest problem faced by all fence types that involve a post set in the ground is rot and decay. An observer in 1947 remarked that fence posts lasted only four to eight years (Larsen and Kalm 1947:77). The problem of rotted wooden fence posts was overcome by the practice of charring the post, as well as using rocks, ash, charcoal, or lime in the backfill (Adams 1990: 94). The presence of these attributes on a fence post are indicators of a historically older fence line. Raup (1947:4) recommends soaking the posts in creosote for five hours to increase the life of the post by eight years. Treated pine posts in the 1965 Sears Roebuck Catalog are advertised as able to last 30 years (Sears Roebuck & Co 1965:949) as a result of the creosote process. Future research could establish the validity of distributers' claims in these practices.

During the surveying of various sites in the San Emigdio Hills, I observed both wood and metal fence posts. The wood posts include rough, locally produced oak branches and mechanically milled lumber posts in round, rectangular, or railroad tie variants (Shier 2016). The metal posts include several different types of hollow pole posts, self-fastening metal posts, T-posts, and two "lasagna" posts. The T-posts alone were used to create a sheep corral in the San Emigdio Hills (Sheep Corrals, SEAH2014-002), consisting of 146 metal line posts in 11 different variations in red, green, or gray (Shier 2016). When I attempted to date the posts, I found little to no information on the metal line posts, even though some were stamped with a Soule brand mark.

I undertook a typography study of metal line posts by gleaning advertisement information from the Sears Roebuck & Company Catalog published over the course of about a century from the fall 1896 catalog to the 1993 catalog (Sears Roebuck & Co 1896–1993). Most of the catalog years have both a spring and fall edition, and both were inspected for fencing materials. The two gaps in Figure 4.1 coincide with World War I and World War II.

Metal posts do not feature in the catalog until 1909, when they appear in two varieties: one is a smooth metal pole with a base designed to splay open as it is installed, to provide anchoring, and the other is an angle post (the steel is bent to a right angle to be set in concrete) with punch fastening technology (Sears Roebuck & Co 1909:1076). Over the next 70 years, three types of line posts were advertised: the angle post, the channel post, and the T-post (Figure 4.1, Numbered 3, 2, and 1 respectively). All three post types used punch and self-fastening wire (Sears Catalog terminology), fastening techniques that secure the wire to the post in different ways (Sears Roebuck & Co 1896–1993). Fastening technology included punch, self-fastening, and studded (Sears Roebuck & Co 1896–1993). Both line post shape and fastening method together should be recorded for dating purposes in the field.

Recording the shape alone is not enough. For example, the T-post was advertised as early as 1924 (Sears Roebuck & Co 1924:1046), but the studded T-post was only manufactured after 1948 (Sears Roebuck & Co 1948:1273). Both the studded T-post and the self-fastening channel post are still in production. However, the studded T-post is advertised toward use in agricultural area while the self-fastening channel post is for use in lawn and garden (Sears Roebuck & Co 1965:949).

Further research into the posts themselves needs to be done to determine regional variability (as suggested by Glassie 1968) and identification of other chronologically significant features, such as anchor plate design or line post coloration. The earliest color-tipped metal line post was trademarked in 1918 (consisting of a red line across the top of the post) by the Chicago Steel Post Company (Chicago Steel Post Company 1919). The research potential is significant enough that fence lines could provide numerous new lines of insight into placemaking practices and identity formation performativity.

Fence Lines in San Emigdio

These various fence components—post, railing material, and anchoring materials—are used to build a fence line. Particularly helpful in defining different fence types is the 1969 work of Martin Primack. Primack (1969) researched the historiography of different fence types and when they were most common from the 1850s to 1910 (Table 4.1). The types most commonly found within the contemporary past in the United States include worm, post and rail, board, stone, hedge, and wire fences (with both strand and woven wires). All of the types of fence lines discussed by Primack can be found within various California contexts, and most can be found in the San Emigdio Hills, such as the post and rail, stone, hedge, and wire. The discussion of different fence lines is laid out in the same order as presented by Primack since his research follows a loose temporal timeline. The wire fence lines are more heavily discussed than the other types as they are the most common in the project area.

Each of these fence lines had slightly different historical narratives and performative ideology associated to them, which will be briefly discussed. Not only will an understanding of

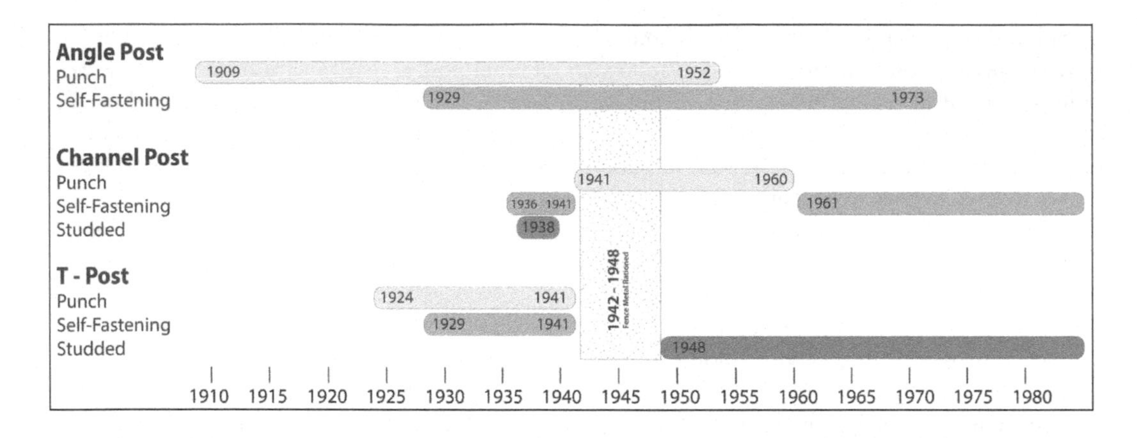

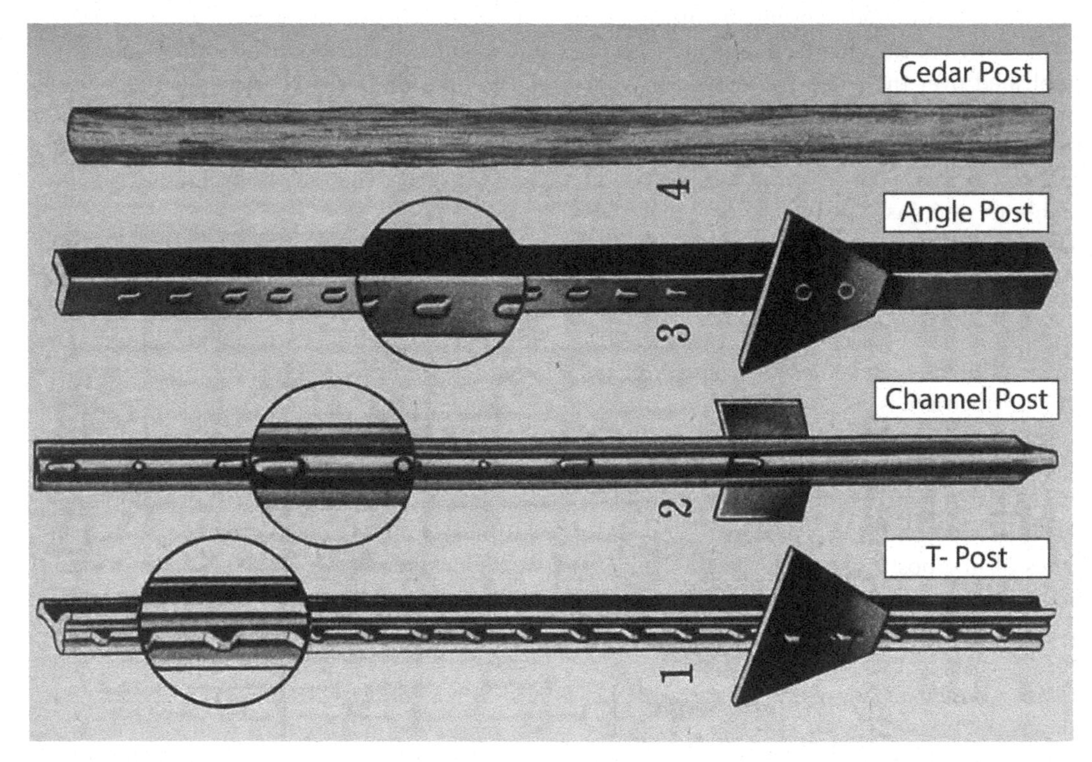

FIGURE 4.1. Fence post typography. *Above*: Date ranges for the three metal post varieties sold by Sears & Roebuck Catalog between 1909 and 1980 (Sears Roebuck & Co. 1896–1993). From 1942 to 1948 the catalog did not sell metal fence posts as supplies were rationed during World War II (Sears Roebuck & Co 1942:1003F). The self-fastening channel post sold after 1961 had an alternating punch and self-fastening wire installation system. *Below*: Line post variety of wood and metal for sale from the Sears Roebuck & Co (1965): 1 is a studded T-Post sold 1948 to modern; 2 is an alternating punch and self-fastening channel post sold 1961 to today; 3 is a self-fastening angle post sold 1929 to 1973; 4 is a white cedar post.

TABLE 4.1. Percent of Each Kind of Fence.

Fence	1850	1860	1870	1880	1890	1900	1910
Worm	79	73	64	58	18	12	*
Post and Rail	9	9	9	8	12	*	*
Board	5	8	12	17	21	13*	15*
Stone	7	6	5	4	—	—	—
Hedge	—	2	3	4	—	—	—
Wire	—	3	7	9	49	67	85

Note: Data from US Department of Agriculture statistics (Primack 1969:88); blanks indicate insignificant percentiles.
* Data combines worm, post and rail, and board fence lines.

the general performative nature of fence lines be understood, but how this related to placemaking within the San Emigdio Hills.

Post and Rail

Edmund Burnett (1948) became so distressed by a newspaper article that encouraged the burning of old rail fences as agriculturalists installed barb wire that he sent his views to the media. He lamented:

> The widespread adoption of wire instead of rails for making fences has already played havoc with farm life. It has gone far toward transforming the farmer, from a neighborly, sociable, reflective person, into an unsympathetic, unprogressively uncivil being, the clodhopper, the hayseed of urban gibe [Burnett 1948:31].

Fence choice for Burnett, was more than an economical one, but driven by a particular ideology linked to the performative activities that occurred at the post and rail fence. The activities that created community also served to express the placemaking ideology of the community and of Burnett.

Burnett further reminisces that upon the top of a rail fence, men of a community could come "sit on the fence, whittle a rail apiece, smoke a pipe apiece, [and] hold delightful and unhurried discourse" (Burnett 1948:31) about any given topic. Post and rail fences were communal space in which neighbors worked together in the placemaking activity.

Post and rail fence lines were used historically in the San Emigdio Hills. During the visit of photographer Carleton Watkins, more famously known for his Yosemite photographs (Loeffler 1992), to southern Kern County in the 1880s on behalf of the Kern County Land Company, Watkins took images of the San Emigdio Hills. Of these images, several show post and rail fence lines in the background (Brewer 1999). The overview of the "Headquarters" image shows three different post and rail fences. The fence lines near the barn and residence are painted white to match the coloring of the barn and house, while the sheep coral lines are left "natural." The painted post and rail fences define the domestic place, while the natural lines define the working place. The visual cue of painted versus unpainted provides a performative differentiation between the two places that would have been recognized by visitors to Headquarters as synonymous with the corporate identity of the Kern County Land Company.

Other Kern County Land Company agriculturally related properties also include white post and rail fence lines near domestic locales with the same patterning and rail distancing (Brewer 1999). The repetition of a particular visual cue is performative. The placemaking association with the construction of the post and rail fence lines of Headquarters presents a particular outward expression of identity and agricultural gentility that was repeated across all Kern County Land Company agriculturally related properties. Through the repetition of color and style, the company created a sense of place through physical features to connect their corporate spaces and identity together, creating a unique landscape identifiable as the Kern County Land Company. This shows how placemaking occurs for groups not only on "small scale" (93,000 acres, Kern County Land Company 1969) ranches but across the entire infrastructure of the Land Company (Shier 2016).

Stone

Historically, stone walls are probably more common in areas characterized by particularly rocky soil (Raup 1947). Rock wall building may also be a part of field clearing for crops, as the rocks can cause expensive damage to machinery (Shier 2016).

Within the San Emigdio Hills, all the stone fences are modern builds of the Wind Wolves Preserve, an organization continually developing their placemaking in the landscape. The stone fence lines are at the Preserve entrance and locations frequented by the public during visitation. The stone fence lines signal a major performative shift in land usage, away from an agriculturally focused locale to a landscape reflecting modern ideologies of nature.

The performativity of the stone walls implies a rustic/natural feeling to the Wind Wolves Preserve that purposefully invokes a visual similarity to the National Parks System, particularly Yosemite National Park (Dan York, personal communication 2014). The Preserve actively uses the stone fence lines to connect with a distant landscape that is laden with performative and ideological narratives of placemaking association with the preservation of "natural" landscapes for the use and enjoyment of future generations of people in the Western United States.

Hedge

Hedge fences are constructed from living trees and shrubs of various species (Mather and Hart 1954:209–210). The hedge fence is the least common fence type within the United States, particularly after the invention of wire fencing methods (Mather and Hart 1954:211). During westward expansion throughout the 1800s, experiments occurred with trees and shrubs, such as the Osage orange (*Maclura pomifera*), honey locust (*Gleditsia triacanthos*), and multiflora rose (*Rosa multiflora*) (Mather and Hart 1954:210). In Southern California, cacti variants such as the prickly pear (*Opuntia tuna*) or octotilla (*Fouquieria splendens*) were used particularly during the Mission Period of California history (Raup 1947:2). Cacti hedges are still commonly seen in Kern County and much of southern California, but are not found in the San Emigdio Hills.

In addition to the cacti hedge fence, eucalyptus tree lines are a common hedge fence of Southern California (Farmer 2013, Santos 1997). Brought from Australia in the early 1850s, these trees had a particular heyday between the 1880s and the 1930s (Santos 1997) as a replacement for native species for firewood and lumber (Farmer 2013). The tree was commonly used along roads and boundaries (Farmer 2013; Santos 1997). The tree is so common it has developed a performative association that is synonymous with California identity (Farmer 2013). To experience the eucalyptus in California is to experience the placemaking of Euro-American Californians.

Within Feature #1 at Headquarters (SEAH 2013-HQ) is a dumping event that consists of seven piles of tree remains (equating to about 26 trees), a rock pile, a cement pile, and an incised boulder. Before their removal, the eucalyptus trees (Figure 4.2) lined the entrance road to Headquarters for about a quarter mile (Dixon 1918).

As with the post and rail fence, the eucalyptus tree line hedge was a performative choice to link the San Emigdio Hills to other Kern County Land Company properties. Even within the San Emigdio Hills several secondary domestic locales spread across the range include eucalyptus trees (Shier 2016). Not only did the eucalyptus line provide a performative visual cue but an olfactory element as well. The distinct aroma of the eucalyptus links the tree to a general California placemaking ideology (Farmer 2013), which the Kern County Land Company utilized in their own placemaking activities to highlight the "clean" mountain air of the ranch (Shier 2016).

FIGURE 4.2. The eucalyptus-lined road leading into Headquarters in San Emigdio Canyon of the Wind Wolves Preserve (Moser 1989). The tree lines are a type of hedge fence. Courtesy of Wind Wolves Preserve.

Wire

Wire fences are by far the most common fence type encountered during field archaeology in the American West. Wire fence types include plain wire, woven wire, and barbwire technologies. All three of these types can be found in the San Emigdio Hills, although neither plain nor woven wire are as common as barbwire.

Plain wire fences were used as early as the mid-1800s (McFadden 1978; Pickard 2005:30), copying in form the post and rail fence structure. Early wire fence lines were unsuccessful as the wire was susceptible to weathering (Primack 1969:287), and livestock routinely "loosened the posts and broke the wire by constantly rubbing against it" (Hayter 1939:189–190). With the advent of the Bessemer process, wire was produced more cheaply and made more rust-resistant (Primack 1969:287).

Certain types of woven wires are known for the animals they are marketed toward, such as chicken or hog wire (McFadden 1978). Various types of woven wire are found in the Sears Roebuck Catalog from 1897 (Sears Roebuck & Co 1897:41–43), but may have been on the market as early as the 1880s (McFadden 1978). Images from Rancho El Tejon, in the canyon east of the San Emigdio Hills, show chicken wire in an image also taken by Carleton Watkins in the 1880s (Latta 2006:76). In urban settings, woven wire would make way for chain-link fences, available in the Sears Roebuck Catalog in 1935 (Sears Roebuck & Co 1935:938).

Chain link on metal pipe posts is observed in images of Headquarters from the 1980s (Moser 1989). By this time there were about half a dozen individual residences and a bunkhouse (Shier 2016, Moser 1989). The chain link replaced the white painted post and rail fence line of a century before, reflecting contemporary placemaking attitudes of the 1980s. The residents of 1980s Headquarters made performative choices in fencing material to link their placemaking behavior and sense of community to urban dwelling spaces, even though the homes were still situated in a rural setting.

The Wind Wolves Preserve has reconfigured Headquarters by removing almost all former agricultural vestiges from the vicinity. All the chain-link fence lines were removed during the transformation from an urbanized residential company headquarters to an administrative center for the Wind Wolves Preserve staff. However, the Wind Wolves Preserve utilizes many of the historical barbwire fence lines put into place by the Kern County Land Company (Shier

2016). A 1969 map of the Kern County Land Company used to show the locations of watering troughs and pipes also illustrates the extent of the fence lines in that period (Kern County Land Company 1969).

While the Wind Wolves Preserve seeks to link Headquarters to the National Parks system, the more expansive barbwire fence lines continue to link the San Emigdio Hills to its agricultural past. Its history of pastoral animal husbandry makes the San Emigdio Hills well suited to be a nature preserve. This placemaking fact is not erased by contemporary use of the landscape but is embraced through the performative usage of barbed wire lines to protect the landscape. The Wind Wolves Preserve is continuing to create place and develop landscape identity through fence line choices, which are rooted in performative decision-making processes.

Conclusion

As biographies of homesteads in the American West are identified, a greater understanding of how people made place in the American West is understood. Glassie (1968) surmised that fences identified locales, and as the seemingly endless vista of barbed wire is recorded, new trends in Western placemaking will come to light. The more work that is undertaken in recording and dating of both fence lines and their components will strengthen future dating of all fence types.

Beyond the use of component material to date construction and alteration of fence lines, the component materials show regional placemaking practices and preferences. The seriation study from the Sears & Roebuck Catalog concerns shipped line posts from Chicago, Illinois (Sears & Roebuck 1941:967F). The posts from Sheep Corral in the San Emigdio Hills are manufactured by a California-based company no longer in production (Jim Soule, personal communication 2014). Through further work in fence lines and fence line construction, new understanding of regional variations and production methodologies can be learned.

This chapter has sought not only to understand fence lines as datable features in a landscape, but also to suggest how choices in construction material and typography are used to outwardly express particular ideologies. The ideological background that both motivated and encouraged the construction of different fence types is important. The ideas that underpin the choices made by people in the past have been influenced by the outward performativity expressed to the community through repeated symbols.

The placemaking identity of Headquarters in the San Emigdio Hills is experienced in part through the performativity of fence lines. The fence lines are bodily experienced as performative communications through visual, olfactory, and physical means (Rodaway 1994). The eucalyptus hedge fence is both a visual and an olfactory experience, informing visitors they are about to enter Headquarters. Within Headquarters, space was distinguished through fence lines. In the 1880s, the coloration of post and rail lines differentiated where the domestic and agricultural spaces merged but also linked Headquarters to the multinational Kern County Land Company corporate identity. By the 1980s, chain-link fences were used to distinguish the small rural collection of houses as a community akin to those found in urban settings. Today, rock fences and barbwire fences continue to define the space of the Wind Wolves Preserve as both rural and natural.

Rooted in the iconography of the American West, fence lines define placemaking practices within the American West. Additionally, fence lines have a unique ability in informing how place was made beyond domestic sites, particularly in agriculturally situated homestead sites. As observed by Adams (1990), the entire 640 acre homestead is the site of placemaking. In the case of the San Emigdio Hills, the 93,000 acres of preserve is a site with an abundance of performative linear features and placemaking markers which are equal parts typical and unique to the American West.

5

Axes and Agency

Chinese Choices at Mineral County, Nevada, Woodcutting Camps, 1880–1920

Emily Dale

From the 1880s to the 1920s, Chinese workers around Aurora, Nevada and Bodie, California successfully entered the woodcutting industry. Based out of Chinese-owned and Chinese-operated rural woodcutting camps in the mountains surrounding the mining towns, Chinese woodcutters supplied urban families and businesses with cordwood and, in some cases, charcoal. In this chapter, I examine the ways Chinese woodcutters displayed purposeful labor strategies at their woodcutting camps and explore the connections between these rural spaces and urban centers. The agency and choices of the Chinese are written on the landscape in the decisions they made concerning their site placement and construction, expressions of labor and masculinity, and consumption habits.

History

Aurora, Nevada and Bodie, California were established as important social, economic, and political centers in the late 1800s. Drawn by promising gold and silver deposits, Aurora's population reached at least 5,000 by 1863 (Shaw 2009:14), while Bodie's peaked around 10,000 hopeful inhabitants by 1878 (Jimenez 2000:2–3).

Among the towns' populations were numerous Chinese residents. Aurora's Chinese population was small, at around 30 individuals (Alta California 1863). The number of Bodie's Chinese inhabitants was much larger, consisting of over 250 individuals, or nearly 5% of the town's entire population in 1880 (United States Census Bureau, 1880a), most of whom lived in the sizeable King Street Chinatown.

Chinese inhabitants of both towns lived under the constant presence of discrimination (see Dale 2011, 2015, 2019). The Chinese community was harassed, threatened with violence, and, in some cases, physically attacked by their Euro-American neighbors. In 1864, Aurora's Board of Aldermen passed Ordinance 32, which required the Chinese to relocate to Spring Street (Esmeralda Daily Union 1864). The attempt to create a Chinatown was seemingly short-lived. Archaeological investigations of Spring Street indicated that the area was largely abandoned by the 1870s, and historical records from the 1880s demonstrate that the Chinese were living scattered throughout the town (Dale 2011, 2019). Similarly, numerous attempts in Bodie to boycott Chinese labor, rally support for the anti-Chinese Workingman's Party, or establish a League of Deliverance failed to generate lasting interest.

Meanwhile, the growth of the two urban centers created opportunities for businesses in the rural areas surrounding the towns. Ranchers

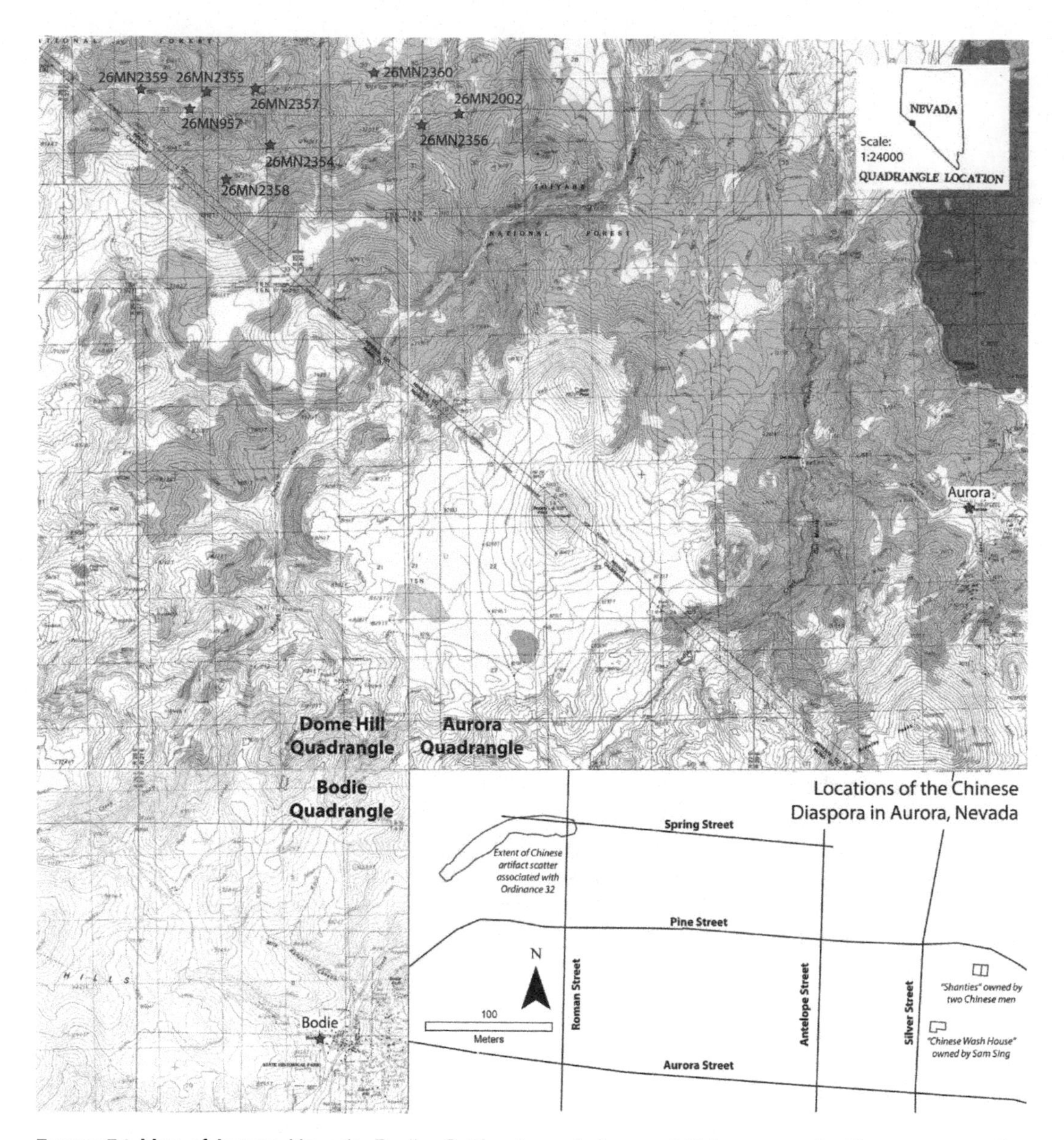

FIGURE 5.1. Map of Aurora, Nevada; Bodie, California; and nine rural Chinese woodcutting camps north of the urban centers. The inset shows the location of prominent Chinese sites in Aurora.

congregated around the nearby Sweetwater and Walker Rivers and their smaller tributaries. Miners prospected further out along Rough and Arrastra Creeks. And Chinese entrepreneurs entered the woodcutting industry on Table Mountain, located to the north of Aurora and Bodie, to harvest cordwood to sell to residents (Figure 5.1).

Chinese Woodcutting Camps

Wood was a scarce commodity in Aurora and Bodie due to the enormous demands of the mines and mills, and Chinese businessmen quickly identified the growing need as an economic opportunity. South China had a long history of logging and woodcutting, so the occupation was likely familiar to some of the Chinese immigrants (Chung 2015:3–4). Bodie especially required imports of wood as the hills surrounding the town were naturally barren. Wood camps operated by Euro-Americans, Mexicans, and Chinese sprang up to meet the demand in the two towns. The census records reported approximately 35 Chinese workers in the woodcutting industry over the years (United States Census Bureau 1870, 1880a, 1880b, 1900a, 1910b, 1910c). It is likely that many of the "laborers" recorded by census takers were also in the wood business, particularly the 17 Chinese laborers recorded on Table Mountain in 1880 (United States Census Bureau 1880b) (Table 5.1).

The earliest account of Chinese individuals successfully entering the woodcutting business was in 1878, when Sam Chung employed several Chinese men to bring wood into town (Bodie Weekly Standard, 4 December 1878). From 1880 to 1881, the appearance of a Chinese mule train laden with cordwood was a common occurrence in Bodie, as noted in the local newspapers and recorded by photographers. Success in the industry was based on various factors, including the amount of wood cut, the ability to bring the wood to customers, and the general price of cordwood.

The newspapers frequently commented on the productive harvests of the woodcutters as they brought their wares to town for sale to households and businesses. One Chinese woodcutter stored over 300 cords of wood on his Bodie Chinatown lot, with an expected profit of $3 per cord once winter arrived (Daily Free Press, 16 July 1881e). Another Chinese man estimated that he had over 1,000 cords of wood ready for delivery to Bodie (Daily Free Press, 10 March 1882b). In 1881, Chinese woodcutters were rumored to have harvested over 20,000 cords of wood (Daily Free Press, 3 September 1881h). As previously mentioned, several members of Aurora's and Bodie's communities viewed the possibility of being surpassed by Chinese businesses as threatening. Perhaps as a compromise, in 1882, Chinese woodcutters chose to sell wood to Bodie families for a set price of $9.50 per cord (Daily Free Press, 31 August 1882e). As average prices hovered around $10, but could reach as high as $20 or $25 during harsh winters (Bodie Morning News, 22 April 1880), entrepreneurial woodcutters willingly sacrificed some profits for the assurance of a friendlier market and more predictable sales. Such a strategy may also have averted race-based violence and resentment from the town's white residents who often called on the inhabitants to purchase from white businesses only.

Agency and Rural Labor

In order to meaningfully address the Chinese roles in Aurora, Bodie, and the rural camps, it is important to address the choices they made in these places. At its heart, agency is the ability to act and self-determine. Lesure described agency as allowing for "creative, strategizing subjects" (2005:237), while Silliman (2001:192) maintained that agency permits people to act freely and strategically while simultaneously requiring some concessions that allow them to survive. In other words, agency is subject to both freedom and limitations. Agency is rarely discussed explicitly in the archaeology of the Chinese diaspora. The recent incorporation of transnationalism (e.g., Hsu 2000; Kraus-Friedberg 2008; Ross 2012, 2013; Voss 2016) and diaspora (e.g., González-Tennant 2011; Voss 2005) invites the use of agency in the field, but it is not intrinsic to these theoretical approaches. Still, agency is critical for an emic understanding of Chinese behavior that fully realizes the Chinese as active participants in social and economic systems, and, therefore, is a key aspect of my approach to understanding Chinese placemaking.

As the agency of the Chinese laborers in this case study centers on both urban and rural spaces, it is also important to address how those places relate to one another. As such, I situate Chinese agency and place within a framework derived from World Systems Theory. World Systems Theory (Wallerstein 1974, 1980) relies on the assumption that labor is a commodity existing on the periphery, ripe for exploitation by the core (Silliman 2006:148). Archaeologists who contextualize the American West as a periphery (e.g., Farnsworth 1989; Hardesty 1991b) have unsurprisingly situated the labor found at the mines, mills, railroads, cattle ranches, missions, and other Western industries they study within economic core/periphery systems drawn from Wallerstein.

The study of 1800s and 1900s Chinese migration filtered through the lens of World Systems Theory necessitates a transnational, transpacific approach (Voss 2016). The shifting labor market from China to the United States provided opportunities for Chinese workers to relocate their labor from one set of cores and peripheries in China to others, including the United States, Australia, Canada, and South America (e.g., González-Tennant 2001; Ross 2012). Yet, while Chinese immigrants emigrated from their homes, they were still connected to their culture and traditions, bringing parts of their own cores and peripheries with them.

World Systems Theory can also account for connections between local cores and peripheries that impacted Chinese labor and agency. Dixon and Smith (2017), for example, argue that rural Chinese wood camps in the Sierra Nevadas cannot be divorced from their association with the distant boomtowns of Nevada's Comstock era.

Even though World Systems Theory inevitably assigns the majority of power to the cores, the relationships between core and periphery are more complex, with agency present in both. As a result, Chinese immigrants became part of local economic, political, and social World Systems while still a part of the larger, transpacific World Systems that connected them back home. Their agency, then, is displayed through numerous choices that hinged on both global and local relationships.

In combining agency with a localized model of World Systems Theory, this chapter positions the urban mining towns of Aurora and Bodie as local cores, with the rural woodcutting camps serving as their peripheries. Three key components to this assessment are explored here. First, the Chinese woodcutters of Mineral County, Nevada and Mono County, California were agentic actors whose actions and choices are visible in the archaeological record. Second, while Chinese choices were constrained by the economic fates of the urban centers and anti-Chinese discrimination, they were not solely dependent on those factors. Third, Chinese workers at the rural woodcutting camps were not passive victims of urban exploitation. Rather, they actively seized upon economic trends and exploited demand for cordwood for their own benefit, simultaneously embracing and inverting the power dynamics between the core and periphery. As a result, the core was dependent on the Chinese labor produced at the woodcutting camps. In other words, this chapter puts Chinese people residing and working in the social, economic, and geographic periphery in the role of exploiter, rather than exploited.

The interplay between urban and rural and related evidence for Chinese agency are visible in the landscape and the places the Chinese constructed to conduct their woodcutting. Specifically, Chinese construction methods and architecture, gendered labor, and consumption habits demonstrate the choices Chinese woodcutters made and the economic and social power of these rural places.

Nine sites were surveyed, mapped, and photographed in 2013 and 2014 in conjunction with the Forest Service's Passport in Time program and University of Nevada, Reno field schools. Excavations were conducted at one woodcutting camp in 2014. Additional artifacts used in this research were donated by Robert Morrill, a private collector who visited eight of the camps in the 1960s and 1970s, in a productive collaboration between collector, the Forest Service, the Nevada State Museum, and myself.

Architecture and Construction

The location and construction methods of Chinese laborers in the rural woodcutting camps clearly display agency and choices made by the woodcutters. While Chinese residents of urban centers largely moved into preexisting lots with preexisting structures, at the woodcutting camps, they had more freedom to construct spaces from scratch. As a result, the rural structures display the personal choices, idiosyncrasies, and con-

FIGURE 5.2. Dugout cabin at one of the Chinese woodcutting camps. Note the rock walls, gabled roof, and thatching. Photograph by Robert Morrill in May 1967 or 1969. Courtesy of Robert Morrill.

struction knowledge or building capabilities of the individual camp owners and laborers.

The primary motivator for camp location was proximity to essential resources for their businesses, and the Chinese woodcutters selected places for a variety of necessary features. First, neighboring timberlands were vital for efficient labor. Second, the Chinese laborers placed their camps near streams and springs for the abundance of water in the dry mountain environment. Finally, the woodcutters chose locations near trails that led to the main roads to Aurora, Bodie, and other towns which allowed for easy access to urban markets. All the camps were located near at least one of these features, and most were sited adjacent to multiple resources.

In addition to similar location features, Chinese woodcutters employed consistent architectural methods. Structures, for example, demonstrate both a sense of permanency and expediency. Sizeable dugout cabins were supported with dry-laid rock walls and key timber supports. Roofs were constructed from wooden beams, many with the bark still attached, and thatched with willow and earth (Figure 5.2). The calculated use of stone over wood likely represents both economic and practical strategies. Stone was abundant in the area, and wood was more valuable as a commodity to sell than as a building material.

The innovations present at the camps may be the result of individual ingenuity or more practical needs. For example, one camp had a large corral, constructed with dry-laid rock walls, into which juniper posts were placed and strung with wire. It may be that the owner had a large herd of mules or raised pigs and so constructed a permanent feature to contain them. This camp was also one of the largest in terms of area and number of structures, suggesting the owner of the camp was more successful and had a larger operation.

Three of the rural camps exhibited heightened attention to security measures. The Chinese woodcutters placed locks and chains on their dugouts, a practice singular to three sites and absent at known urban Chinese sites. The

TABLE 5.1. Location and Number of Chinese in the Woodcutting Industry, 1870–1910.

Year	Location	Job Description	Number
1870	Aurora	Wood Chopper	3
1880	Bodie	Wood Hauling	12
	Table Mountain	Laborer[a]	21
1900	Bodie	Wood Cutter	1
	"Wood Camp about 10 miles North of Bodie"	Wood Cutter	6
		Wood Packer	5
		Wood Chopper	3
		Coal Burner	1
1910	Aurora	Wood Chopper	2
	Bodie	Wood Chopping-Cord	2
		Wood Dealer	1
		Wood Chopper	1

Note: As recorded in the United States Census (1870, 1880a, 1880b. 1900a, 1910b, 1910c).
[a] There are no Chinese individuals listed in the wood industry on Table Mountain, a major location of woodcutting, in 1880. Instead, they all appear to be recorded as laborers.

camps were seasonally occupied, meaning they could be abandoned for long stretches of time. They were also isolated, making the possessions and safety of the laborers more vulnerable. Competition between woodcutters or the presence of nomadic Paiute in the area may have spurred these precautions. Several newspaper articles indicated economic tensions between the Paiute and Chinese (Daily Free Press, 1 October 1882f), and both groups worked in the woodcutting industry, occasionally competing for customers (Bodie Weekly Standard, 4 December 1878; Daily Evening Bulletin, 16 April 1862; Sacramento Daily Union, 24 February 1868). Chinese woodcutters also had antagonistic encounters with trespassers. In one such encroachment, Sam Chung, one of the first Chinese businessmen to enter the woodcutting industry, shot and killed a Mexican woodchopper whose mules trampled Chung's unfenced gardens on his Rough Creek property (Bodie Daily News, 9 July 1880). While confrontations with Euro-Americans in the urban areas were a constant threat to Chinese residents, the rural camp employees may instead have been concerned for their safety or the security of their goods from other populations who had also been pushed to the margins by discriminatory practices and attitudes.

Labor and Masculinity

The gendered labor performed by the Chinese in both the urban and rural places impacted the lives of the individuals in numerous ways. Williams (2008:54) argued that since Chinese diaspora sites are often primarily male communities, men's activities and ideologies are central to archaeological interpretations. In Aurora and Bodie, Chinese men, women, and children operated in a variety of industries, catering to both Chinese and non-Chinese customers. The labor at woodcutting camps, on the other hand, centered almost entirely on tasks related to woodcutting and thus performed almost exclusively by men. The jobs for the Chinese community at the woodcutting camps and throughout the rural areas around Aurora and Bodie were associated with the wood industry. Wood chopper, wood hauler, wood cutter, wood packer, coal burner,

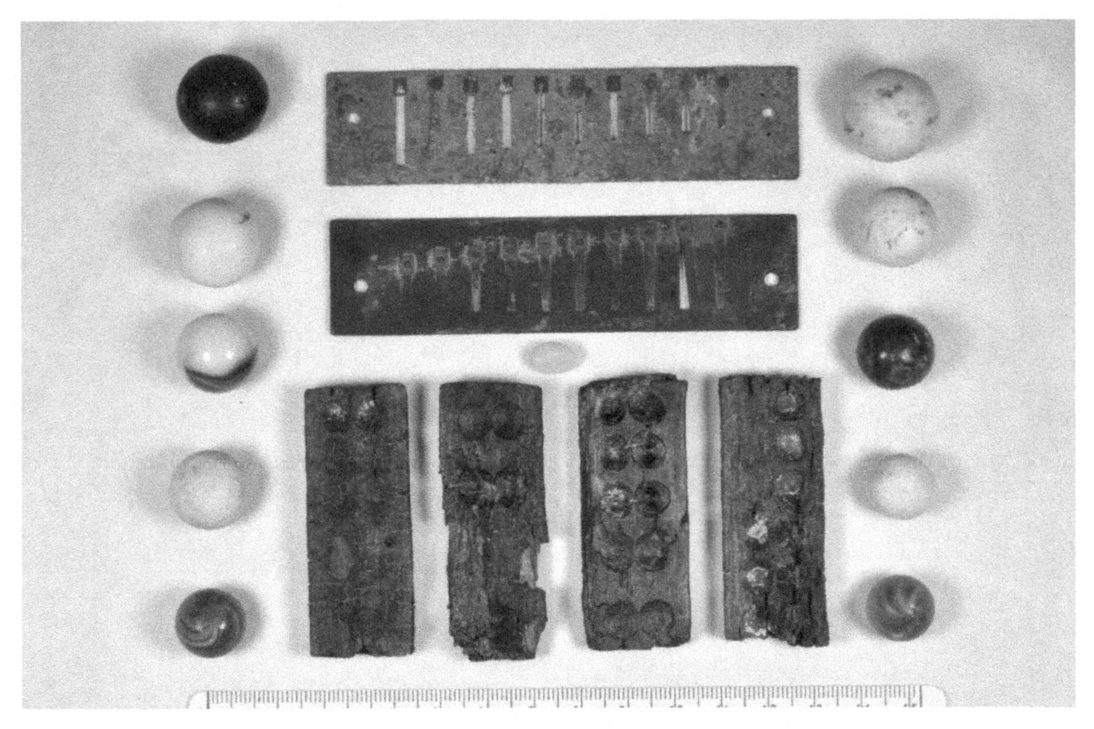

FIGURE 5.3. Artifacts of recreation and entertainment from various woodcutting camps. Artifacts include glass and clay marbles, harmonica reed plates, a possible quartz gaming token, and dominoes with extant red, white, and black paint. Photograph by Emily Dale and Leo Demski.

and wood dealer were common occupations listed in the census records (Table 5.1; United States Census Bureau 1870, 1880a, 1880b, 1900a, 1910b, 1910c). With the exception of one Chinese female recorded in 1880 on Table Mountain, all of the workers were adult males (United States Census Bureau 1880b). The newspaper accounts about Chinese woodcutters described only adult males. As a result, the woodcutting camps were male spaces.

Woodcutting camps were places of labor, and the artifacts identified there reflect the focus on work, dramatically contrasting with other Chinese sites in the urban centers that possess more domestic materials and few work-related artifacts. Axes, saws, mattocks, work gloves, and a pair of shoes with caulked soles were recovered from the camps, reflecting labor in the woodcutting industry, as well as masculinity, as these objects were made for, advertised to, and used by men.

Still, the woodcutting camps were not simply locations of labor. Beyond basic domestic chores like cooking and cleaning, they were places for men's social activities, and the material record reflects those activities. Chinese workers at the woodcutting camps did not have the same opportunity to frequent the opium dens, brothels, gaming parlors (all noted in the historical documents of Aurora and Bodie), and other entertainment establishments available to the urban Chinese. Instead, they built their communities at the level of the camp. Marbles, dominoes, harmonica parts (Figure 5.3), alcohol cups, and large, communal ceramic serving vessels found at the camps suggest some of the activities and shared meals taken up by the workers at the camp during their leisure time. The rural nature of the camps granted an opportunity for the men to socialize in an environment free from the fear of judgement, raids, or attacks that permeated Aurora and Bodie's Chinese communities.

FIGURE 5.4. Chinese brownware ceramics used for storing and shipping food found at various woodcutting camps. Vessels include two soy sauce jars, a globular jar, a straight-sided jar, ginger jars, and lids. Photograph by Emily Dale and Leo Demski.

Consumption Habits

Consumer choice is another aspect of agency recovered in the artifacts and sites of the Chinese. Archaeology is uniquely positioned to discuss consumption since archaeologists study material objects, allowing them to "confront the multivalent meaning of goods, probe the ideological roots of material symbolism, and emphasize that even the most commonplace objects provide insight into meaningful social struggles" (Mullins 2004:195). In the case of Chinese immigrants living in the American West, the material culture found at the woodcutting camps reveal a transnational strategy of combining traditional and new goods, a typical pattern of behavior seen at Chinese sites across the American West (for more on the application of transnationalism to Chinese diaspora sites, see Kraus-Friedberg 2008; Ross 2012, 2013; Voss 2005, 2016). They also demonstrate the connections between the rural camps and the urban cores, where the woodcutters would have purchased both Chinese and non-Chinese goods from Chinese merchants, as well as the larger ties back to China.

Most of the traditional Chinese goods were related to food shipping, storage, and service. All the camps had an abundance of traditional Chinese ceramics, including Chinese brown-glazed stoneware spouted, wide-mouthed, straight-sided, and globular jars (Figure 5.4); Double Happiness and Bamboo bowls; Four Seasons bowls, saucers, plates, alcohol cups, and spoons; Celadon bowls, alcohol cups, and spoons; and ginger jars. One campsite had a Sweet Pea liquor warmer or server. Another campsite yielded a Chinese inkstone, indicating the presence of at least one literate individual. Basic choices, like what to eat, were intrinsically connected to the larger transnational ties between Chinese immigrants and their home culture.

Many of the Euro-American goods were seemingly chosen for their practicality. Levi's buttons and a Levi's overalls patch reveal the presence of denim work clothing, while shoe soles showed a preference for sturdy rubber and leather footwear. Such clothing was more practical in the labor-centric environment than traditional Chinese clothing.

The Chinese laborers seamlessly integrated new goods alongside their traditional cultural elements as well. Baking powder tins, Lea & Perrins' stoppers, and lard pails demonstrated an incorporation of Euro-American foods into meals also consisting of Chinese foods. Euro-American medicines—like Perry Davis & Son Vegetable Pain Killer, Florida Water, and Saxlehner's Bitterquelle—were used alongside Chinese toothbrushes and medicines from traditional vials. Opium and tobacco, as evidenced by tins and pipes associated with both, were smoked together at the same Chinese lumber camps.

Finally, Chinese woodcutting camps relied on artifact reuse, usually of metal artifacts. Nearly every woodcutting camp had metal barrels with knife cuts sliced into the lids and sides, possibly used to sift charcoal. At one camp, a tin can was deftly repurposed into a candlestick holder, complete with holes on a tab to hang it from the wall. At another camp, a shipping crate from the China Nut Company, based out of Hong Kong, was attached to the interior wall of a dugout for use as a shelf. Another camp owner placed a large Chinese brownware globular jar in the ground next to the camp spring, ostensibly to filter and collect water (Figure 5.4). At least two of the camps had blacksmithing shops, as evidenced by blacksmithing tools, including tongs, files, grindstones, iron stock, crucibles, and a bullet mold.

Indicative of the limited access to goods and the economic realities of daily life at rural locations, the Chinese camp workers devised inventive cost-cutting measures designed to maximize profits. Based on necessity and design, the rural Chinese woodcutters appear to have repurposed goods rather than purchasing new items. For example, when a mule needed reshoeing or an axe needed sharpening, the camps had the ability to perform these tasks themselves. Such reuse was present at urban sites, but to a much lesser degree. Reuse of artifacts also meant the Chinese laborers working in rural spaces spent less time in the urban environments, where the possibility of discrimination and either verbal or physical assaults were ever-present. The strategy of reusing goods, then, had both economic and safety benefits.

Connected Places across Spaces

Despite the distance and distinctive places, urban and rural Chinese residents' lives were connected. In fact, the urban and rural people were often one and the same. Chinese woodcutters owned lots and houses in Aurora and Bodie where they lived in the winter and stored their wood prior to sale. They bought goods in the urban centers, where Chinese businesses sold imported Chinese goods transported from San Francisco. When woodcutters were injured on the job or their pack trains got caught in the snow, the Chinese woodcutters often relied on friends in town for assistance.

Thus, the relationship connecting urban and rural spaces, and Chinese people who occupied them, is more complex than a flow of goods and people between rural and urban. Instead, the agency of the rural, woodcutting Chinese laborers is visible in the historical and archaeological records. The key question, then, is not one of more or less agency, but of the different array of choices available to and necessitated by the rural nature of the woodcutting camps.

The camps allowed the woodcutters to create a physical and metaphorical distance between themselves and the perceptible aura of discrimination against the Chinese constantly present in Aurora and Bodie. Yet, this distance separated them from the sense of community and access to the social aspects of Bodie's Chinatown, encouraging the men of the camps to create social camaraderie through communal meals, games, and drinking. The woodcutters also actively deployed their purchasing power by bringing an array of traditional, new, and adapted goods to their camps. The reliance of the core centers on the rural camps for wood allowed Chinese woodcutters to set prices, make a profit, and create new choices based on the power of place.

6

Persistence and Place among the Northern Paiute in Aurora, Nevada

Lauren Walkling

Cultural persistence is a concept touted in archaeological studies of colonialism as an alternative to reductive studies of Indigenous-colonial experiences. Studies about persistence are seen as a response to simple dominance and resistance studies and add nuance to the lives of Indigenous groups in colonial environments. One approach of interest within archaeological studies of persistence focuses on colonial landscapes and how they affect the cultural values and lifeways of colonized groups. This particular method addresses concepts such as double consciousness, which describes the internal conflict of oppressed groups who feel that their identity is split into multiple forms. Double consciousness is presented in actions ranging from colonized peoples basing their actions off colonizers' attitudes of the occupied to the creation of public and private cultural identities.

One example of persistence as a theoretical framework that analyzes the formation of colonial and Indigenous landscapes is persistence as defined by Lee Panich (2013). This approach focuses on how identity and cultural practices are modified or preserved as they are passed onto future generations (Panich 2013:107). In this chapter, Panich's (2013) definition of persistence provides the conceptual basis for examining the archaeological and historical evidence of persistence strategies. Persistence is used to study how a sense of place is formed within a colonial context and along with the adaptation of double consciousness in connection with place and identity. In particular, the concept will be applied to the Mono Paiute or *Kutzadika'a* of Pyramid Lake and Winnemucca Valley, who currently reside on the Yerington Paiute Tribe Reservation.

While the location of interest is Aurora, Nevada, a Comstock-era mining town along the California-Nevada border, the study focuses on a Paiute campsite located in the piñon forest foothills northwest of this area. These historic Paiute campsites provide an archaeological sample of how persistence was cultivated in the colonial mining context of the Nevada Silver Rush from the 1860s through to the 1920s.

Persistence: Theoretical Background

Studies of cultural persistence began in earnest during Columbus's quincentennial anniversary in 1992, which encouraged postcolonial critiques of previous simplistic archaeological studies of colonialism (Wylie 1992:591). One approach suggested during this time centered how physical and cultural landscapes are tied with the perpetuation of colonized cultural identities. Specifically, how cultural landscapes formed by colonized groups facilitated the continuation, or persistence, of cultural lifeways and ideals (Silliman 2004).

This definition of persistence as a concept to be researched in the archaeology of colonialism has varied since the postcolonial critiques of the 1990s (Wylie 1992). The approach and definition used for this chapter come from Panich (2013).

In his article "Archaeologies of Persistence: Reconsidering the Legacies of Colonialism in Native North America," Panich defines persistence as the ways that colonized groups change their cultural presentation and actions to survive and preserve their culture (Panich 2013:107). To study persistence holistically, archaeologists must study three aspects: identity, practice, and context (Panich 2013:107).

Identity, in the present and past, is socially constructed through active decision-making processes on both collective and individual levels (Panich 2013:107–108). Here, studying identity means tracking changes in the choices made by specific cultural groups and seeing how these decisions are reproduced by future generations. Practice—derived from practice theory—is the use of an item and how its use informs the symbolic and cultural meanings behind said objects (Silliman 2009:215). Practice acknowledges the ways that social and material situations restrain or empower social agents and explores how daily practices can change because of those situations (Pauketat 2001:80). Finally, context is the group of historical events that inform the change or retention of cultural lifeways among colonized groups (Panich 2013:109–110; Silliman 2009:215–216).

A concept I address in conjunction with persistence is double consciousness. W.E.B. Du Bois describes double consciousness as "this sense of always looking at one's self through the eyes of others, of measuring one's soul by the tape of a world that looks on in amused contempt and pity" (Du Bois 1897:194). While Du Bois discusses double consciousness as an African American in turn-of-the-century America, his concept is applicable to the lived experiences of many colonized groups. Double consciousness is particularly appropriate when applied to the creation of public and private identities, the question of which cultural practices are retained or altered, and the context of how strategies of persistence are adopted.

My study of six historic Northern Paiute, or Kutzadika'a, sites in Aurora uses persistence and these three underlying concepts. Using archaeological survey and analysis, local journals and newspapers, and descendant oral narratives, I explore persistence and its role in connection with the cultural landscape of the Northern Paiute.

Historical Background

According to Marlin Thompson, a Northern Paiute Master Artist from Yerington, Nevada, the Aurora Paiute descended from the *Kutzadika'a*, or *Koo'saa'vii'tu'ka'du*. The *Kutzadika'a* originated from the Mono Lake Paiute and were known for collecting, drying, and consuming *kusa*, or brine fly maggots (Marlin Thompson 2015–2017, personal communication; Shaw 2016). The group was primarily situated at Pyramid Lake and Winnemucca Valley and migrated into the mountains seasonally for pine nut harvests (Parks 1965:1, 6; Pritzker 2000:2; Schrader et al. 2016:114–115; Shaw 2016:174).

Great Basin Indigenous groups did not contend with European Americans until the 1800s. The most notable encounters were the expeditions of Peter Skene Ogden and Joseph Walker, which occurred in 1829 and 1834 respectively (Hattori 1975:3; McBride 2002:3). Both were highly violent, resulting in the deaths of several Mojave during Ogden's expedition and about 47 Paiute during Walker's encounter. While Native American activists, such as Sarah Winnemucca and Captain Truckee, attempted to ease the tensions between white settlers and Great Basin Indigenous groups (Michno 2007:5; Stewart 2004:56), racial tension eventually erupted into the Owens Valley Indian War during the early 1860s.

Due to the overexploitation of Owens Valley by European American cattle herders, together with the harsh winter of 1861 to 1862, the Paiute turned to cattle raiding to offset lost resources. Eventually, the cattle raiding led to armed conflict between white cattle herders and the Paiute and Shoshone (the Shoshone were also blamed) (Chalfant 1933:172; Walton 1992:17). Aurora was a particular point of anxiety due to white settlers wondering whether the Paiute there would join the fight. This fear was compounded by Aurora's role as a supply hub for cattle drivers (Walton 1992:17). Following the Paiutes's surrender during this conflict, the tribes were escorted to military forts or set up camps around white settlements (Shaw 2009:29–30; Stewart 2004:57; Walton 1992:21–22).

The Paiute encampment around Aurora is an example of one of these camps. To set the encampment in context, Aurora was a boomtown resulting from the mass migration in the Nevada territory during the Silver Rush of the 1860s. While other boomtowns, such as Virginia City, were the consequence of the silver ore of the Comstock Lode, Aurora resulted from the Esmeralda Lode. Aurora began as a mining camp in early 1860 and, by the fall, was established as a town within the Esmeralda Mining District. At its peak, the town consisted of a diverse population of 5,000 residents, 1,500 of which were Paiute (Shaw 2016:307–314; Stewart 2004:2). Due to the Esmeralda Lode's shallow mines, yielding at most $16 million total, the town quickly went bust. While there were brief booms during the 1870s, 1880s, and World War I, the town was abandoned by 1920 (Shaw 2009:153–158; Shaw 2016:89–112, 183–188; Stewart 2004:71, 75–76).

During Aurora's heyday, the Paiute set up home camps outside Aurora, as seen in the aftermath of the Owens Valley Indian War. Articles from Bodie's Daily Free Press from September 30, 1881, and another from the Sacramento Daily Union from July 3, 1873, written by Colonel Samuel Youngs, describe the existence of Northern Paiute camps in foothills north of Aurora (Daily Free Press, 30 September 1881g; Sacramento Daily Union, 3 July 1873:2; Shaw 2009:89). The location of these campsites provided a lookout point over the valley, the brush and trees acted as shelter from the valley's prevailing wind, and the mountains had warmer temperatures than the valley floor on which Aurora was located. The presence of piñon pine trees within the hills also offered easy access to the Paiutes' traditional food source.

The Paiute's involvement in the Aurora economy increased as mining and development around the town diminished the piñon pine forests and overhunted fauna necessary to the Paiute diet (Shaw 2016:167). To compensate for this loss, the Paiute took up labor such as panning for ore, postal service, firefighting, fishing, cutting and selling lumber, laundry work, selling pine nuts and hunted or trapped game for food or entertainment (Daily Free Press, 8 May 1881a, 20 January 1882a, 15 April 1882c, 25 June 1882d; Shaw 2016:175–176). Outside of wage labor, the Paiute also performed war dances for the general populace of Aurora for pay (Daily Free Press, 29 May 1881b). While integral to the town's economy, these actions did not diminish the racism towards the Northern Paiute. Xenophobia was systematic, ranging from the Paiute being portrayed as inherently drunk or "savage" in the Aurora and Bodie newspapers to interracial violence towards the Paiute (Daily Free Press, 1 July 1881c). In the latter case, the Northern Paiute were either the targets of brawls or killed by Euro-American settlers, who in some cases were acquitted (Daily Free Press, 11 August 1880b; Bodie Standard News, 10 August 1880:3). For white settlers, the Paiute simply existing in this colonial context was enough for Euro-Americans to contest their existence in Aurora, often brutally.

Site Survey Summaries

The sites analyzed for this research were first identified by U.S. Forest Service volunteer Clifford Shaw and brought to my attention by Eric Dillingham, the district archaeologist at the Bridgeport Ranger District of the Humboldt-Toiyabe National Forest. Six sites were surveyed and mapped in 2015 and 2016 (Figure 6.1). Each site was coded AN-CC (Aurora Neighborhoods, Culture Contact) followed by its site number. I grouped each site around one or more features, such as *wiqiups*, Great Basin Indigenous residential features, or metates, groundstone implements used to process seeds and nuts such as piñon pine nuts.

The sites were surveyed and recorded through photographic cataloging and tape-and-compass mapping. Features were mapped using tape-and-compass and grid methods, while site boundaries were recorded with a Garmin Oregon 400t and a Garmin Portland.

The six sites include: one wiqiup rock ring and piñon cache, four singular wiqiup rock

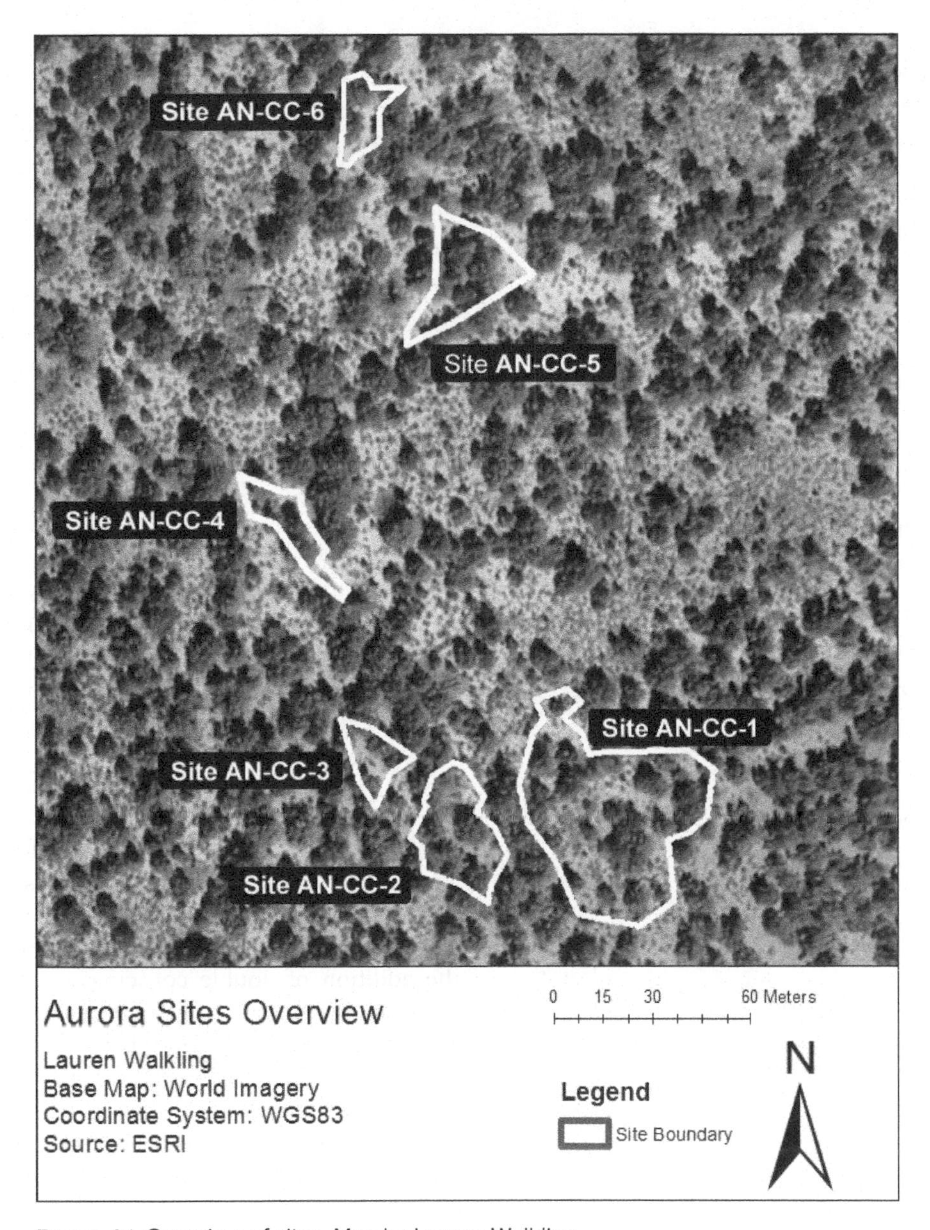

FIGURE 6.1. Overview of sites. Map by Lauren Walkling.

rings, and one non-portable metate with an artifact scatter. Using artifact totals alone, the sites could be interpreted as historic rather than prehistoric. The combined archaeological, documentary, and oral historical evidence suggests an ethnohistoric origin.

Nine features are present within all six sites. These features include five wiqiup rock bases, two metates, one piñon cache, and the remains of one lean-to constructed from a tree branch and wire. The artifact total between the sites is 270. The artifacts were split between three categories: lithic artifacts ($n = 66$), historic artifacts[1] ($n = 196$), and ecofacts ($n = 8$). Tables 6.1, 6.2, and 6.3 contain summaries of the recovered artifacts. Notable diagnostic artifacts include hole-in-top cans (1900s–1990s), a can with an external friction lid (1880s–present), hole-in-cap

TABLE 6.1. Historic Artifact Count, Total, and Types of Sites AN-CC-1 through AN-CC-6.

Category	Artifact Total
Beads	2
Bucket/Bucket Fragments	4
Buckle/Belt Buckles	2
Buttons	3
Cans	65
Can Lids/Fragments	24
Combs	1
Fry Pans	1
Glass Bottle Fragments	55
Glass Fragments	3
Horseshoes	2
Lumber Fragments	3
Metal Bands	1
Metal Caps	2
Metal Fragments	3
Mining Pans	1
Modified Tree Limbs	1
Muleshoe	1
Nails	1
Pipe Fragments	2
Safety Pins	1
Shoe Leather Fragments	11
Wash Bin	1
Whiskey Flask	1
Wire Fragments	5
Total	196

TABLE 6.3. Ecofact Count, Total, and Types from Sites AN-CC-1 through AN-CC-6.

Category	Artifact Total
Burnt Faunal Remains	1
Charcoal Fragments	4
Fire Cracked Rock (FCR)	2
Shell Scatter	1
Total	8

TABLE 6.2. Lithic Artifact Count, Total, and Types from Sites AN-CC-1 through AN-CC-6.

Category	Artifact Total
Bifaces	3
Cores	7
Individual Flakes	26
Flake Scatters	15
Flake Tools	2
Projectile Points	5
Scrapers	1
Utilized/Retouched Flakes	7
Total	66

cans (1823–1940), sanitary cans (1904–present), olive amber bottle fragments (1815–1885), aquamarine glass fragments (1800s–1920s), olive green glass fragments (1860s–present), amethyst glass fragments (1880–1920), and a key-opened can (1926).

Persistence and Place through Identity, Practice, and Context

The archaeological and written histories of the Paiute are analyzed through the subconcepts of persistence: identity, practice, and context with the addition of double consciousness. From there, I discuss how the Paiute created their sense of place, vis-à-vis their sphere of influence, within a colonial environment. I argue that the Northern Paiute used strategies of persistence to survive within the colonial sphere of Aurora, Nevada. I examine how double consciousness and the Paiute's creation of their own place, a space where they could practice their cultural lifeways outside of Aurora's colonial system, informed by said tactics.

Identity

Two types of identity are essential for persistence: public and private spheres of identity. Public identity, especially for the Paiute around Aurora, was expressed through large public gatherings such as fandangos, parades, and war dances to the town collective, not to themselves

(Johnson 2000; Shaw 2009). Compared to the private identity expressed within the Paiute camps, their public identity was informed and promoted by Aurora's white settlers.

Paiute war dances and their participation in Fourth of July parades reflect the Paiute's conscientiousness of Aurora's colonial landscape. The Paiute put on public displays known as "war dances" for the Aurora Euro-American populace. According to Samuel Youngs, a war dance was

> "an Indian feast dance in town to amuse the citizens, who gave them a few shillings…20 to 30 Indians form a circle, commence singing a humming nasal tune, stamp first one foot then the other, shaking their arms. Painted on faces, backs and bodies naked except cloth around their loins" [Sacramento Daily Union, 7 August 1861:1].

These war dances reflected a trend found among Native American groups in other mining town settings. Multiple Indigenous groups, such as the Miwok in Susan Lee Johnson's *Roaring Camp*, exploited white spectatorship to make a profit from white romanticization and fetishization of Indigenous groups (Johnson 2000:307).

The Paiute dancers of Aurora adopted this idea towards entertaining white colonizers. These war dances were often advertised as a show for the mostly European American population of Aurora (Figure 6.2). As seen in Young's journal description (Sacramento Daily Union, 3 July 1873:2), the Euro-Americans of Aurora viewed the Paiute as an "exotic other," usually through a racist lens as the "Noble Savage" stock character. It is possible that the Northern Paiute of Aurora utilized these viewpoints to earn a profit, given that their circumstances matched that of the Miwok.

The Fourth of July parade in Aurora, much like the war dances, illustrates how the Northern Paiute adjusted their public identity in relation to Aurora's white audience. One of the anticipated attractions of the parade was the Paiute volunteers who marched during the event (Daily Free Press, 6 July 1881d; The Esmeralda

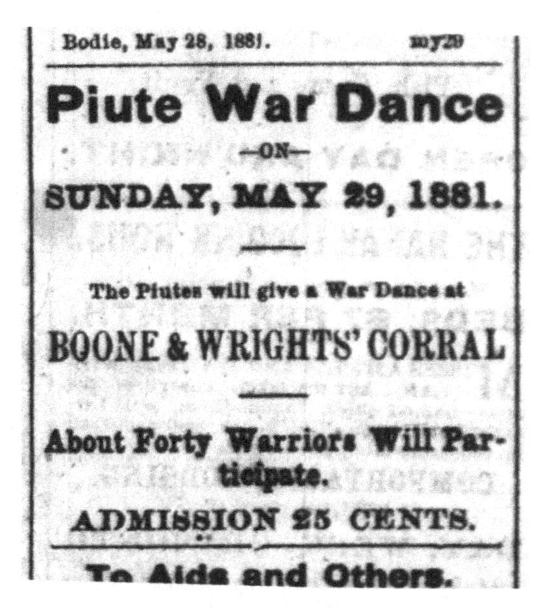

FIGURE 6.2. Advertisement for Paiute War Dance at Boone & Wrights' Corral (Bodie Daily Free Press, May 28, 1881).

Herald, 3 July 1880:2). The event proceeded as such:

> "Each [Paiute] with a red ribbon tied around his arm, carrying the Stars and Stripes and a banner labelled 'Heap Good Union Piute.' At the hall [armory] they marched in and gave their primitive style three cheers for the union. They attracted much attention and applause" [Daily Bodie Standard, 5 July 1879a:3; Shaw 2009:65].

The reasons for Paiute participation in the parade included appealing to Euro-American nationalism, trying to ease racial tensions between the groups, forging peaceful relations, presenting a positive image to European American settlers, and satirizing American presentations of patriotism. Regardless, the public presentations of both war dances and the Fourth of July parade shared a similar thread of intent. Both activities represented an attempt by the Northern Paiute community to attach themselves to the Aurora community and become associated with it. By connecting themselves to the public image of Aurora as a place, not only did these performances have economic intent behind them, the performances could also be seen as a way to continue their cultural connection to their traditional home despite the drastic changes taking place.

Consulting examples of private identity presented a crucial juxtaposition to the public persona that the Northern Paiute put on in Aurora. Private forms of identity could be seen in the Paiute's continued use of lithic and stone technology. The continued use of lithic and stone tools was driven by the practical need for subsistence and the need to continue cultural practices in a colonial context. Tools for hunting and pine nut gathering were documented in both the archaeological record and newspapers of Aurora and Bodie (Daily Free Press, 3 March 1880a, 19 November 1880c, 28 August 1881f, 8 February 1883b; Daily Bodie Standard, 24 October 1879b:3). Items at the sites that were related to piñon nut gathering included a piñon cache, a non-portable metate, and two portable metates. Hunting tools include five projectile points: one corner-notched Great Basin point, two cottonwood triangular points, one large side-notched point, and one Elko Corner-notched projectile point. Other lithic tools included a scraper, cores, and retouched and utilized flakes. Within Aurora's colonial context, the Paiutes' main purpose for hunting and gathering changed. Subsistence activities switched from providing only for the Paiute camps to supplying sustenance for themselves as well as selling the same goods for profit. Despite the motivation for sustenance lifeways changing, the tool use did not.

This retention and adjustment of cultural practices were fostered in spaces like Paiute campsites. Their proximity to Aurora allowed Paiute's access to Euro-American goods including canned food, buttons, buckets, mining pans, frying pans, Euromerican clothing and shoes, and combs. However, the campsites in the foothills also allowed a degree of privacy away from Aurora's white gaze. This private sphere of influence meant that traditional Northern Paiute lifeways could be preserved or modified and thus transmitted in a secure space without the worry of colonial influence on Paiute identity.

Practice

The subconcept of practice is evident through two important activities for the Paiute community in Aurora: economic lifeways and consumption practices. Labor activities were highly varied, ranging from wage labor, gathering and selling pine nuts, and lumber work to hunting and selling game. Popular game included ducks, jackrabbits, coyotes, and badgers, which were then either sold, retained, or used for animal fights (Daily Free Press, 20 January 1882a, 15 April 1882c, 25 June 1882d, 6 February 1883a, 21 February 1883c, 8 March 1883d; Daily Bodie Standard, 27 May 1880a:3; Shaw 2009:86, 91). Journal accounts substantiated the Paiute's wage labor, specifically gathering lumber, shoveling snow, and delivering water from the town's well (Ackley 1928; Shaw 2009:86–87). Archaeological evidence of these activities included tools relating to piñon nut gathering and integrated Euro-American technology such as two horseshoes, a mule shoe, a mining pan, and two lumber fragments.

While the labor practices described were undoubtedly influenced by the colonial economy, the practices are inherently connected with Paiute identity and their relationship to their environment. Although hunting and gathering were modified to participate in the Aurora economy, the type of activities was consistent. As discussed, war dances as a practice were influenced by economic need. The Northern Paiute changed war dances both to cater to white residential consumption and to protect the dances' more sacred aspects. Within a colonial sphere like Aurora, the Northern Paiute would adjust their cultural practices for their economic survival, as they could not live on their previous lifeways alone, due to radical environmental changes.

The acknowledgement of white settler attitudes and the need to keep and protect cultural ideals is consistent with the definition of double consciousness. The removal of sacred details in war dances and the accommodation of white spectatorship is further proof of that phenomenon. In a space such as the campsites, the Paiute were allowed reprieve from this double consciousness, integrating new technology and retaining cultural items and lifeways without the pressure of the white gaze.

Context

According to Panich (2013), context is the series of historical events that inform the present or a specific era. The context behind the colonization and establishment of Aurora informs the sense of place taken up by the Paiute of Aurora and their strategies of persistence. The context specifically focuses on the first Euro-Paiute interactions in Nevada and the Paiute's occupation of the area.

Based on the presence of two Elko projectile points within the campsites, the oldest point of occupation is between 3300–1300 BP. Another datable lithic artifact is a Cottonwood Triangular projectile point dated from 700 BP to the present. The presence of both point types reflects the long-term settlement continuity within the foothill campsites. That is not to say that the use of the area stopped with the end of Aurora as a mining town. Marlin Thompson (personal communication, 2015–2017), for example, stated that he and his family used the area for piñon nut harvesting into the present. The enduring settlement and use patterns attest to this continuity as being the biggest form of resistance for the Paiute.

While the campsites and the associated artifacts inform a sense of place and continuity, first contact with Euro-Americans influenced Paiute strategies of persistence. The initial violence of the Peter Skene Ogden and Joseph Walker expeditions were a precursor to the systematic racism of Aurora towards the Paiute. This oppression ranged from causal racist attitudes to interracial violence committed by white settlers towards Paiute citizens, where even though colonization was complete, violent altercations over who could occupy space "normally" were constant. Between the racism in Aurora and the decimation of their traditional subsistence environment, the Paiute began to rely on double-consciousness, persistence, and their created sense of space within the campsites to survive and resist when able.

These three tactics were integrated in response to an instance of interracial violence. In the summer of 1880, a Paiute man was killed during a shootout between an Aurora gardener and a group of Paiute. When the gardener was not charged for the killing, the Paiute community refused to take part in the Fourth of July parade that year (Daily Bodie Standard, 15 June 1880b:3, 16 June 1880c:3).

As discussed previously, the Paiute were popular participants in the parade among white settlers, which helped give their threat to boycott the parade more weight if the wrong done by the court was not corrected. This popularity was based on the Paiute's double consciousness, as they played towards the attitudes held by Aurora's white settlers. The modification of the public cultural aspects of this performance also reflected the Paiute's willingness to change cultural presentations to survive in a new economy and attempts to garner respect from a possibly hostile audience. This power play could not have been made without a support system among the Paiute, which was nurtured by the private nature of the foothill campsites and unavailable in the public sphere of Aurora. These three factors allowed the Paiute in this situation to use the pleasure created from their performances as a form of collateral against potential violence and injustice.

Conclusions

The archaeological and written history of the Paiute of Aurora presents a solid argument that the construction of a sense of place within a colonial sphere was integral to the formation of strategies of persistence. Specifically, how the creation of their own place was important to ideas of identity, practice, and context in relation to persisting and resisting in a colonized environment.

The double consciousness seen in the Paiutes' public identity reflects a need to find alternative modes of employment, as seen in the war dances and Fourth of July Parade. In contrast, by establishing their own space in the form of their campsites, the Paiute could retain or modify aspects of their culture and technology away from Aurora's colonial gaze.

Practice is seen through the various economic lifeways taken up by the Aurora Paiute and the highly diverse consumption practices in order to survive in a drastically changing environment. The historical context of these persistence strategies, between the violent first encounters and the destruction of the valley's environment, informs why and how certain cultural features were altered or preserved. These events also inform how the incorporation of a place of community, double consciousness, and strategies of persistence encouraged the survival of the Paiute within Aurora. The integration of double consciousness, the archaeology of Aurora, and the written and oral history of the Aurora Paiute strengthens the connection between the Paiute's sense of place and cultural persistence in a space where their own presence was constantly challenged.

Notes

1. Although the term "historic" has been critiqued for its arbitrary use on postcontact items (Lightfoot 1995), it is used in this context for items of European or Euro-American origin until a more appropriate term is coined.

7

Sisneros and Cisneros

Place-Based Community Development among Hispanic Homesteaders in Northeast New Mexico

Erin Hegberg

This chapter is a story of place and a Hispanic homesteading community near the town of Mosquero in northeastern New Mexico, between 1890 and 1940. This community, sometimes known as lower Mosquero, was defined and bounded by the landscape and topography. While the community initially had strong ties to the valley settlement of Gallegos, by the 1930s relationships had shifted to the mesa-top railroad town of Mosquero. At the same time, homesteaders sought to anchor their own place and identity through interpersonal relationships and support networks, drawn together around a Works Progress Administration (WPA) school house. In this chapter, I explore how residents of the lower Mosquero homesteading community saw themselves and their community, how this changed through time, and how residents' place on the New Mexico landscape shaped their allegiances and community ties. I do this using the architecture and artifacts of 10 homestead settlements documented during an archaeological survey, together with homestead case files, census data, and other archival data.

In the American West, questions of community are inextricably tied to ideas about race and ethnic identity, place, settlement, narratives of expansion and loss, and movement. How did communities form on the Western landscape? What were the important social bonds? What kept communities together through time and social change, or why did they disperse? These questions are primary within Western historical archaeology in the context of mining booms, homesteading migrations, and other forms of "westward expansion" (Branton 2009; Clark 2012; Hardesty 2002; Purser 2017).

In New Mexico, research related to community development and resilience must also be understood within the context of layered conquest and colonialism (Deutsch 1989; Forrest 1998; Gonzales-Berry and Maciel 2000; Kutsche 1979). For centuries, the New Mexico territory was a multiethnic contact zone. By the late nineteenth and early twentieth centuries, northeastern New Mexico was a region where the eastward expansion of Hispanic villages overlapped with the westward expansion of Euro-American ranchers. Hispanic and Euro-American settlers met within the canyons and plains of the Canadian Escarpment and negotiated and redefined themselves in terms of place and community.

The range of ethnic nomenclatures used in New Mexico over time also reflects this long period as a multiethnic (and multiracial) contact zone. In particular, the rise in popularity and change in cultural meanings behind the label "Hispanic" has occupied several scholars (Healy et al. 2018; Montgomery 2002; Nieto-Phillips 2004; Salgado 2018). Terms such as Hispanic, Hispano, Nuevomexicano, Mexican-American, and Manito are each "contingent, strategic, and performative" (Cisneros 2014:xi) and existed within a larger nexus of self- and group-identification, history, and governmental control. In this chapter I use the term "Hispanic" to refer to the Spanish-speaking persons in lower Mosquero, who, according to the United States Census Bureau (1900b, 1910d, 1920b, 1930b, 1940b), are at least second-generation New Mexicans. I use this term rather than other common terms, such as Mexican-American, due to its growing frequency during the 1900–1930 period and its common usage by Spanish-speaking persons in northeastern New Mexico today.

Background

Using assessment and analysis of baptismal and marriage records, homestead patents, post office data, and title records, Pratt and colleagues (Pratt 1990; Pratt et al. 1986) developed a model of Hispanic expansion and permanent settlement in northeast New Mexico. In the second half of the 1800s, a variety of forces brought Hispanic settlement eastwards. Communities grew, migrated, and settled, only to grow and splinter again, moving farther east in a series of settlement stages (Figure 7.1). Forces behind the change included population pressure and growth, the need for more sheep grazing land, Navajo raids from the west, and competition for grazing land with Texas cattle ranchers pushing from the east (Baxter 1987; Deutsch 1989; Remley 1993).

The Mosquero study region is located at the edge of the Canadian Escarpment, between the mountains of the upper Rio Grande and the vast open plains of the Llano Estacado, in a broken landscape of steep canyons and rolling plateaus. Topographic distinctions played an important role in defining place and community within the canyonlands along the Canadian River. Settlers here had "up top" strategies of farming or ranching large areas on the mesa tops and plateaus, alongside "down below" strategies of subsistence agriculture and self-sufficiency in the canyon bottoms. Pratt (1990) noted this dual pattern in the study region, and homestead patents and oral histories from a similar landscape along the Purgatoire River in southeastern Colorado also demonstrated this pattern of land-use (Clark 2012:25–26). Around 1890, Hispanic homesteaders began claiming tracts in the well-watered lowlands and canyons of Mosquero Abajo, also known as Lower Mosquero or Old Mosquero. In the early 1900s, there was a Euro-American homesteading pattern on the uplands of Black Mesa, also known as Upper Mosquero, Mosquero, or Gould (Pratt et al. 1986). While several researchers have noted differences in patterns of homesteading and land-use among Euro-American and Hispanic settlers (Van Ness 1976), Church (2002:226) summarizes them as "the grant and the grid," in part because many differences are rooted in the different historical land tenure systems of each group. She notes that Hispanic settlers—coming from a historical tradition of large Spanish and Mexican land grants with mixed economic uses, and both communal and private ownership—tended to bend the Homestead Act to support settlement in family groups, distributed in a dendritic pattern along drainages and waterways, with extended family plazas. Euro-American settlers came from a historical tradition of cadastral grid settlements. They were more likely to maintain independent homesteads, to settle in uplands, and to pursue single-use strategies like homogenous farming *or* stock-raising (Church 2002).

Another early community in the area was Gallegos, located in the Ute Valley at the base of the mesa escarpment. Gallegos was tied to the Comanche trade and sheepherding in the late nineteenth century. The Gallegos family appears to have utilized a mixture of Mexican and American period land-use practices to develop a settlement similar to a community land grant, like those offered by the Spanish and Mexican governments, which included provisions for both privately held land and land that was shared among the grantees for grazing, firewood, and

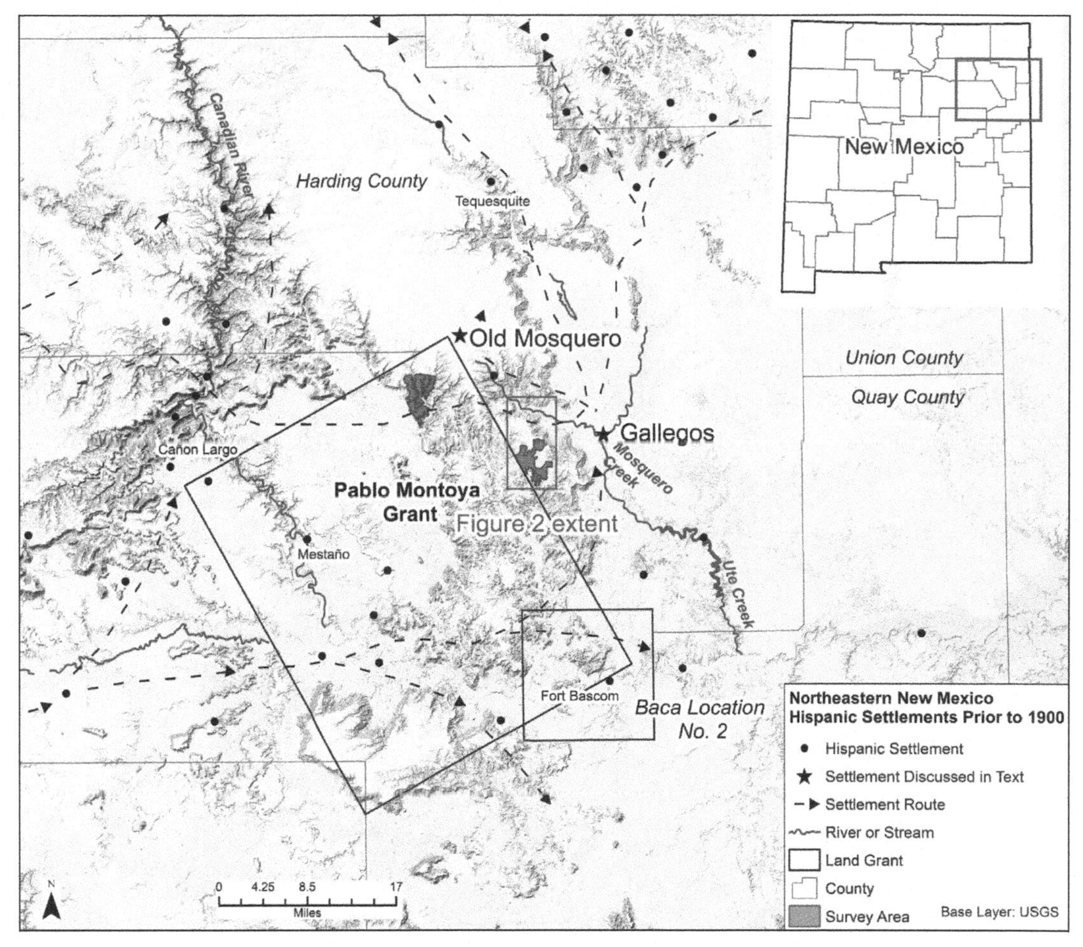

FIGURE 7.1. Hispanic settlement patterns surrounding the project area. Map by Scott Gunn, based on the research of Boyd C. Pratt (with contributions from Jerry L. Williams) in *Gone But Not Forgotten* (Pratt et al. 1986: 220, Map 35).

other resources (Karpinski 2007). Francisco and Emiterio Gallegos received homestead patents in the 1890s, and their settlement contained corrals, a mercantile, and a church (Bickers 2010).

Initially, Hispanic homesteaders in the Mosquero study region chose "down below" strategies, aligning themselves with sheep-raising operations at Gallegos. In the 1920s and 1930s, as the American economic system of wage labor became all-pervasive, lower Mosquero residents shifted their primary relationships "up top" towards the town of Mosquero, which was beginning to grow thanks to the construction of a railroad siding in 1903 by the El Paso and Northeastern Railway. Mosquero also became the seat of Harding County and local bureaucratic center for Depression-era federal assistance.

Homestead Sites

In 2016, the University of New Mexico's Office of Contract Archeology surveyed nearly 3,500 acres on a privately owned cattle ranch near Mosquero (Cordero et al. 2016). The extensive study area encompassed some homestead allotments in their entirety and allowed archaeologists to identify all remaining structural features within the allotments. The study area has abundant water in easily accessible seasonal creeks,

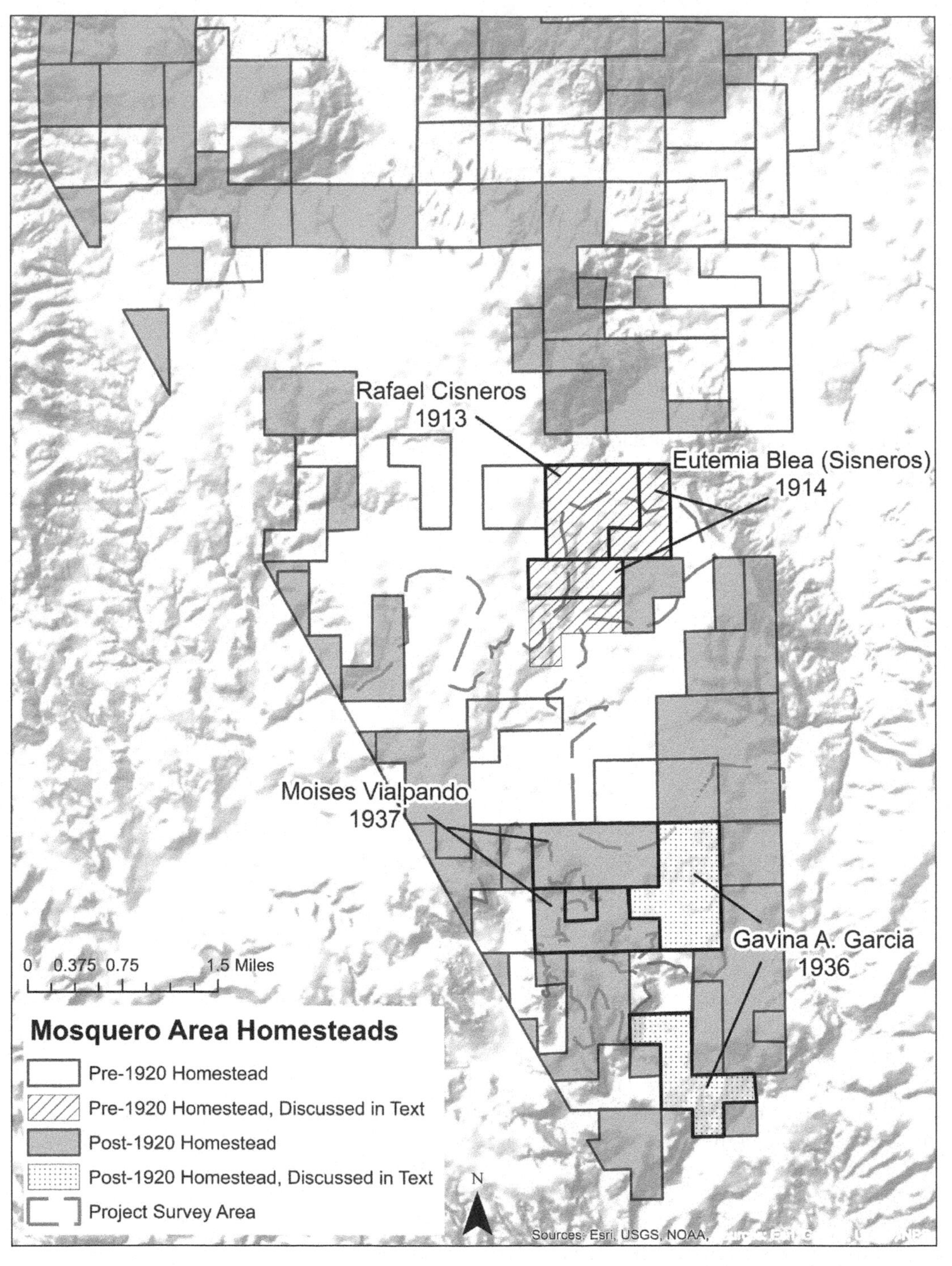

FIGURE 7.2. Homesteads in the survey parcel and surrounding area. Areas with no homestead claims are New Mexico state land. Map by Scott Gunn.

sufficient open grassland for grazing, and woodlands to provide some building material and fuel. The area is defined by a rolling plateau that overlooks Mosquero Canyon to the north and Ute Valley and Gallegos to the east. The town of Mosquero (Upper Mosquero) is approximately 16 km to the north. The study area was the focus of at least two phases of homesteading activity, one in the first two decades of the twentieth century, and another in the 1930s (Figure 7.2). Three specific homesteads will be discussed here to highlight changing community ties and relationships that the homesteaders maintained with the landscape, surrounding settlements, and each other.

Eutemia Blea née Sisneros maintained an original homestead and an enlarged homestead allotment, both patented in 1914.[1] A site with a residential structure was recorded on each allotment. The site documented on her original homestead consisted of a full settlement complex with a one-room stacked-rock house with a prepared terrace, a barn, a rock-lined dugout, and at least two small artifact concentrations. The site documented on the enlarged homestead consisted of a one-room structure with several unique architectural features, a stacked-rock corral, and an artifact concentration (Table 7.1). Diagnostic artifacts from both sites suggest they were occupied in the first two decades of the twentieth century. Eutemia Blea née Sisneros could not be located in the US Census (1910d, 1920b) for the area.

Directly north of the Eutemia Blea née Sisneros allotment, another large residential site was occupied by homesteader Rafael Cisneros and his family, beginning in approximately 1907 and lasting until at least 1913 (United States Bureau of Land Management 1914). In his final proof, Rafael Cisneros listed structural improvements made to the patent: a three-room rock house, a chicken house, a shed and corral, 50 acres under fence, and a well (United States Bureau of Land Management 1914).

Based on the 1910 US Census, Rafael Cisneros and his family moved to the region from Colorado City, Colorado prior to 1901. Between 1907 and 1910, Rafael Cisneros worked several miles away in Gallegos as a salesman in a store and as a school teacher (United States Census Bureau 1910d). Rafael Cisneros' distant employment suggested that the majority of the artifacts and features at the site are related to his wife Marina Cisneros and their two sons and two daughters. Diagnostic artifacts at the Cisneros homestead consisted of glass, ceramic, and metal artifacts that generally indicated manufacture and use between 1895 and 1920. Artifacts such as porcelain doll arms reflected that there were children at the site. As a salesman in a store, Rafael Cisneros would have had regular access to manufactured products and goods. The small number of cans or metal fragments at the site, however, suggested that the Cisneros family may have raised most of their own food rather than purchasing canned or bottled goods.

A second surge in homesteading occurred in the project area in the 1930s. Several sites were associated with the 1936 Stock-Raising Homestead allotment of Gavina A. Garcia, including the primary homestead settlement and a 1936 rural school house built by the WPA and designed by Gavina Garcia's eldest son, Julian Garcia (Table 7.1; Figure 7.3). According to her homestead case file, Gavina Garcia first occupied her allotment in January 1930. In her March 1936 claimant testimony, she listed over $1,000 in improvements made to the homestead allotment, many of which were relocated during survey. Neither Garcia nor her witnesses mentioned a WPA school house on the property (BLM 1936).

Gavina Garcia was an elderly widow at the time she applied for her homestead patent. Much of the construction and use of the allotment was probably by Julian Garcia and his family. Gavina Garcia lived in (upper) Mosquero since at least 1935 and probably only maintained livestock on the allotment (United States Census Bureau 1940b).

The Garcia family was impacted by drought and the economic conditions of the Depression. Gavina Garcia returned to land offices in (upper) Mosquero and Roy approximately 16 times between her initial application and final proof to have the land qualified as a stock-raising

TABLE 7.1. Homestead Sites and Features.

Eutemia Blea née Sisneros (Occupation 1906–ca. 1920s)		
LA Number	**Feature Number**	**Feature Type**
185271	1	Barn
	2	One-room habitation with prepared terrace
	3	Rock alignment
	4	Rock pile
	5	Rock alignment
	6	Rock-lined dugout
	7	Small rectangular outbuilding
	NA	Two artifact concentrations and general artifact scatter (n = 508)
185276	1	One-room habitation
	2	Stacked-rock corral
	NA	Artifact scatter (n = 227)
Rafael Cisneros (Occupation 1907–ca. 1920s)		
LA Number	**Feature Number**	**Feature Type**
185270	1	Three-room habitation
	2	Small rectangular outbuilding (chicken house)
	3	Outbuilding (shed?)
	4	Rock alignment
	5	Rock alignment
	6	Rock terrace
	7	Rock pile, function unknown
	8	Rock pile, function unknown
	9	Rock pile, function unknown
	NA	One artifact concentration and general artifact scatter (n = 659)
Gavina A. Garcia (Occupation c. 1930–1936)		
LA Number	**Feature Number**	**Feature Type**
185283	1	Half dugout (animal shed?)
	2	Small rectangular structure
	3	Earthen dam, possibly WPA
	5	One-room habitation with prepared terrace
	7	Half dugout
	8	Juniper post corral
	10	Three-room habitation
	11	Check dam
	NA	Artifact scatter (estimated 1000s, n = 73 diagnostic artifacts)
185286	1	Dugout
	2	Small rectangular structure
	NA	Artifact scatter (estimated less than 100, n = 16 diagnostic artifacts)
185295	1	Well
	NA	No artifacts associated with the well feature
185318	1	WPA school house
	NA	Artifact concentration within 15 m of the school house (n = 1,445)

FIGURE 7.3. LA 185318 Feature 1, Works Progress Administration schoolhouse: (*a*) south elevation, (*b*) east elevation with entrance, (*c*) interior, view from entrance looking west. Schoolhouse is on the Gavina A. Garcia homestead allotment. Photograph by Erin Hegberg.

homestead (therefore avoiding the cultivation requirements) and to receive an extension on her final proof due to economic circumstances (United States Bureau of Land Management 1936). The homestead was an important source of additional income or subsistence for the Garcia family between 1930 and at least 1940.

Architecture, Place, and Community

Residents of the lower Mosquero homesteading community built their own homes using locally quarried stone, and their homes exhibited New Mexican vernacular building traditions that were rooted in place and local topography. By the 1930s, residents also incorporated some aspects of postrailroad national building styles. These stylistic adoptions were limited and only retained if they were compatible with local community needs.

Archaeologists recorded 93 structures and features related to homesteads in this area, 30 of which are within homesteads discussed in this chapter (see Table 7.1). They consisted of residences, barns, corrals, and a range of less easily identified outbuilding types that probably functioned as chicken coops, loafing sheds, privies, cold storage, or smokehouses. All of the residential structures were stacked-rock masonry with little to no adobe remaining. The buildings were constructed between approximately 1900 and 1935.

In a survey in the Pinyon Canyon Maneuver Site in southeast Colorado, Carrillo and others (2011:56) noted that the rural vernacular architecture there showed very little change even into the 1920s when nearby towns included bungalows, frame houses, and other varieties imported on the railroad. In some ways, this is true for the residential structures and outbuildings in the lower Mosquero homesteading community. Despite changes in national styles and available architectural materials, buildings in lower Mosquero maintained characteristics of New Mexico vernacular style architecture, such as stacked-rock masonry and local materials rather than milled lumber, room organization in linear or L-shaped arrangements, and use of the natural landscape to provide wind protection, passive solar heating, and other benefits (Wilson 1997).

Still, this community also displayed subtle influences from nearby towns, especially in the second wave of homesteading in the 1930s. Residential buildings from this period had the highest proportions of quarried stone with rusticated finishes (Figure 7.4), possibly indicating an interest in postrailroad trends in similar stone buildings in (upper) Mosquero. The use of rusticated stone finishing was especially prominent in the 1936 WPA school house. Like other buildings in the project area, the school house was built from local stone. The interior core of the walls was stacked tabular sandstone and the exteriors were dressed with rusticated quartzitic sandstone. The exterior of the school house was not intended to be covered with adobe, and other nearby residential structures with rusticated stone dressing possibly were also left uncovered on the exteriors in an evolution of the local vernacular style.

The stacked-rock house on Eutemia Blea née Sisnero's enlarged homestead allotment is another example of the local incorporation of some national architectural features. The one-room structure has several characteristics atypical of New Mexico vernacular architecture from this period. First, the remaining walls suggest a single-story structure with ceilings nearly 3.5 m high (Figure 7.5). Additionally, window/door openings are present in all four walls and are also very tall (at least 1.16 m). Such large windows would have been cold and inefficient for a habitation in this climate, but possibly ideal for a public structure such as a post office or store. The openings in the structure were later filled in with rubble masonry, which may indicate careful seasonal abandonment or remodeling by later occupants. The coursing, stone size, and rusticated dressing of the masonry have some similarities to buildings observed in (upper) Mosquero. Swan and Martinez noted in (upper) Mosquero that many structures illustrated "the blending or hybridization that occurred when Hispanic and Anglo building traditions interacted on the plains" (1994:52). Similar hybridization can be observed in the structure on

FIGURE 7.4. Masonry styles: (*a*), (*b*), and (c) are from pre-1920 structures; (*d*), (e), and (*f*) are from post-1920 structures; (c) and (*f*) are wall dressed wall profiles. Photographs by Erin Hegberg.

Eutemia Blea née Sisnero's property, especially in the window size and placement.

Lower Mosquero residents adapted traditional architecture and incoming national styles to meet their local needs relative to place and microtopography. Among the residential structures, the orientation of windows, doorways, and corner fireplaces varied considerably. Previous work suggested that the southeast corner was preferred for fireplaces (Boyd 1974) while

FIGURE 7.5. LA 185276 Feature 1, west wall exterior with doorway blocked by masonry, Eutemia Blea neé Sisneros enlarged homestead allotment. Photograph by Erin Hegberg.

south and east sides were preferred for entryways in Hispanic homes (Bunting 1976). Lower Mosquero residential structures, however, were often placed just below the crests of small hills with entries oriented towards seasonal springs, regardless of the direction. Overall, postrailroad architectural styles did not lead to large changes in the vernacular residential architecture in the community, but neither were the residents completely unchanged or unaware of changes in regional building trends.

Unlike many "traditional" Hispanic villages, the lower Mosquero homesteading community had a dispersed settlement pattern. The large sizes of stock-raising homesteads and enlarged homesteads precluded settlements clustered around a plaza or community buildings, or along waterways and irrigation networks. The lives of residents in the study area were still closely integrated and retained the mutual dependencies that defined communities, especially during the difficult years of the 1930s. These relationships can be traced through witness statements in homestead case files.

The lives of Gavina Garcia's family and their neighbor, Moises Vialpando, appear to have been especially intertwined. Two of Gavina Garcia's sons, Gregoro and Julian Garcia, served as witnesses to Vialpando's application for a leave of absence. As a witness to Vialpando's claimant testimony, Julian Garcia stated that he saw the claimant 200 times a year, suggesting a very close association. Joe Garcia, a third son of Gavina Garcia, had an arrangement with Vialpando to graze six head of cattle on his allotment. Joe also served as a witness to Vialpando's application for stock-raising designation for his allotment (BLM 1937). In return, Vialpando served as a witness in Gavina Garcia's final proof as well (BLM 1936).

Generally, homesteaders in lower Mosquero chose their close neighbors and peers to serve as witnesses. They were often of a similar age to the homesteader, and all of the named witnesses had Hispanic surnames. In the case of Gavina Garcia, the many witnesses involved in her homesteading process were of similar age to Julian Garcia, her eldest son, further suggesting that he was the primary force behind the application and resident on the allotment.

These three homesteads demonstrate that although their allotments were dispersed, Eutemia Blea née Sisneros, Rafael Sisneros, and Gavina Garcia maintained connections with surrounding settlements, through labor, architecture, and family networks.

Community Affiliations

Gallegos is a possible candidate as the parent village of the Hispanic homesteaders who came to lower Mosquero. The village is located 9.7 km directly east of the study area (as the crow flies) at the bottom of the escarpment. Mosquero Canyon opens into the Ute Valley approximately 12.9 km northwest of Gallegos (see Figure 7.1).

In the US Census, Gallegos and (upper) Mosquero were enumerated separately beginning in 1900 (United States Census Bureau 1900b). Despite the distinction, consistent confusion appears to surround how the population in the study area should be documented in the census. Most often when homesteaders or witnesses in the community were recorded in the census rolls between 1900 and 1930 (United States Census Bureau 1900b, 1910d, 1920b, 1930b), they were enumerated in Mosquero, or, as of 1930, in Lower Mosquero. One witness was listed in Gould (an early name for upper Mosquero). In the homestead case files, however, 19 out of 37 people with listed locations self-identified as being from "Gallegos." All of these individuals were associated with patents prior to 1930.

By the 1930s, the orientation of the lower Mosquero homesteading community shifted northwards. A narrative history of Mosquero, collected by the Works Progress Administration (WPA) Federal Writers' Project in July 1936 described Old Mosquero as:

> a little Mexican settlement located several miles southeast of the present town, and down in the canyon. This little village consisted of a few stores, saloons, and a post office...There are still a number of inhabitants in old Mosquero although there is no business maintained there. The people all own a small herd of goats, and some have a few cows; they raise small gardens and do a little farming; most of the men work on the big ranches of the Gallegos', the de Bacas', and the Mitchels' [Emery 1936].

The narrative suggests that by the 1930s the idea of lower Mosquero/Old Mosquero as related to the (upper) Mosquero railroad community, rather than being affiliated with Gallegos, had solidified and was being incorporated into descriptions of the town's historic roots. The homestead community had not moved, but the social relationships homesteaders maintained with surrounding settlements had shifted away from Gallegos towards Upper Mosquero.

The 1936 WPA school house on Gavina Garcia's allotment is another example of community development among this group of homesteads. The school was designed by Gavina's son, Julian Garcia, and was built by a work crew of local men. In small rural communities, a school house served not just educational needs, but was also as a place to host many community events and functions. Having the school house as a community space further integrated the homesteaders in the area and established their local identities as independent from, but integrated with, Upper Mosquero and Mosquero Canyon. On a 1938 state highway map, the immediate community is labeled "Garcia." This may have been a cartographer's confusion of the community name and landowner's name, but it also reflects that the area had the population density and social cohesion outsiders might have associated with an independent community (New Mexico State Highway Department 1938).

Discussion

Office of Contract Archeologist crews documented at least 10 distinct homestead settlements during the survey project. The settlements reflected two different homesteading periods: the first in 1900–1920 and the second in 1920–1930s. The second period was concentrated on stock-raising homestead patents, primarily in the drier southern portion of the study area.

Homesteaders in the community had Hispanic surnames, and their parents were born in New Mexico. Census records indicated many residents spoke Spanish and could not read or write (United States Census Bureau 1900b, 1910d, 1920b, 1930b). Most residents were involved in ranching or stock-raising, either as employees of larger ranches or independently. The US Census falls short in adequately reflecting the range of activities Hispanic settlers used to maintain a living on their allotments. For example, Rafael Cisneros also taught school in Gallegos and kept a store. Julian Garcia was a carpenter/architect, while his mother, Gavina Garcia, kept a herd of 100 goats.

Homesteaders in the community worked hard to maintain ownership of their allotments. Gavina Garcia made at least 16 trips to the land office before she was finally able to prove up on her allotment. Access to land was an important part of the Hispanic economic and subsistence base in this region, whether for household gardens, livestock, or small-scale economic activities such as selling milk or eggs. While many farmers and ranchers sold or lost their property during the Depression, most Hispanic homesteaders in the area did not sell until the 1940s.

Homesteaders in this community demonstrated again and again their determination to define their own community and relationships. Despite census enumeration patterns (1900b, 1910d, 1920b) associating the settlement with upper Mosquero in 1900 to 1920, the homesteaders chose to work, travel to, and socialize in Gallegos, down in Ute Valley. They consistently self-identified as being "from Gallegos" throughout the early homesteading period.

During the 1930s homesteading phase, the community narrative shifted. Now some community members lived at least part-time in upper Mosquero and drew on the railroad town's architectural styles and access to bureaucratic services. Euro-Americans attempted to integrate lower Mosquero into the historic narrative of the town, even as the U.S. Census Bureau (1930b) identified it as a separate settlement for the first time. Residents again defined their own community narrative, however, by leveraging WPA funding for their own rural schoolhouse and maintaining local support networks through the Depression such that they could each keep access to their land. The community continued to underscore its independence to the degree that it was mapped as "Garcia" in 1938.

New Mexico has few fully documented Hispanic homesteads, and archaeological survey conducted under the auspices of cultural resource management rarely provides the opportunity to examine entire homestead allotments. Comprehensive survey, combined with census data and homestead case files, has allowed archaeologists to chart the shifting relationships within the lower Mosquero homesteading community, how community definitions changed over time, and how homesteading residents created a place for themselves on the landscape and among surrounding settlements.

Acknowledgments

This work was possible through a contract between the Office of Contract Archeology and the New Mexico Department of Game and Fish, and with the support of Trigg Ranch and the Trigg family who allowed us to work on their land and visit their family home. Francisco Uviña, Patricia Crown, and Robert Dello-Russo made helpful comments on drafts of this chapter and the original report. Scott Gunn gave essential graphical support.

Notes

1. Between 1862 and 1916, Congress passed seven different homesteading acts that established several avenues for citizens to claim public land. Some patents in the project area were filed under the original 1862 Homestead Act, while others were filed under the Enlarged Homestead Act of 1909, which allowed up to 320 acres, or the Stock-Raising Homestead Act of 1916, which allowed 640 acres. Each type of homestead had slightly different residency and development requirements.

8

Writing on the Trees

Observing the Marks Left by Hispano Sheepherders in New Mexico

S. Joey LaValley

People deliberately leave traces of their identities on the landscape, whether it be through place names, petroglyphs, or graffiti on a train, and the American West is no exception. The traces of human existence may be as visible as Wheeler Peak, the highest mountain in New Mexico, named after Euro-American explorer and surveyor George Wheeler. Still, the materiality of many of history's participants is easily overlooked, unnoticed, or seen as inconsequential.

Nearly two miles above sea level in the rugged but beautiful mountains of northern New Mexico stand ancient aspen groves marked by visitors both historic and modern (Figure 8.1). Along dirt roads, dispersed campfire rings litter the ground and scars on the trees bear witness to those who have recently passed. "Gina + Mark 4 ever" and "Paul was here 1997" remind newcomers that others have visited this place. Beyond these modern camps, tucked away in thickets of mixed conifer, rest countless other messages left from people and times nearly forgotten.

Previously undocumented aspen carvings illuminate how one particular group, twentieth-century Hispano sheepherders, interacted with their landscape. Also referred to as dendroglyphs, these carvings represent a medium through which Hispano sheepherders expressed their identities and provide insight into how this community viewed place at home and away. The carvings document names, hometowns, dates of authorship, and artistic impressions made during the 1930s, 1940s, and 1950s. This chapter highlights one way Hispano sheepherders from Arroyo Seco, a small village in northern New Mexico, left their trace in the American West, while also shedding light on the demographics, economics, and motivations of these herders.

Dendroglyphs and Herding Sheep in the American West

In general, dendroglyphs are made on aspen trees, as the soft wood and smooth bark is easy to carve, and the resulting black scars contrast against the snow-white bark. A glyph will last for the remaining life of the aspen and, depending on rates of decay, can be visible on the dried bark for some time after the tree is dead or fallen. Many variables affect aspen growth rate and a tree's life span, including elevation, aspect, slope, soil, and wind (Connolly 2012). Aspens grow in clonal colonies connected via an underground system of roots, a network that under certain conditions can persist for thousands of years. Generally, a healthy individual tree will live between 80 and 120 years, with some reported cases of trees living up to 200 years (Mueggler 1989). As such, dendroglyphs represent a written history that will invariably disappear.

Dendroglyphs are not unique to the highlands of New Mexico, but are found throughout the American West wherever aspen grow.

FIGURE 8.1. Typical aspen grove encountered in the Sangre de Cristo Mountains. Photograph by Lisa Carter. Courtesy of the Carson National Forest.

Arguably the most well-documented and prolific aspen tree carvings are those produced by Basque sheepherders in the mountains of Nevada and California, and, to a lesser extent, in Oregon and Arizona. Typical Basque inscriptions include names, dates, hometowns, poetry, and art—the latter sometimes depicting erotic scenes or provocative sketches of women (Connolly 2012; Mallea-Olaetxe 2008, 2009). The life of a sheepherder was one of solitude and it is generally thought that carving was practiced to pass time or to project the herder's thoughts in the moment.

While the Basques immigrated primarily to Nevada and the surrounding states, sheep ranches in southern Colorado and northern New Mexico were owned by and employed a mostly local Hispano labor force. Hispano, used here and throughout, refers to persons descendant from settlers of New Spain living in the southwestern United States. This group is differentiated from Hispanic, a term that encompasses a broader community, and the Basques who hail from the Basque Country in northern Spain. According to Reyes Martinez (2012:64), "a great part of the adult male population of Taos County [where Arroyo Seco is located] chose or adopted…[sheepherding] as their calling or main occupation," following family and regional traditions, and sheepherders from this area were preferred in other sheep-raising areas such as Colorado and Wyoming. In *Stories from Hispano New Mexico*, Martinez (2012) describes the typical year for a sheepherder. During the winter months, sheep were pastured in the lowlands where temperatures were warmer and grass more plentiful. The lambing period was typically in late April or early May, and the owner of the herds hired more men during this period than they would employ the remainder of the year. After lambing, the flock was moved to corrals where the ewes could more easily be sheared. Soon after, the flock began a multiday trek to summer pastures in the surrounding mountain ranges via well-established stock driveways. If too large, the flock was split into smaller, more manageable ones, and one man oversaw each flock until the beginning of fall. On some occasions, a second man, referred to as a *mayordomo*, broke and set camp, scouted new pastures, and prepared meals, while the first man tended the flock. In September, the sheep were driven back to the valleys where lambs were separated and shipped to market. Rams and ewes were then pastured together and the cycle began again.

While the yearly sheepherding cycle played out in this order, sometimes variation in the timing of the cycle was necessary due to yearly discrepancies in the seasons and the environmental conditions of the places important to sheepherders and their flocks. For example, a wetter than average winter or late snow melt at higher elevations might delay the drive, resulting in a late July or early August arrival to summer pastures. Conversely, a previous dry season would affect the amount of grass available at lower pastures, making it advantageous to move the sheep to greener grounds sooner in the summer. Such variations, as explored below, are reflected in the dates of newly identified dendroglyphs.

Like the Basques, Hispano sheepherders left their mark on the aspens along sheep driveways (Boster 2017). James DeKorne's (1970) *Aspen Art in the New Mexico Highlands* documents a variety of dendroglyphs depicting names, dates, and various artistic representations. Examples of art include horses, birds, crosses, and houses. Unlike the Basque examples, however, Hispano aspen carvings exhibit very few lewd or erotic depictions (Boster 2017; DeKorne 1970; De Yoanna 2014). While dendroglyphs are very common along sheep driveways, they are also found wherever a herder grazed or rested their flock.

The Newly Recorded Dendroglyphs

In July 2014, contract archaeologists, including the author, identified numerous previously undocumented historic dendroglyphs on trees in the Carson National Forest in northern New Mexico. These carvings are located between 3,109 and 3,353 m above sea level in the Sangre de Cristo Mountains near the headwaters of Upper Bitter and Cabresto Creeks. These creeks likely provided well-watered and relatively easy access routes into and out of the high elevation pastures that herders considered ideal for summer grazing. While historic cabins and mining features are also present in the surrounding area, there are only two examples of these features *and* dendroglyphs occurring at the same location within the project area; therefore, these activities appear to be unrelated. Unsurprisingly, due to the ephemeral and ever-moving nature of sheepherding, none of the dendroglyphs have observed artifacts directly associated with them. A lack of associated artifacts at these sites makes it difficult, if not impossible, to identify the carvers without further research. Archival documents, however, tie the carvings to Hispano sheepherders. These carvings represent the only physical evidence that sheepherders once passed here.

Carved dates observed range from 1931 to 1954, but most were carved during the 1940s

TABLE 8.1. Summary of Names, Dates, Places, and Presence of Art.

Names		Dates	Hometown	Presence of Art
Garcia	Fernando	—	—	No
Martinez	Crisoforo	1944, 1945, 1946, 1949	Arroyo Seco, NM	Yes
"	Eloy	1940	Arroyo Seco, NM	No
"	Epifanio	—	—	No
"	Ernesto	1949, 1950	Arroyo Seco, NM	No
"	Gilberto	194?, 1954	Arroyo Seco, NM	No
"	Nicolas	1944, 1946	Arroyo Seco, NM	No
"	Ruben	1944, 1945, 1948, 1949	Arroyo Seco, NM	No
Pacheco	Benero	—	Arroyo Seco, NM	No
Romero		1934	—	No
Sanchez	Felix/Phil	—	Arroyo Seco, NM	No
"	J A	—	Arroyo Seco, NM	No
"		1931	NM	No
Valencia	Patrocinio	1942, 1945, 1949	Arroyo Seco, NM	Yes
M S	M S	—	Cerro, NM	Yes
Zeries	Zeries	1950	—	No
—	—	1933	—	Yes

and early 1950s by a small group of socially and familially connected individuals, the Martinez family. In fact, only eight examples of dendroglyphs not associated with the Martinez family were located. For the purpose of this study, these examples will not be discussed any further. Table 8.1 contains a summary of the data collected from the dendroglyphs, including names, dates of inscription, hometowns, and the presence or absence of associated art.

Dendroglyphs associated with the Martinez family were produced by individuals from Arroyo Seco, New Mexico. This small community was established in 1806 on a Spanish land grant approximately 12 km north of Taos, near the mouth of Hondo Canyon and located at 2,316 m above sea level. Arroyo Seco was and still remains today a largely agricultural community, although sheepherding is no longer as common an industry as it once was. As the crow flies, Arroyo Seco lies roughly 32 km southwest of the newly documented dendroglyphs, well within the range of a seasonal sheep drive. Its location at the foot of the Sangre de Cristo Mountains provided the sheepherders of Arroyo Seco easy access to warmer winter grazing pastures in the valley bottom and lush summer grazing pastures high up in the mountains.

Sheepherders of Arroyo Seco

While most studies of sheepherders solely focus on the dendroglyphs they produced, little has been discussed about the demographics or economics of the everyday sheepherder. These factors can play a significant role in determining how this particular demographic views and interacts with the places they live and work. A review of 1940 United States Census Bureau data for Arroyo Seco allows for such a discussion. Relevant census data gathered in 1940 includes age, sex, highest grade of school completed, ownership and cost of housing, occupation, number of months employed in 1939, estimated salary from 1939, and current status of employment (United States Census Bureau 1940c). Since the census was conducted in the spring, it is likely that most sheepherders would have been present in town rather than at camps in the mountains, making this an important and inclusive source of information.

Based on the data, herding sheep in Arroyo Seco was a major industry in 1940. The 1940 United States Census, identified at least 51 men as sheepherders and many more as farmers or stock raisers (United States Census Bureau 1940c). A cursory glance at available census data prior to 1940 shows that sheepherding had been a significant industry for Arroyo Seco since at least the mid-nineteenth century. The reason for this is likely its location on the landscape, at the base of the mountains with easy and abundant access to both winter and summer pastures. As Arroyo Seco was comprised of 163 households in 1940, nearly one in every three households held a sheepherder.

All 51 individuals recorded as sheepherders in the 1940 US Census for Arroyo Seco identified as Hispano men between the ages of 17 and 74, with a median age of 43, and Spanish appears to be the primary language spoken in their households (United States Census Bureau 1940c). Of these 51 individuals, 36 reported being fully employed while 15 were reported as under- or unemployed. It is also likely that the number of working sheepherders was higher, since herders were not always listed as such and children of stock raisers often were not considered employed or paid if underage and working for the family farm.

This trend of children working for the family business is possibly represented in the levels of education reported in the census data (United States Census Bureau 1940c). The median highest grade of school completed for sheepherders was third grade. In fact, only one herder out of 51 reported attending a grade higher than eighth. Similar trends are apparent in other parts of Arroyo Seco's non-herding industries as well. It appears that in Arroyo Seco, like many rural farming and ranching communities, a higher education level was not necessarily required or prioritized as children could be pulled from school to provide additional labor on the farm. Among sheepherders, a slight correlation can be found between age and highest completed grade in school. On average, the older generation had less schooling than the younger generation, indicating a potential shift over time in prioritizing education. Additionally, level of education did not appear to affect the number of weeks worked annually or previous year's income.

Not surprisingly, a positive correlation can be found between income and number of weeks worked. On average, sheepherders reported being paid $11.27 per week in 1939. Those employed at the time of the census reported working 70 hours during the week of March 24 to March 30. If accurate, the average sheepherder's hourly wage would be $0.16, nearly half that of the country's minimum wage at the time (United States Department of Labor 2009). Moreover, sheepherders were considered "on the clock" 24/7 when tending sheep in their summer pastures. A 40-hour work week would bring their wage up to $0.28 per hour, only two cents below the minimum wage, but none reported working less than 70 hours. While it is easier to think in terms of hourly wage, sheepherders may have been paid a salary or flat rate instead. Since a sheepherder's schedule fluctuated throughout the year, working 70 hours a week makes sense during lambing season or summer grazing, while fewer hours might be worked during the winter.

Another interesting economic measure for sheepherders is the value and ownership of property. In Arroyo Seco, most heads of household owned their own property. Homes/farms ranged from $80 to $4,000, with a median value of $300, well below the median cost of $656 for a home in New Mexico in 1940 (United States Census Bureau 1940c, 2012). Although below the state's average, the median cost of non-herders' homes was also $300, suggesting that Arroyo Seco had a lower cost of living than other parts of the state, potentially due to the town's rural location and reduced amenities and industries as compared to more urban centers such as Santa Fe or Albuquerque. However, the 36 fully employed sheepherders and the 15 who were under- or unemployed display a visible distinction in their income and home values. Those employed at the time of the census averaged a previous year's income of $356.75 over 31.2 weeks for an average of $11.43 per week. Those under- or unemployed at the time of the census averaged a previous year's income of $238.27 over 24.3 weeks for an average of $9.81 per week. That difference resulted in a disparity of $1.62 per week or $118.48 for the year. This disproportionate income is also represented in the average value of homes or properties. The value of homes owned by those fully employed averaged $342.70, while properties of the under- or unemployed sheepherders averaged $271.43, for a difference of $71.27. Although no correlation between age or highest grade of school completed can account for this gap, fluctuations in labor demand could. As typical in the sheep-raising industry, seasonal employees would be hired during the spring for lambing and shearing, as well as in the fall when lambs were shipped to market. Those men under- or unemployed at the time of the census may represent this seasonal workforce. Additionally, families may have been more inclined to employ their own sons during the summer drives, as indicated by the Martinez case.

Who Are the Martinez?

The Martinez family serves not only as a case study of the demographics of Arroyo Seco's sheepherders, but also provides tangible links between specific people and the archaeological marks they left on the landscape. As discussed above, the surname Martinez accounts for a majority of the dendroglyphs and includes seven brothers: Crisoforo, Eloy, Epifanio, Ernesto, Gilberto, Nicolas, and Ruben. Additionally, of all the names carved on aspens, only the seven Martinez brothers and Patrocinio Valencia occur more than once in the project area. Based on this observation, the Martinez family likely held a grazing permit for these particular pasturelands, potentially making them a prominent sheepherding family in Arroyo Seco. Evidence for the Martinez and their relationships to each other is also found in several historic documents, including World War II military records and the 1940 US Census (1940c).

Table 8.2 lists all members of the Martinez family household as reported in the 1940 US Census for Arroyo Seco (and provides a few of their responses to the main questions asked of each census participant) (United States Census Bureau 1940c). In addition to these questions, two out of every 40 individuals were also asked supplementary questions, including Luiza Martinez, the youngest Martinez daughter. Her responses indicated that Spanish was the primary language spoken in the Martinez home and that both parents were born in New Mexico (United States Census Bureau 1940c).

The family of 14 reported living on a farm valued at $1,000, which was owned by the head of household, Toribio Martinez. As established above, this home value is well above the median for Arroyo Seco during that time and supports the idea that the Martinez family operated a successful enterprise. Toribio and his two eldest sons, Juan Francisco and Juan Reyes, are listed as farmers/stock raisers, working full-time all 52 weeks in 1939. Toribio also worked on his own account (i.e., self-employed), and both sons were reported as unpaid family workers. All three reported zero for wages earned in 1939, and other than Celina Martinez (matron of the family) whose reported occupation is "house wife," no other family members were listed as working. Though none of the seven brothers who carved dendroglyphs were employed in 1940, census data indicates they followed in their father's and elder brothers' path and eventually worked as sheepherders in the high mountains. Based on their ages as reported in 1940 and known dates in which they carved dendroglyphs, the Martinez brothers were between the ages of 13 and 20 when they herded sheep (see Table 8.2; United States Census Bureau 1940c).

The other individual prominently featured in the dendroglyphs, Patrocinio Valencia, though not affiliated with the Martinez household in the 1940 US census, appears in the 1930 US Census

TABLE 8.2. Martinez Family Details as Reported in the 1940 US Census.

Individual	Relation to Head of House	Sex	Age	Highest Grade Completed	Working	Occupation/ Industry	Appears in Dendroglyphs	Age When Carved
Toribio	Head	M	55	4	Yes	Farmer/ Stock raiser	No	—
Celina	Wife	F	46	4	Yes	House wife	No	—
Juan F.	Son	M	27	7	Yes	Farmer/ Stock raiser	No	—
Juan R.	Son	M	22	10	Yes	Farmer/ Stock raiser	No	—
Divian E[loy]	Son	M	20	9	No	—	Yes	20
Celestina R.	Daughter	F	18	11	No	—	No	—
Jose Epifanio	Son	M	16	7	No	—	Yes	?
Luiza E.	Daughter	F	14	7	No	—	No	—
Santiago N[icolas]	Son	M	12	5	—	—	Yes	16–18
Crisoforo B.	Son	M	11	4	—	—	Yes	15–20
Ruben R.	Son	M	9	1	—	—	Yes	13–18
Ernesto T.	Son	M	6	—	—	—	Yes	15–16
Gilbert[o] C.	Son	M	4	—	—	—	Yes	13–18
Jose Elias	Son	M	1	—	—	—	No	—

Note: Data from United States Census Bureau (1940c).

for Arroyo Seco and in the 1940 US Census for the neighboring village of Valdez (United States Census Bureau 1930c, 1940d). Furthermore, Patrocinio's World War II draft registration card from 1941 specifies him as a "sheepherder," working out of Arroyo Seco for Toribio Martinez (United States World War II Draft Registration Cards 1941). Based on his age reported at the time these documents were completed and dates associated with his carvings, he was between 22 and 29 when he herded sheep with the Martinez brothers, making him older than them by several years. Interestingly, Patrocinio's draft registration card notes the "registrant unable to read or write," and many of his carvings contain small inverted or misplaced letters (Figure 8.2; United States World War II Draft Registration Cards 1941).

While his own children left herding by the age of 20, why Toribio Martinez employed Patrocinio, at least into his late 20s, is unclear. Possibly Toribio needed someone older than his youngest sons to manage operations away from the ranch when the oldest Martinez sons were no longer available to work sheep for their father. The eldest Martinez brother, Juan Francisco, moved to Douglas, Wyoming, by 1941 (United States World War II Draft Registration Cards 1941), and the next eldest Martinez son, Juan Reyes, served in the Navy between January 1944 and April 1946 (New Mexico World War II Service Records 1946).

Seasonality, Revisiting Place, and the Nature of Art

As discussed above, herding sheep is cyclical with specific events happening at specific times and places. Due to this predictability, specific places were revisited during similar times of year, sometimes by the same individuals. The

FIGURE 8.2. Dendroglyphs by Patrocinio Valencia. Note small handwriting, backwards "S" in "ASNM" motif, and inverted "AIC" at end of name. Photograph by Lisa Carter. Courtesy of the Carson National Forest.

FIGURE 8.3. Partial view of dendroglyphs that completely read "7/2/46 / CRISOFORO / MARtlnez / ARROYO / Seco / n.M." Photograph by Lisa Carter. Courtesy of the Carson National Forest.

project area in which these new dendroglyphs were identified consisted of several discontinuous parcels spread across a 5 × 5 km area. As not every sheepherder produced dendroglyphs and additional dendroglyphs, probably occur in the unsurveyed areas between and around the parcels, an exact quantity of people present any given season and finite patterns of movement cannot be precisely attained. Still, larger patterns can be ascertained regarding the nature of dendroglyphs as placemaking and community-building activities.

Some of the dendroglyph sites within the project area show evidence that individuals returned in a later year and carved on a different tree. This duplication, however, is rare, and no instances were found of more than one person carving on the same tree or more than one date occurring on the same tree. Along with the year, some dates observed also include the month and day on which they were carved (Figure 8.3 and Figure 8.4). Of the 33 aspen carvings with detailed dates, six were made in June, 23 in July, and four in August. The earliest is June 17 and the latest is August 7, though the former was from 1933 and has no associated name or place. The dendroglyphs, then, provide further insight into the behaviors of Arroyo Seco's sheepherders

FIGURE 8.4. Partial view of dendroglyphs that completely read "Ruben MArTiNeZ / Arroyo Seco / New Mexico / 6/30/44." Photograph by crew member. Courtesy of the Carson National Forest.

and their connections to the landscapes of their labor in general and the Martinez family specifically.

The earliest time of year a Martinez is known to have been in the immediate area was June 29 (Crisoforo in 1946), indicating that on average they arrived during a four- to five-week period in peak summer. This time span conforms to the known seasonal cycle for herding sheep in the highlands of New Mexico, as sheep were typically moved in late spring from the valley bottoms to higher pastures for grazing.

The route from Arroyo Seco that the Martinez followed to drive their sheep is unknown, as is the length of the trip to the pastures, but these aspen groves were part of their seasonal round. In fact, at least one member of the Martinez family returned here nearly every year for more than a decade. While the general area was revisited year after year, specific aspen stands appear to have been reoccupied more than once over several years. Carvings from up to four different summers at the same dendroglyph site indicate that the Martinez were tied to these places. Repetitive use of place could be attributed to constraints beyond one's control, such as resource availability or government-mandated grazing allotments, but another factor might be the security, which comes from being in a familiar place. While government permits may have defined the general area in which sheep could be grazed, the repeated use of particular aspen groves is likely the result of individual agency rather than external forces. Revisiting a specific place from years past might have invoked nostalgia for the Martinez brothers, and, while witnessing their brothers' past inscriptions, might have provided them solace at times of loneliness. Although the exact motive for revisiting these places is not entirely clear, the purpose could be practical, psychological, or maybe a combination of both.

Based on the carved dates and their locations, most of the herders appear to have visited specific groves alone on any given year. This is not to say that they were alone the entire time, as evidence indicates that several herders occupied the same general area at the same time. In 1944, Crisoforo, Nicolas, and Ruben herded, while Crisoforo, Patrocinio, and Ruben and were present in 1945, and only Crisoforo and Nicolas herded in 1946. In 1949, Crisoforo, Ernesto, Patrocinio, and Ruben herded sheep in the area. In rare cases, the Martinez brothers appear to have either worked in pairs or at least met during their stint in the mountains. On June 30, 1944, Nicolas and Ruben, aged 16 and 13 at the time, both carved their names and the date at the same site. At another site, Crisoforo and Ruben, aged 16 and 14 at the time, carved their names and "7/26/45" on separate trees. And, on July 6, 1946, Crisoforo and Nicolas, aged 18 and

FIGURE 8.5. Partial view of dendroglyphs made by Patrocinio Valencia. Artwork includes houses (visible), a turnip (partially visible on left), and corn stalk (not visible). Photograph by Lisa Carter. Courtesy of the Carson National Forest.

FIGURE 8.6. Art motifs including a five-point star, swastika, and hat associated with a second aspen (out of frame) with a bull and the letters "FM." Photograph by Lisa Carter. Courtesy of the Carson National Forest.

16 at the time, carved their names and the date at the same site. These examples could indicate the Martinez family employed an apprenticeship or *mayordomo* method of herding in which one brother trained the other brother how to tend sheep. In each case, one of the brothers is at least two years older than the other. In the latter two examples from 1945 and 1946, each brother had already experienced at least one season and, therefore, would not have required oversight. More likely, these instances represent a casual meeting to exchange information or supplies. Also worth noting, each of these sites has evidence for at least one later occupation by one or both of the original participants and/or a different brother.

Names, dates, and towns are the most prevalent carvings currently observed with the dendroglyphs reported herein, while artwork is typically lacking. When present, artwork is predominantly associated with two individuals, Crisoforo Martinez and Patrocinio Valencia, as indicated by their full names or initials on the same tree (Figure 8.5). Motifs include hands, birds, houses, and possible vegetables such as corn and turnips. Art produced by other individuals, not definitively associated with the Martinez family or Patrocinio, include a horse, a bull, a skull, stars, a hat, and a swastika (Figure 8.6).

While similarities exist in the artwork produced by these Hispano herders and Basque sheepherders from elsewhere in the American West, the Basque are well-known for carving poetry, portraits, and both tasteful and lewd depictions of women, motifs not currently observed in our study area. A young teenager, in the case of Crisoforo, may not yet have been exposed to such images or experiences. Additionally, since he was sometimes accompanied by a sibling, he might have been less inclined to express his feelings in a poem or to carve such coarse illustrations. In Patrocinio's case, he was an employee of the Martinez family and would be expected to behave in a professional manner. As illustrated above, there was a strong likelihood that the place in which they carved would be revisited by someone familiar, potentially curbing the nature of their art.

Place as a Rite of Passage

. . . *And Now Miguel*, a historical documentary film turned children's novel by Joseph Krumgold (1953a, 1953b), is a first-person nonfiction account of sheep raising in northern New Mexico during the 1940s. The film is narrated by Miguel Chavez, a 12-year-old Hispano boy living in Los Cordovas, New Mexico, a small town only 10 miles southwest of Arroyo Seco. Upon watching the film, one cannot help but draw comparisons between the Chavez and the Martinez families. For much of the film, Miguel takes the viewer along for the daily chores of living and working on a sheep ranch, all the while yearning to be treated as a man. Miguel romanticizes the day when he can accompany his father, uncles, and older brothers on the summer sheep drive to the Carson National Forest and into the Sangre de Cristo Mountains. He longs for the day that he will be able to carve an aspen, as the men in his family have done before him. After his eldest brother is drafted into military service, a replacement herder is needed, and Miguel's dream of joining the summer drive becomes a reality. Along the way, he notes his grandfather's and father's aspen carvings from July 1901 and June 1919. The story culminates when Miguel, finally recognized as a "grown up" by his family, carves his own name into an aspen high up in the Sangre de Cristo.

While determining such a motive may be unattainable, the Martinez brothers conceivably also saw the summer drive and the act of aspen carving as a rite of passage. Traveling to aspen groves high in the mountains away from home and parental oversight, along with witnessing their predecessors' marks, could have imparted onto them a similar attachment to family tradition and place, while also guiding them into maturity. Their inspiration to carve may not have been born out of loneliness, as is often an interpreted motive for the Basque, but rather pride, custom, and an innate deference to the places through which their father passed. The people of Arroyo Seco, and specifically the Martinez family, had a long history of sheepherding. We may never know if Toribio Martinez also carved his name into aspen, and, if he did, it would be impossible to know if he visited the same groves in which his sons carved, since those trees are likely long dead. But it is possible.

The subject of their art may also have been informed by the sanctity of their trip. . . . *And Now Miguel* makes it clear that Miguel romanticized the Sangre de Cristo Mountains, and throughout the film, he revered the journey as sacred. Such feelings might dissuade a young herder from scarring these holy places with offensive images. Consequently, the physical expression of an individual's or group's identity on the landscape can be informed by numerous variables not necessarily obvious from what they physically leave behind.

Conclusion

Dendroglyphs have the ability to shed light on nearly overlooked histories and to reflect the ways people identify themselves on the landscape. While the carvings observed in the Sangre de Cristo Mountains had limited context and associated archaeological signatures in the field with which to frame them, the addition of historical documents helps situate these places within a larger context. The project area was revisited as part of a yearly cycle, largely by a group of related individuals. From a stock raiser's perspective, this place was likely ideal for summer grazing with its lush pastures and cool temperatures, but to the individuals returning it may have represented something more. The independence and personal freedom that these teenage sheepherders gained each summer may have been a highly anticipated yearly event.

These groves provided a place to transition between adolescence and young adulthood. The aspen carvings may represent a continuation of family tradition, while also exhibiting a sense of hometown pride and a way to connect themselves to multiple places on the landscape. Lastly, the repetitive use of the area, especially by family members, as well as an intrinsic respect for this place, may have influenced the style and substance of their art.

As demonstrated by the above analysis of the 1940 US census for Arroyo Seco (1940c), supplemental information pulled from historic records sheds light on the demographics and economics for some of these sheepherders, adding new layers to the story told in the trees. Sheep herding, a profession in decline since the 1950s, used to be more widespread, as the consumption of lamb and use of wool in clothing was more prolific and profitable. As the industry shrank, traditions that were entrenched for many generations were quickly lost and any personal significance of these places was left in the past. While the marks made on aspens by herders will last longer than the people who made them, they, too, will eventually be lost to time. Recording these glyphs in detail not only preserves them in perpetuity, but also preserves an ever-dwindling tradition while illuminating a method with which groups and individuals interacted with place. Nonetheless, dendroglyphs (and their associated stories) represent just one account in a web of narratives that has shaped the American West into what it is today.

When one sees a place name on a map or graffiti on a rushing train, there is a lot more to those marks than can be gathered from a quick glance. Some may be easily unraveled, while others may lead to a complex network of relationships both amongst people and between people and place. Despite our best efforts, we may never know the history behind someone's representations or identify that person's intentions. However, one truth is constant: wherever people venture, traces of them and their identities remain.

9

Gathering Places

Alsatian Migration and Placemaking on the Texas Frontier

Patricia Markert

"Places gather," Edward Casey writes in Feld and Basso's *Senses of Place* (1996:27). By choosing a verb to characterize the nature of places, Casey makes place active. He frames it as a process, rather than a point on a map or location on a landscape. This chapter addresses this process of gathering in two towns that emerged from a nineteenth-century migration from Alsace to Texas (Waugh 1934; Weaver 2005). The two towns, known as Castroville and D'Hanis, were settled by Alsatian migrants in the 1840s on the westernmost border of Texas, 48 and 97 km west of San Antonio, respectively (Figure 9.1). By examining the narratives, strategies, and desires that brought the towns into existence and shaped them as places on the landscape, I explore how they are "gathered," or continually brought together, from their shared origins to their eventual divergence.

Casey's treatment of place is phenomenological, focusing on the way places transpire from dwelling in the world. His use of the term "gather" indicates that places are constantly in some state of emergence:

> Rather than being one definite sort of thing—for example, physical, spiritual, cultural, social—a given place takes on the qualities of its occupants, reflecting these qualities in its own constitution and description and expressing them in its occurrence as an event: places not only are, they happen. (And it is because they happen that they lend themselves well to narration, whether as history or as story) [Casey 1996:27].

Therefore, places reflect the communities that dwell in them, giving shape to the narrative ways people remember, narrate, and express them as situated histories on a landscape. The two towns I discuss here illustrate how migrations can constitute acts of gathering, and how different sorts of places can emerge from the same migration event through time. The places themselves take on storied qualities that illustrate and inform the strategies people use to root themselves in remembered pasts, imagined futures, and physical landscapes.

Alsace, a narrow region between the Rhine River and the Vosges Mountains, is currently a province of France, but has famously (along with its neighbor Lorraine) been a contested territory between France and Germany during the wars of the nineteenth and twentieth centuries. While the region has exhibited both French and German influences, it has a distinct language and culture that are a source of pride in both present-day Alsace and Alsatian Texas. The Alsatian migrants who settled in Texas during the mid-nineteenth century brought with them their language, Catholic religion, local food,

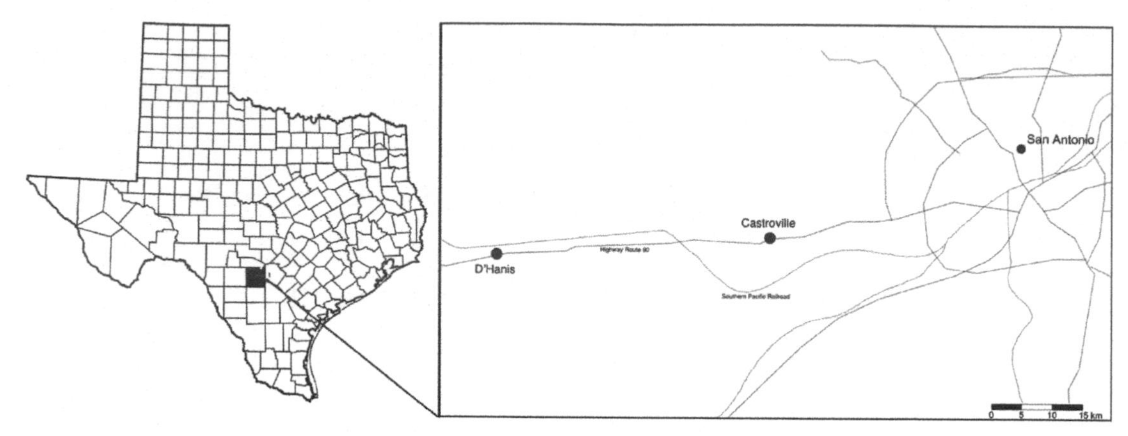

FIGURE 9.1. The location of Castroville and D'Hanis, Texas, in relation to San Antonio. Map by Patricia Markert, 2018.

and building styles. However, Castroville and D'Hanis have become very different places throughout a century and a half of placemaking, despite their shared origins as nineteenth-century Alsatian colonies.

The distinctions between the towns are visible in their built landscapes: Castroville presents itself as the "Little Alsace of Texas," while D'Hanis resembles an American railroad town. Their distinctive built landscapes convey storied understandings about history, identity, and memory in the communities of each town. In this chapter, I begin with a discussion of some of the observable differences between Castroville and D'Hanis, as well as two examples of material interventions on the landscape that illustrate placemaking strategies in the present. I will then turn to a discussion of their shared nineteenth-century origins to examine how "gathering" brought them into existence as places on the Texas landscape. Since, as Casey suggests, places emerge as events, I will present two encounters with these towns that illustrate how they have come to be expressed today.

Encountering Place in D'Hanis and Castroville, Texas

I returned to D'Hanis, Texas (pronounced *De-Hennis*) in August of 2017. I had first visited the town the year prior while working on an archaeological project directed by Ruth Van Dyke of Binghamton University in the town of Castroville, approximately 48 km east of D'Hanis. A year separated these two visits, but during that time D'Hanis had visibly changed. Photographs I had taken on the first visit in 2016 showed a single-sided main street with a block-long series of brick facades and false storefronts facing a railroad track and highway. It looked like a railroad town of the American West. What was striking about this first encounter was that the brick buildings on east side of the block were largely in ruin (Figure 9.2). On the west side of the block, just yards from the collapsed storefronts, a general store and post office continued to operate as usual. Conversations with local residents revealed that a tornado had struck part of the small downtown area in 2015, damaging the historic building used as the bank, a saloon, and a double-celled jailhouse. Each of these buildings dated to the turn of the twentieth century. My visit was brief, but this image of a small Texas town operating in the midst of its own ruins stayed with me.

Returning a year later, I found myself confronted by a different D'Hanis: a series of pristine and intact storefronts along the block's east side, newly constructed of brick and indistinguishable from the older buildings to the west (Figure 9.3). Local residents had invested in reconstructing the buildings to match their historic predecessors as closely as possible, reusing the old bricks and consulting old photographs to recreate the interior molding. Behind the

FIGURE 9.2. D'Hanis, Texas, in July 2016. The storefronts, constructed in the late nineteenth and early twentieth century, sustained tornado damage in 2015. Photograph by Patricia Markert.

FIGURE 9.3. D'Hanis, Texas, in August 2017. Taken a year later than Figure 9.2, this photograph shows the outcomes of a local effort to reconstruct the buildings as they would have appeared in the early twentieth century. Photograph by Patricia Markert.

buildings, the jailhouse still sat in ruin, but all signs of destruction had disappeared from sight along the main highway. In fact, D'Hanis looked new, as it might have in the early twentieth century when the residents constructed the downtown area along the Galveston, Harrisburg, and San Antonio Railroad (Castro Colonies Heritage Association 1994).

Of course, places change. They proceed, disrupt, transform, and emerge from places that have come before them (Bender 2001; Feld and Basso 1996; Munn 2013). But as Casey notes, they are *always* changing, continually happening, made and remade by the people who inhabit them (1996:27). This process of continual placemaking does not occur simply on the material landscape but is also inherent in the ways people come to think about, understand, and narrate place. D'Hanis did not just build a new bank along its main street—it rebuilt it in the image of the bank that had come before. It is not enough to say that residents used bricks during the reconstruction, because they used many of the *same* bricks and, when those were not available, bricks fired at the same D'Hanis brickyard or specifically chosen to match the original construction. This sameness characterizes the building material as much as fired clay or architectural functionality. The reconstruction of downtown D'Hanis illustrates how places are built from materials as much as histories, memories, and narratives.

As Basso noted in *Wisdom Sits in Places*, "placemaking is a way of constructing history itself, of inventing it, of fashioning novel versions of 'what happened here'" (1996:6). In D'Hanis and elsewhere, history becomes entangled with the constructed landscape. In (re)building its structures, D'Hanis constructed and maintained a narrative of place and history, drawing from the identities and desires of the people that make up its community. As Basso argues, making place and making history can be conceived as a single process.

I turn now to Castroville, the larger of the two towns, which is known locally and in Alsace as "The Little Alsace of Texas."[1] I first encountered Castroville in November 2015 during a short trip to give a public presentation for the Castro Colonies Heritage Association on an artifact assemblage from excavations at a local historic home known as the Biry-Ahr House, now the site of a local living history center and museum. Ruth Van Dyke of Binghamton University directed the excavations between 2013 and 2016, and I joined the project as an archaeological lab manager in 2015 (see Van Dyke 2017). When arriving in Castroville from the direction of San Antonio, visitors are confronted by a historic Alsatian-style townhouse that sits to the south of the highway that runs through town (Figure 9.4). This building is striking; it stands out in what otherwise might be considered a typical Texan-American landscape with a four-lane highway, traffic lights, and a Bill Miller's barbeque restaurant across the street. The house signals that a traveler has entered a particular kind of place as they moved west through South Texas: the "Little Alsace," a place that blurs the geographic and cultural distance between Texas and Europe.

The historic house is not simply built in Alsatian-European style. It is, in actuality, a seventeenth-century Alsatian townhouse on the Texas landscape. Known as the Steinbach House, it serves as Castroville's visitor center and a small house museum dedicated to presenting daily life in old Alsace (Steinbach Haus & Castroville Visitor Center 2018). Between 1998 and 2002, a team of Alsatian students, faculty, and craftsmen dismantled the three-century-old house in Alsace, transported it to Texas, and reconstructed it along the Medina River in Castroville. The movement of the townhouse constitutes a fascinating series of material engagements across time and space, illustrating placemaking across national borders, centuries of history, and regional and ethnic identities. Over a century and a half after Alsatian migrants made the journey to Texas, an entire dwelling followed. It is worth noting that the structure predates Castroville by nearly two centuries and would have been both socially and economically inaccessible to many of the Alsatian migrants, many of whom were farmers, prior to their migration (Weaver 2005). Nonetheless, the building was "gathered" to the

FIGURE 9.4. The Steinbach House, a seventeenth-century Alsatian townhouse that was dismantled, transported, and reconstructed in Castroville, Texas, between 1998 and 2002. Photograph by Patricia Markert, November 2015.

town, its dismantling and reconstruction an explicit act in an ongoing process of placemaking. I touch briefly on this act here to illustrate how history, narrative, and identity intertwine with the material constructions of place in Castroville. In this case, the movement of the Alsatian townhouse conveys a set of choices and material strategies mobilized to convey a particular narrative of Alsatian Texas.

Different Places, Shared Origins

The encounters described here, I hope, demonstrate what Casey means when he says "places gather" by illustrating these processes on a contemporary stage (1996:27). Both Castroville and D'Hanis continue to gather, as seen in the reconstruction of a historic storefront or a seventeenth-century house from Alsace. Narratives take physical shape as people make place, but they also serve to situate those places in dialogue with other histories, identities, and places. The landscapes of D'Hanis and Castroville position the towns within broader narratives that extend beyond the local, drawing on images of small towns in Texas or cities in Alsace, France. But despite the differences Castroville and D'Hanis exhibit today, the fact that the towns share nearly identical origins in the mid-nineteenth-century requires attention. The question I would like to address now is how Casey's notion of gathering can be used to identify and understand acts of placemaking in the more distant past, in order to address the towns' origins as well as their eventual divergence.

Following Basso's assertion that place and history emerge simultaneously, an investigation of placemaking in Castroville and D'Hanis starts well before the towns exist as they do today. At their beginning both towns originated from a nineteenth-century migration from Alsace to Texas, but over time developed different landscapes and narratives that characterize them as distinct places, products of distinctive processes of gathering. In the following sections, I highlight a few moments in the towns' histories that illustrate how Casey's concept of gathering works to illuminate how the towns have developed as places over time. First, I explore how these moments have the potential to shed light on the ideas and processes that contributed to the towns' origins as places on the Texas frontier. Then, I turn to a discussion of divergence, in order to explore some of the ways the communities of Castroville and D'Hanis have built their own narratives into their landscapes through time.

Gathering Places on the Texas Frontier

Alsatian migrants settled Castroville and D'Hanis in 1844 and 1847, respectively (Castro Colonies Heritage Association 1994; Weaver 2005). To examine the towns as places-in-progress, it is important to look to the political and ideological forces that set their existence in motion and made them "happen," so to speak (Casey 1996:27). Before they became physical places on a landscape, the idea of the towns as *potential* places in an imagined future began the work of placemaking. Like an imported Alsatian townhouse or a reconstructed historic building, the towns themselves did not simply begin with the first brick or stone laid. They coalesced around and within existing narratives and expectations, which brought together people, resources, and ideas to create colonies on a contested landscape. Three factors contributed to this initial gathering of Castroville and D'Hanis: Texan Anglicization and the Republic's desire to settle its western lands; the entrepreneurial imagination of the *empresario* who founded the colonies; and a narrative of opportunity and prosperity that prompted Alsatians to migrate to Texas.

Texan Anglicization and Settling Western Lands

Others have addressed the history of Texas and its centuries of colonization in detail (see Campbell 2003; Weaver 2005). Here, my goal is to briefly contextualize the efforts and motivations of the Republic of Texas to settle Europeans on lands to the west of San Antonio. During the first half of the nineteenth century, Texas was undergoing a series of dramatic changes. Within two decades it had taken part in two revolutions: the Mexican Revolution in 1821 and the Texas Revolution in 1835. It also underwent significant shifts to its demographic population as Anglo-Americans[2] crossed into New Spain and later Mexico seeking inexpensive land, resulting in the "whitening" or "Americanization" of Texas (De León 1983:3; see also Campbell 2003; Kökény 2004). These settlers brought with them United States political ideals of democracy and self-government, as well as notions of racial superiority, Manifest Destiny, and slavery (Campbell 2003:110). "By 1830," Randolph Campbell states in his sweeping history of the Lone Star state, "the approximately 10,000 Anglo-Americans in Texas began to give the province an indelible imprint of the southern United States" (2003:110). This created the climate for the Texas Revolution from Mexico. As a province of Mexico, white Texans pushed back against the 1829 emancipation of enslaved individuals by Mexican President Vicente Guerrero and were granted an exemption (Campbell 2003:113). When Santa Anna consolidated and centralized governmental power in Mexico City in 1835, Anglo Texans saw this as a threat to their right to "self government and economic prosperity" (Kökény 2004:285–286). Despite deep divisions in commitment to secession, particularly between Anglo and Mexican residents, Texas declared its independence from Mexico and became the Republic of Texas in 1836, setting the stage for United States statehood nearly a decade later (Kökény 2004: 299). This history is foundational for understanding the Texan path to statehood, as well as contemporary Texan identity (Clemons 2008), but it also played an integral role in shaping the way the government of the young Republic approached space on its western frontier.

Two points are important here. First, even before declaring an independent republic, white, English-speaking Texans, most of whom had migrated from the United States, were already participating in the broader American project of nation-building in Texas. This effort included drawing on notions such as the duty to "tame" a frontier, advance American ideas of democracy, and promote the spread of Protestant Christianity (De León 1983:1). Second, increasingly racialized and hostile attitudes towards both Mexicans and Native peoples, such as the Apache and Comanche in south and west Texas, drove an urgency to settle and, thus, "secure" western lands (Babcock 2016; Campbell 2003; Sowell 1986; on attitudes towards Mexicans and Tejanos, see De León 1983; Kökény 2004). Participation in these broader processes shaped how government in Texas conceptualized space on its frontier, which lay to the west of San Antonio. These ideas characterized the frontier as a space needing to be ordered and controlled, and thus, as racialized attitudes increased, a space ideally settled by people of European ancestry (De León 1983; Edwards 1917). These conceptions of space both prompted and constrained the process of gathering people to the Texas frontier, emerging in practice through the Republic's implementation of an *empresario* system as a means of populating the Republic's open lands.

Empresarios, *Land Grants, and Placemaking through Contracts*

New Spain and Mexico had both contracted *empresarios* to recruit settlers to Texas, though the focus of these efforts prior to the Republic of Texas' secession from Mexico were primarily Mexican and white United States residents. The most effective way to secure frontier spaces for the young government was to settle them, and so the *empresario* system was designed to populate open areas by offering free land to potential settlers. *Empresarios*, simply put, were "colonization agents" charged with settling specific tracts of land granted to them under government contract (Campbell 2003:103; Jordan 1966; Weaver 2005). Stephen F. Austin had served as an *empresario* for the Mexican government to settle Anglo-Americans in Texas, a political choice that had far-reaching consequences as demographics quickly shifted in the province (Campbell 2003:101–103). As an independent Republic, Texas continued the goal of settling its vast lands—but this time, it presented *empresario* contracts to entrepreneurs further afield. Efforts in the 1840s focused on promoting European immigration, and a number of French and German *empresarios* were granted contracts to settle large tracts of land in western Texas (Edwards 1917). The Republic of Texas passed a law called "An Act Granting Land to Emigrants" in 1841 that laid out the details of these contracts, which included stipulations such as persons must be white, must swear allegiance to the Republic, and must cultivate the land provided (Edwards 1917: 341). Other requirements were made as well: migrants should have enough to sustain themselves for a whole year (Weaver 2005), would preferably be farmers (Edwards 1917: 346; Weaver 2005), and would bring their own farming implements (Weaver 2005). Henry Castro, a Parisian entrepreneur of Portuguese descent, became one of the Republic's first and most successful *empresarios*, obtaining a contract from Texas President Sam Houston in 1842 to settle colonists to the west of San Antonio (Cohen 1897; Edwards 1917; Waugh 1934; Weaver 2005). These contracts set in motion the colonization of the area west of San Antonio, predating the first colonies by several years. Both the imagined settlements and the desired qualities of the settlers existed on paper well before the places came to exist in physical space. Therefore, contracts defined the terms of what types of places Castroville and D'Hanis were to be, even before news reached Alsace of the opportunity to migrate.

The details of Castro's efforts to colonize his land grant are lengthy and often colorful in their narration. The story of his colonization efforts, their many obstacles, and the difficulties the colonists endured are detailed in several historical works (see Cohen 1897; Waugh 1934; Weaver 2005). In brief, Castro recruited many of his colonists from the Rhine region in Europe, particularly the region of Alsace as well as parts of Germany. This decision was calculated. In the wake of the Industrial Revolution and political upheaval throughout Europe, farmers, factory workers, and laborers were often marginalized and prevented economically and socially from land ownership, which made the prospect of free land in Texas attractive despite the cost and uncertainty of leaving their homeland (Weaver

2005). Pressured by the terms of his contract and the need to settle the land quickly, Castro recruited somewhat indiscriminately. Though he was instructed by the Texas government to send people with the means to support themselves, many of the Alsatian colonists he sent to Texas were impoverished and ill-prepared for the conditions they faced upon arrival (Edwards 1917:348–349; Waugh 1934; Weaver 2005). Despite early setbacks, he succeeded in establishing four colonies. Castroville, the first and largest, was founded in 1844, followed by Quihi in 1845, Vandenburg in 1846, and D'Hanis, the last and the furthest west, in 1847 (Cohen 1897:42; Edwards 1917:347). While Quihi and Vandenburg were primarily German-speaking, Castroville and D'Hanis were populated by a majority of Catholic, Alsatian-speaking migrants. Of the four initial colonies, Castroville and D'Hanis developed and sustained populations and town centers into the twenty-first century.

Historical sources describe Castro as a champion of Texas colonization (Cohen 1897; Waugh 1934), a single-minded businessman (Edwards 1917), and a man fallen from grace in his later years, bankrupted from the effort and fallen from favor among residents of Castroville (Weaver 2005). Of course, he did not succeed in settling his colonies alone, but enlisted the help of European bankers, local officials, and both Mexican and European residents to carry out his work on the Texas frontier. As an individual, however, he did have a singular influence that characterized the places his colonies would become. His position allowed him to make a series of foundational decisions, such as who to recruit and where to locate the settlements on his land grant, or, as was the case with Castroville, land he had purchased strategically (Weaver 2005). He is often credited locally with a vision and dedication to seeing the colonies he established succeed, particularly in the town that bears his name.[3]

As products of the *empresario* system in Texas, Castroville and D'Hanis emerged in part from the plans, actions, and imagined futures of politicians and businessmen in Texas, Mexico, the United States, and as far afield as Europe. Castro's individual role in shaping the colonies also occupies a prominent space in their historical narrative and development. Materializing as the result of the Republic's political goals and Anglo-American ideals, the contract he signed put the processes that would create Castroville and D'Hanis in motion.

Alsatian Migration to the "Land of Milk and Honey"

Of course, Castro and the government of the Republic of Texas were only two of many players in the process of gathering that created these two towns on the Texas frontier. The settlers themselves, of course, played a key role. Many Alsatian migrants also imagined a place and a future before the series of material interactions that would materialize it on the landscape. Also of note is how Castro *promoted* his land grant in Alsace, because it set the narrative for the type of place prospective colonists would expect to find in Texas. Undoubtedly, complex personal, political, and economic reasons motivated people to choose to leave their home and settle in an unseen land, but Castro's advertisements provided a framework for *imagining* such a place, creating the images that made the unknown knowable. Of course, like many promotional and boosterish materials for the American West, these representations often promoted a rosier, or at times invented, version of the area to be settled that differed markedly from the reality people encountered once they arrived (Wrobel 2002). A traveler passing through Castroville in 1849 detailed in a diary entry this sharp divide between promotion and reality. After two days in the town, he quoted an excerpt of an advertisement for the colony stating that "the prospects... in that beautiful and magnificent state of Texas surpass everything that has ever been offered by governments and individuals" (Jordan 1977:402–403). In his own estimation, he follows, "No matter how wonderful this information may sound, the Society [of the Protection of Immigrants in Texas, H. Castro Concession][4] has brought misery for hundreds of people"

(1977:403), citing crop failures, homesickness, and the lengthy and difficult journey over land to reach the town.

By available accounts, the journeys migrants made were harsh and often life-threatening (Cohen 1897; Domenech 1858; Edwards 1917; Sowell 1986; Waugh 1934). Many lost their lives to disease or conflict, many more gave up on the idea of the Texas colony and settled in cities along the way, and some, when resources were available, abandoned the endeavor altogether and returned to Europe. Descendants of the Alsatian migrants that still live in the towns today often talk about the shock they imagine their ancestors felt upon encountering the harsh reality of the Texas landscape after leaving their home based on the promise of a "land of milk and honey" (Castro Colonies Heritage Association 1994). This narrative of struggle is paired with one of survival, highlighting the perseverance and endurance of the Alsatian ancestors. Together, these narratives have come to characterize the collective history of the colonies and an enduring sense of place among current residents who descended from the migration. West Texas may not have been the promised land Alsatians had imagined, but the sentiment is often that they worked to make it so (see also DeCordova 1856).[5]

The imagined land of "milk and honey" remains in the public memory and represents a form of discursive placemaking that occurred before the material work of placemaking began. Though this imagined future ultimately contrasted with the material reality settlers encountered upon arriving in Texas, the promotional narrative promoted by Castro instilled a sense of place that was powerful enough to move people across a great distance to an unknown landscape.

Gathering Alsace and the American West

So far, I examined two types of gathering that brought Castroville and D'Hanis into existence and shaped the types of places they would become. Underlying a discussion of placemaking in Alsatian Texas are certain themes and narratives: the European migrant, Manifest Destiny, Anglo-American nationalism, *empresario* contracts, and the promise of land, opportunity, and prosperity, among others. These themes constitute a collective imagination that brought these places into being—in other words, gathered them, caused them to happen. While the historical narratives I have discussed above may not be as explicitly stated on the built landscape as an Alsatian townhouse or an American main street, they were fundamental in *placing* places, and the communities that occupy them, in Texas. Places not only take on the qualities of their occupants, but also reflect the qualities of their histories, which are complex, varied, and often contested, particularly in contexts of colonization and migration (Basso 1996; Bender 2001; Casey 1996).

The discussion so far has explored the shared processes and narratives from which Castroville and D'Hanis emerged. To conclude, I will return to a brief discussion of what types of gathering may have contributed to their divergence as places, using an example from each town. How did two Alsatian colonies in Texas end up as the "Little Alsace of Texas" and an American railroad town? My ongoing work looks at these processes in depth. In advance of more fulsome results, I will discuss how Casey's concept of gathering sheds some light on these local processes in the past as well as the present.

In Castroville, a visitor will notice a particular style of house among the more recent homes: stone-walled cottages, often with white plaster walls and steeply sloped roofs. These houses generally date to the 1840–50s and were constructed within a decade after Castroville's settlement, though many underwent later additions and renovations (Figure 9.5) (Van Dyke 2017).

Locally, the cottages are often said to have been built following styles traditionally observed in Alsace. Ruth Van Dyke (2017:15) also points out that they resemble vernacular styles seen throughout South Texas (see also Guerric 1999). Regardless of whether the cottages themselves are historically Alsatian in style, it is possible to find Alsace built into the historic

FIGURE 9.5. An example of the stone cottages that are characteristic of early Castroville architecture. This structure was the site of the 2013–2016 excavations by Binghamton University, directed by Ruth Van Dyke, and is currently the Living History Center for the Castro Colonies Heritage Association. Photograph by Patricia Markert, August 2018.

landscape in distinct ways. During the excavation of an 1850s Castroville home that took place between 2013 and 2016, Van Dyke and students from Colorado College and Binghamton University uncovered a large, walled-in stone fireplace in a room that had been converted to a bathroom by the house's twentieth-century residents (Van Dyke 2017). The fireplace, which may have at one point been an outdoor cooking area before being incorporated into an early home addition, resembled a style one might see in a nineteenth-century Alsatian kitchen, "with large overhead vents and hooks for smoking meats" (Van Dyke 2017:19). Van Dyke noted that early residents drew on what they knew, or what they imaged domestic places to be, by "recreating the familiar, domestic bodily habitus of a home space" (2017:19). These combined strategies likely drew from both Texan and Alsatian architectural styles and represented the type of gathering early Alsatians undertook as they constructed new places in Texas.

D'Hanis underwent a different process of gathering, which significantly reshaped its built landscape, history, and identity as a community. When the Galveston, Harrisburg, and San Antonio Railroad (joining later with the Southern Pacific) was built through the area in 1881, the railroad company laid tracks and placed a railroad stop about a mile and a half from the original settlement of D'Hanis (Castro Colonies Heritage Association 1994). The route had earlier circumvented Castroville by five miles, too great a distance to have a significant impact on its built landscape. Alternatively, over the next few decades, the residents of D'Hanis abandoned the original settlement and reconstructed homes and businesses along the railroad, gathering the town around the tracks and the larger network of American trade, economy, and identity they brought to the small settlement (Castro Colonies Heritage Association 1994; Finger 2012). As the residents of D'Hanis constructed the new town at the turn of the twentieth century, they used bricks from recently established local brickyards and borrowed explicitly from American vernacular styles of architecture, which evoke images that are familiar across the American West. A new community identity, and a new set of community qualities and ideas of place, became part of the "constitution and description" of the town (Casey 1996:27). The decisions made while building the new town, which came to be called New D'Hanis, did not prioritize earlier aesthetics or building styles used by the original Alsatian settlers. In the area of the old settlement, now known as Old D'Hanis, it is still possible to see a few stone homes similar to those found in Castroville, though most are in ruin. Further archaeological study of Old D'Hanis will clarify the choices its early residents made on the landscape, but the move to the railroad appears to signal a shift in the town's vision of itself, prompting a set of material choices that shaped the place its residents imagined and desired it to be.

Concluding Thoughts: Future Work and an Archaeology of Gathering

In this chapter, I have aimed to demonstrate how acts of gathering constitute places on a landscape. These two Alsatian colonies in Texas show that gathering includes the ways places are imagined and desired as much as the ways they are physically constructed.

Clearly history is perceived as a rich, personal, and deeply rooted point of identity in both towns. This identity creation is expressed not only in the anecdotes about placemaking in my introduction, but also through events organized by the local Castro Colonies Heritage Association, the development and maintenance of several local museums and historic sites (e.g., the Castro Colonies Living History Center, Medina County Museum, and Landmark Inn State Historic Site), a diverse array of local publications on the area's history (e.g., Castro Colonies Heritage Association 1994; Finger 2012; Lawler 1974), and the continued speaking of the Alsatian language by several older residents of both D'Hanis and Castroville (Roesch 2012). Through work with both communities, it has become clear that the story of place and history is more complicated than can be learned from the landscape alone. This complexity is further evidenced by the relationships with Alsace maintained by residents of both towns, despite their differences in physical appearance. Since the local heritage association spurred an effort to reconnect with the old country, which began in earnest in the 1970s and 1980s, residents of both towns have made frequent trips to Alsace and hosted Alsatian relatives who come to visit Texas. My ongoing research takes these aspects of placemaking— and of gathering across both time and space—into account as I examine the development of the towns through time.

Of course, with any examination of gathering as a mode of placemaking, other issues must be addressed as well. Studies of the American West in archaeology and related fields must understand processes of placemaking in terms of displacement as well, particularly regarding conflict with and erasure of Native peoples in spaces reclaimed as the colonial frontier. Narration of these conflicts is too easily rendered a one-sided telling of the past, in both written history and public memory. This limitation is seen in Texas history time and time again, from the retold triumphs of the Texas Rangers to the fraught public memories of violence between colonists and groups such as the Comanche and Apache (Sowell 1986). To understand the complexities inherent in places, archaeologists should seek the difficult histories as well as the celebrated ones. Our work can only benefit from multiple tellings of the past and diverse understandings of place. Archaeologists who study place may therefore look at conflict, violence, and erasure as processes of gathering and critical components of places-in-progress (Starzmann and Roby 2016). Placemaking in colonial contexts regularly involves place-unmaking; as Jones and Russell state, it is "impossible to have emplacement and belonging without a kind of displacement" (Jones and Russell 2012:282). While I have not been able to explore these complexities fully here, I end with this as a challenge and a goal in my ongoing work and a provocation for future research. There is more to address and more to learn, but, of course, that is only appropriate. As I quoted Edward Casey in the opening to this chapter, "places not only are, they happen" (1996:27). It seems right that our studies of places do as well.

Acknowledgments

This project has been conducted with the generous support of the Wenner-Gren Foundation, the National Geographic Society, and the Council of Texas Archeologists. I would like to thank my dissertation advisor Dr. Ruth Van Dyke, whose work in Castroville brought me to Texas and whose mentorship has made my dissertation work possible. Many thanks to Dr. Randy McGuire and Dr. Sabina Perrino, who have offered their support and feedback as I explored the theoretical aspects of place and migration. I am profoundly grateful to the Castro Colonies Heritage Association for their help and support throughout every phase of this project, and to my crew members, Hunter Crosby, Nolan O'Hara, and Emily Sainz, who were out there helping me complete fieldwork even as I completed revisions on this chapter. I would also like to thank Jeremy Trombley, Emily Dale, Carolyn White, and my anonymous reviewers, who offered edits, feedback, and advice throughout the writing process. And of course, my most heartfelt gratitude to the communities of Castroville, D'Hanis, and Medina County, who have welcomed us and been incredible partners through this research process—thank you.

Notes

1. Castroville had a population of 2,680, and D'Hanis had a population of 847 as of the 2010 United States Census.
2. Following conventions used by my sources when writing about the history of Texas, I use Anglo and Anglo-American to refer to English-speaking or Anglophone residents of the United States, predominately those considered white or of European descent, though not specifically English descent (cf. the second definition of Anglo-American provided by the Merriam-Webster dictionary: "a North American whose native language is English and especially whose culture or ethnic background is of European origin.")
3. A welcome video at the Castro Colonies Living History Center in Castroville features a young and an old reenactment of Henry Castro, who both express these sentiments and the history of his efforts as *empresario* to visitors as they enter the building.
4. Gilbert J. Jordan translated, edited, and published notes from William Steinert, a traveler through Texas writing in 1849, in *The Southwestern Historical Quarterly*. Steinert used this name to refer to Castro's colonization company. It is referred to elsewhere as Société de Colonisation Europée-Américaine au Texas (Weaver 2005:26).
5. This statement is also expressed as part of the welcome video at the Castro Colonies Living History Center, narrated by the aging Henry Castro as he looks back at his work to establish the colonies.

10

The Ordeal and Redemption of Betsy Brown, Christina Geisel, and Mary Harris

Historical Memory, Placemaking, and the Archaeology of Oregon's Rogue River War

Mark Tveskov *and* Chelsea Rose

In 1971, Stephen Dow Beckham opened *Requiem for a People*, his enduring popular work about the history of settler colonialism in southern Oregon, with an invocation about the importance of place in the ongoing maintenance of historical memory. He started the book with the following passage:

> Within the sound of the constant roar of the Pacific's surf on the southwestern Oregon coast is a dense thicket of spruce, the sharp needles of the trees fold from limb to limb through the moist air to filter out the sunlight which attempts to penetrate the solitude and rain-forest grandeur of the place. The needles falling from these trees, for centuries have carpeted the ground. In a scarcely visible clearing, but one large enough to allow a few pale huckleberry bushes to grow gnarled and gaunt in the shadows, lies flat among the needles a lichen-covered granite marker, lettered in an antique script. It reads:
>
> *Sacred to the Memory of*
> *John Geisel*
> *Also his three Sons*
> *John, Henry*
> *& Andrew*
> *Who were*
> *Massacred by the Indians*
> *Feb 22, AD 1856*
>
> A single fern frond, seldom stirred by the wind, reaches across the top of this marker. The entire scene appears frozen and unreal, but there in the forest deepness is a lingering memory of an era when Indian and pioneer faced each other. This was an era whose story has been told in almost endless fashion as America was settled and the inhabitants of her forests, river valleys, and shores were forced to yield before the strong push of civilization [Beckham 1971:3].

Beckham detailed how, as the Rogue River War erupted along the southern Oregon coast, the Tututni, Joshua, Mikonotunne, and other Indigenous groups that lived around the mouth of the Rogue River attacked settler homesteads and gold mining claims. He described how the men of the Geisel family, like many of their neighbors, were murdered, and how the Geisel women, Christina, Mary (age 13), and Anna (two weeks old) were taken captive (see also Curry Historical Society 2017; Tveskov et al.

2017). The settlers who survived the night retreated into Miners' Fort, a small revetment recently completed near the mouth of the Rogue River. For a month, about 70 settler men and a handful of settler and Indigenous women were besieged inside the fort's walls until rescued by the United States Army.

Historical Memory, Placemaking, and Settler Colonialism

Since the tragic night of February 22, 1856, the Geisel homestead became deeply, recursively, and often luridly inscribed into the phenomenology of local historical memory, landscape, and identity. Earlier popular accounts reported how Mrs. Geisel "was compelled to witness the murder of her husband and children when she was conducted to like horrible scenes upon the persons of many of her friends and neighbors" (Sacramento Daily Union 21 March 1856:1). A later account asked, who "shall tell that mother's anguish?" (Webster 1884:235–240) as the Geisel homestead was burned to the ground, the bodies of the husband and sons still inside. A 1929 newspaper presaged Beckham's description of the site itself, describing the dirt road to the graves as a "dark tunnel cut through the forest of interweaving myrtle, spruce and fir...so dense and matted that a snake hardly could crawl through it" (Thurston 1929:33). By the early 1960s, the place achieved official sanction, memorialized as Geisel Monument State Heritage Site in the newly formed Oregon State Park system and a wayside on the newly completed coast Highway 101 (Tveskov et al. 2017). Beckham's use of the Geisel tragedy as a literary device to preface his telling of the Rogue River War was thus the latest act of placemaking to inscribe the Geisel homestead in the historical memory and identity of Oregon's south coast residents.

Miners' Fort as a place also persisted in local historical memory and identity, and a key facet of this memory is the narrative of how the Geisel women were ransomed from captivity through the efforts of a settler man named Charles Brown. This redemption was memorialized by those trapped in Miners' Fort while the siege was ongoing:

> Charles Brown did...voluntarily leave the fort and go unarmed at the imminent risk of his life, into a large band of hostile and armed Indians, which act was repeated until he succeeded by skillful negotiations in effecting the release of the said maiden, whom he led in triumph into the fort [Berry et al. 1856:2].

Years later, Orville Dodge (1898:347), a compiler of settler memoirs, noted that many "were saved from a horrible death" thanks to the "bravery" of Charles Brown. The fort's turf walls remained visible into the 1960s, and, to the present day, Charles Brown's descendants maintain the oral history of his actions at Miners' Fort, and the local community holds picnics on the site to celebrate their pioneer heritage (Joel Bravo, personal communication 2017; Lundquist 2004).

Just as Highway 101 was being completed along the Pacific coastline, Interstate 5 was being constructed further inland, linking the Portland metropolitan area to southern California through the interior valleys. By the late 1960s, travelers on this new highway were greeted in rural southern Oregon by a wooden sign explaining they had stopped at a rest area located on a place of historical significance:

> This marker is placed near the site of the Harris Massacre of October 9, 1855. The cabin was attacked in the forenoon by 20 Rogue River Indians. Mr. Harris was killed almost immediately. The hired man's body was found one year later. David Harris—9 years old—was never found. Mrs. Harris defended the cabin all night, while her 11 year old daughter, Sophia, although wounded molded lead bullets. Before dawn they hid in a near-by brush pile until rescued by the militia.

This story, like the Geisel Homestead/Miners' Fort narrative, had a long lineage in southern Oregon. Mrs. Harris, after all, had exhibited "one of the most remarkable instances of female heroism and courage upon the record," and even in the 1850s, local settlers knew this story "should be handed down to posterity as an instance of bravery in woman under the most trying and heart-rending circumstances" (Woods 1855; see also Abbott 1913; Clarendon 1855). Like Christina Geisel, Mary Harris survived her ordeal and lived a long life, and both women were identified, in part, by the redemption garnered through their peculiar wartime ordeals. Their fame—and their stories—grew as the years passed. As the twentieth century turned, Oregon Senator Binger Hermann even lobbied Congress for official recognition for both widows, and for years Mrs. Harris's rifle hung with pride in the local pioneer museum (Sutton and Sutton 1969:148).[1]

Southern Oregon long remained free of sustained European American settlement, but the region saw the quick subjugation, murder, and removal of Indigenous people once the gold rush commenced in the 1850s (Beckham 1971; Douthit 2002; Lewis 2014; O'Donnell 1991; Schwartz 1997; Tveskov 2017; Whaley 2010; Wilkinson 2010). Since that time, the Geisel and Harris stories, memorialized in the places where the stories occurred, served to remind the public of the events of that era of settler colonialism. The Harris and Geisel narratives are important peaks in the topography of historical memory and identity, from immediately after the events and continuing to the present day. The stories resonated even in the post-World War II era of optimism, modernism, materialism, and middle class affluence that saw the construction of a vast interstate highway system at public expense and its attendant state parks. The Geisel and Harris places were not left behind, and both were presented to the public as part of this system, complete with historical markers.

Historians in recent years have considered how settler narratives index back to accepted myths, tropes, and forms (e.g., Boag 2014; Buss 2011; Cothran 2014; Kelman 2013; O'Brien 2010; Slotkin 1973; Tate 2006; Tveskov 2017; Whaley 2010). Settler memoirs mask as much as reveal history, serving primarily to rationalize the contradictions and violence of the settler experience and reify a narrative of the triumph of Manifest Destiny, rugged individualism, and Christian heteronormativity. The story of the murder of the men of the Harris and Geisel families and the subsequent travails of the women were not new in the structure of their telling, nor were they factually accurate. The 1850s were incredibly violent in southern Oregon. Thousands of Indigenous people and settlers died from murder, war, disease, lynching, and massacre, but the stories of Mary Harris and Christina Geisel stand out. In telling the story of the war through the lurid victimization of a white woman, the memorialists and historians of the Oregon Territory were using the familiar trope of the captivity narrative, one of "America's oldest" and "most unique" literary genera (Vaughan and Clark 1981:2; see also Sayre 2000, 2010; Slotkin 1973; Tate 2006).

Captivity Narratives

Captivity narratives as a genre of English literature originated in the seventeenth century during the final Indigenous efforts at military resistance to British imperialism in colonial New England. Many settler women were taken hostage, and their memoirs had immediate resonance and popularity (Sayre 2000:9, 2010; Slotkin 1973:95). Captivity narratives provided a Christian allegory as Puritan (and later, pioneer) settlers, like Jesus himself, were redeemed through trial in an undomesticated and thus morally profane wilderness (Slotkin 1973; see also Tate 2006:4). Captivity narratives are heralded as seminal feminist literature, presenting first person accounts of women required to be resilient, strong, and self-sufficient (e.g., Andrews 1990:4; Sayre 2000:16; see also Derounian-Stodola 1998). That these women exhibited plucky frontier courage was a New World bonus, and captivity narratives set the stage for ruggedly individualistic cowboy epics that "captivated the popular imagination and translated America's frontier experience to the world" (McMichael 1985:198–199; see also Slotkin 1973; Vaughan and Clark 1981; Sayre 2000, 2010).

The popularity of captivity narratives persisted through the nineteenth century as the frontier moved westward, appearing in ever more prescribed forms, serialized in almanacs, or mass produced in sensationalized "dime western" novels (Eaton and Morgan 2000:382–385). Thousands of Americans preparing to cross the Great Plains to the Oregon Territory or California consumed these narratives along with romantic fictions or adventurous tales of fur trappers and explorers (Tate 2006:4–9). This literature helped rationalize the settler experience in the moment and, in retrospect, helped form an American origin tale that smoothed over the moral contradictions of settler colonialism through, in the case of the captivity narratives, the ritualized ordeal of a virtuous and brave settler woman.

Captivity narratives remain resonant in the present day, in one form or another. Sayre (2010:337) and others (cf. Kumar 2004; Balode 2013) point out that the sustained appeal of the form was demonstrated by the media presentation and public consumption of the story of Private Jessica Lynch's captivity and subsequent rescue during the Iraq War in 2003. HBO's recent hit television show *Westworld* (Season 1, Episode 8, "Trace Decay") indexed the trope again. An episode during the first season features a scene that in almost all of its details might just as well represent what happened to Mary Harris and Christina Geisel in southern Oregon in the 1850s, presented with the cinematic power of contemporary Hollywood.

Landscapes of War—Women in Battlefield Archaeology

The Southern Oregon University Laboratory of Anthropology (SOULA) investigated the Geisel and Harris family homesteads as part of a public archaeology project researching the settler era of Oregon that includes collaboration with federal and state agencies, local communities, and descendent Indigenous and settler communities (e.g., Rose 2013; Rose and Tveskov 2017; Tveskov 2007, 2017; Tveskov and Cohen 2014; Tveskov and Johnson 2014; Tveskov and Rose 2019). The Rogue River War was unlike Napoleonic-style conflicts where state-sponsored armies faced off across broad fields. Instead, the violence that characterized Oregon's gold rush settler era is more akin to the Pequot War, King Philip's War, or more recent wars in Vietnam, Iraq, and Afghanistan, where colonized people employ guerilla tactics against a professional state-sponsored army. As such, the Rogue River War had only a handful of set-piece battles and instead took place within a larger landscape that lacked front lines and embroiled, in the most visceral ways possible, women, children, and entire families.

An archaeological perspective that interrogates the dynamic construction of historical memory can acknowledge this dynamism and the placemaking within these landscapes. The genocidal violence of settler colonialism or the ordeals and triumphs of people other than white men are generally not part of popular narratives, and the experiences of women in particular are often muted (Jetéé 2010; Tushingham and Brooks 2017; Tveskov 2007, 2017; Tveskov and Rose 2019). When portrayed in captivity narratives, women are instead signifiers of the nobility and stability of the settler enterprise and of heteronormative domesticity. Alternatively, in a structural mirror of the noble savage/ignoble savage dichotomy, they are fantasized as harlots or Annie Oakley-style gunslingers that signify the entrepreneurial ruggedness of the frontier (Johnson 2000, 2004; Rose 2013).

The influence of these archetypes extends within historical archaeology, where research into sites that index popular mythologies of settler colonialism resonate strongly with the public (Schablitsky 2007). In archaeological analysis, glass trade beads are often simplistically equated with the presence of Indigenous women in gold rush or military contexts, furthering many stereotypes that women were prostitutes in an erroneous beads-equals-babes equation (Rose 2013). The material culture of pioneer women is likewise circumscribed by deliberations over dish patterns and clothing fasteners. While domestic items certainly can lead to discussions about identity, choice, and control, when used uncritically, they can reinforce stereotypes that confuse the actual experience of women.

Settler women were most likely as skilled at loading and firing a weapon as they were at baking a flaky biscuit, and traces of women can be found everywhere in the Rogue River

FIGURE 10.1. A sample of the domestic artifacts recovered from the Geisel homestead excavations, including a variety of heat- altered leaded glasswares (left) and a blue transfer-print serving dish with a romantic scene. Courtesy of Southern Oregon University Laboratory of Anthropology.

War of the 1850s and not simply as prostitutes, Indian Princesses, or virtuous homemakers. Indigenous women were particularly adept at negotiating colonial contexts creatively, serving as cross-cultural intermediaries, political or military leaders, wage laborers, or matriarchs of multiethnic families (Douthit 2002; Jetéé 2010; Rose 2013; Tushingham and Brooks 2017; Tveskov 2007, 2017; Tveskov and Rose 2019; Wasson 2001). A Takelma woman named Mary (frequently referred to in contemporary documents as "Queen Mary") is particularly noteworthy. She participated in the negotiation that led to signing of the Table Rock Treaty of 1853 and later helped lead the Takelma to victory over a much larger force of US Army dragoons and settler volunteers at the Battle of Hungry Hill in the fall of 1855 (Tveskov 2017). The shame of that defeat at the hands of a woman fostered the suppression and misrepresentation of this event by both the United States military and later settler memorialists (Tveskov 2017).

The Archaeology of Captivity and Redemption

Excavations undertaken in 2016 and 2017 at the Geisel and Harris homestead sites and at Miners' Fort help interrogate the historical memory of these events, which has traditionally been presented uncritically through the problematic lens of the captivity narrative. Both homestead sites revealed austere architectural remains and rudimentary artifact assemblages befitting the life of immigrant families living in the gold-rush Rogue River area. At the same time, the choice made by the Harris family to situate their homestead immediately adjacent to the well-travelled wagon road linking California and Oregon, and the choice made by the Geisel family to bring transferware dishes and leaded glass tableware to an extremely isolated mining community on the Oregon coast bespeak the desire to reproduce more cosmopolitan facets of civilization in their new homes (Figure 10.1). Many artifacts recovered from the Geisel homestead were melted by a very hot fire, complementing the documentary record that indicates that the Indigenous assailants set fire to the house, cremating the bodies of the Geisel men.

In contrast, the monthlong occupation of Miners' Fort left a much more robust archaeological signature comprised of intact architectural remains and thousands of artifacts reflecting a war-ravaged domestic space. Transferware dishes and robust leaded glass vessel fragments similar to those from the Geisel homestead were found within the Fort's walls, suggesting that, even in a moment of extreme duress, settlers

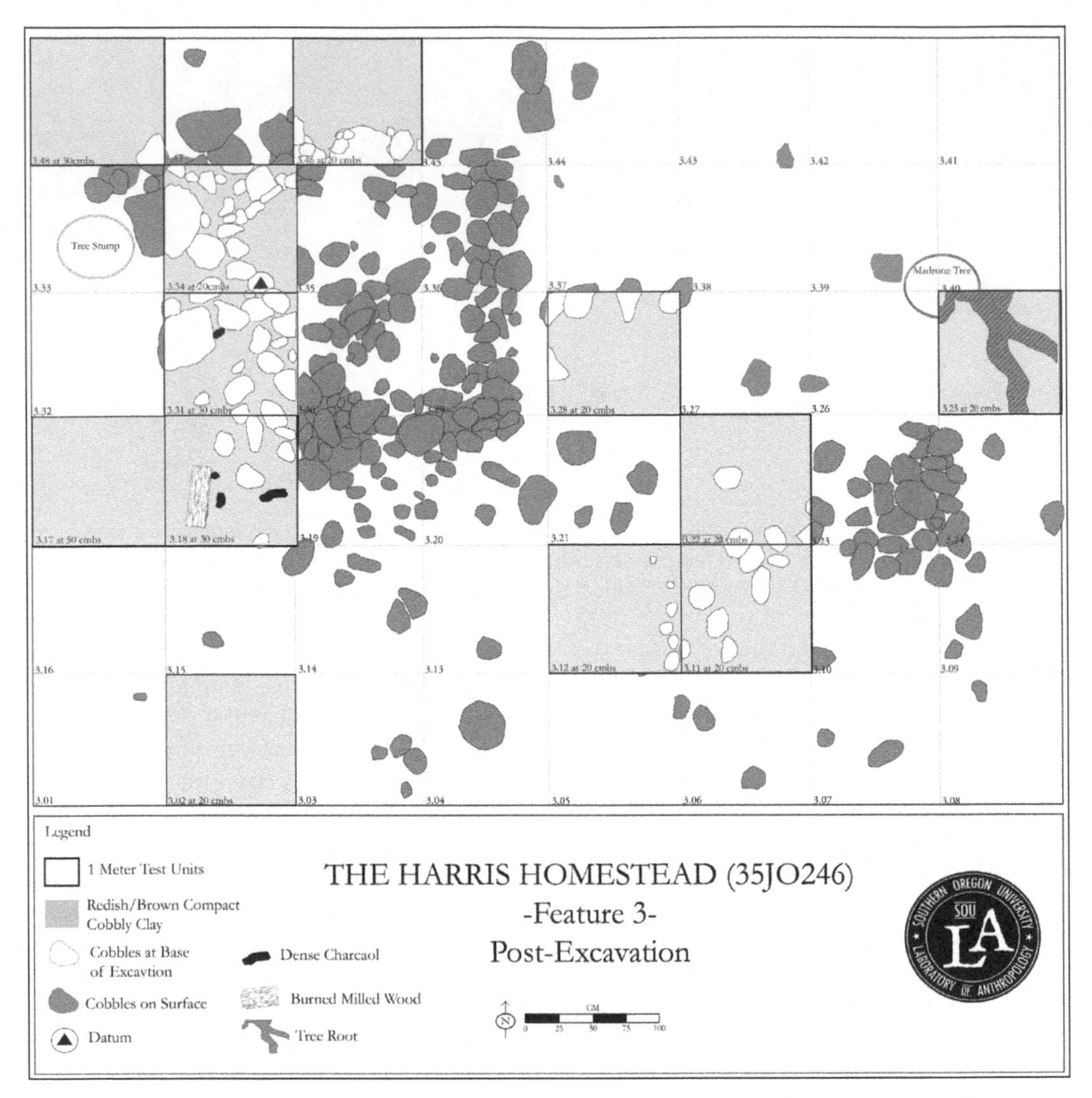

FIGURE 10.2. A plan view of the Harris Cabin excavations (Feature 3), which focused on the chimney foundation and associated rubble. Excavations also recovered cut nails and chinking from the log cabin walls (Southern Oregon University Laboratory of Anthropology).

prioritized the preservation of material items that symbolically, if not practically, reinforced the domestic comforts.

Coupled with documentary accounts of near starvation within the fort, the recovery of large numbers of tiny fragments of calcined mammal bone, and material evidence that the trapped denizens of the fort resorted to burning their own wagons to keep warm, provides a garish example of the archaeology of desperate times (cf. Dixon et al. 2011). Befitting siege conditions, freshly molded lead shot, sprues, and the crucibles, scales, and lead used in their manufacture were suffused across the site (Figure 10.2). Likewise, the distribution of fired musket balls within the site walls indicates, again in agreement with the documentary record, that the fort was under fire from the outside. In contrast, little evidence of a gunfight was found at either the Geisel or Harris homesteads.

Only a single percussion cap and one musket ball were recovered from the Harris Cabin, despite systematic testing, excavations, and metal detector survey of the surrounding land-

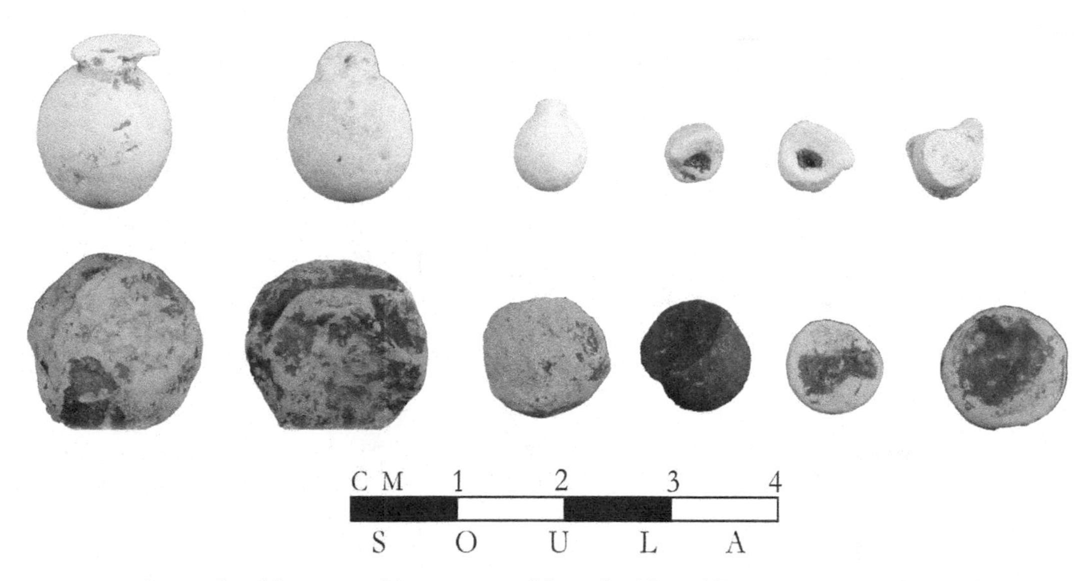

FIGURE 10.3. A sample of the ammunition recovered from the Miners' Fort excavations. The artifacts on the top row represent the variety of homemade musket balls recovered from the site. The three molded musket balls on the upper left have the mold sprue still attached. Three sprues are shown on the upper right. The bottom row shows fired musket balls in a variety of calibers. Courtesy of Southern Oregon University Laboratory of Anthropology.

scapes (Baxter et al. 2011; O'Neill et al. 2014; Rose et al. 2018; Tveskov et al. 2017). Particularly in contrast to the material evidence found at Miners' Fort, the paucity of ammunition or other material evidence of armed conflict at the Harris homestead challenges the very narrative of the events that transpired there (Figure 10.3).

Despite being outnumbered by 70 men, the five white women and five Indigenous women dictated the domestic arrangements inside Miners' Fort. Documentary evidence indicates that the settler women segregated themselves away from the Indigenous women (who, like the white women, had come to the fort alongside their settler husbands), choosing to live with some balance of the men in the larger of the two overcrowded cabins within the fort's walls (Jones 1856:522–26). Within the smaller cabin, the agency of the five Indigenous women was indicated by the archaeological work (Figure 10.4). While each of the two cabins had a distinct hearth, the feature in the smaller cabin was formed by a concentration of beach cobbles known generally in the Far West as a camas oven. Thus, one of the cabins within a pioneer fort, recalled in the placemaking of local historical memory as a bastion of settler colonialism literally surrounded by hostile Indians, contained a feature designed and likely manufactured by Indigenous women. These cross-ethnic families employed Indigenous technology to cook food, manufacture ammunition, and warm their household in a time of extreme duress.

Betsy Brown is the only Indigenous woman whose actions in Miners' Fort are described in the primary documentation (Jones 1856:522–526).[2] Mrs. Brown is recalled in her family's oral history as being of Tolowa/Dee-ni' and Chetco origin. She came to Miners' Fort as a wife of a settler, an arrangement reciprocally arranged in Indigenous fashion through the agency of her family. In Betsy's case, her mother, Lossegingn, and her father, Kwut'tl-Ne'-Son, betrothed her to a Russian immigrant from Saint Petersburg[3] named Charles Brown, the very same gold miner celebrated in the historical memory of the fort for negotiating the release of the Geisel women from captivity on March 7, 1856 (Slagle 1985:26–36; Joel Bravo, personal communication 2017). The Tututni, Joshua, and Mikonotunne who murdered the Geisel men and the other settlers and held the Geisel women captive shared

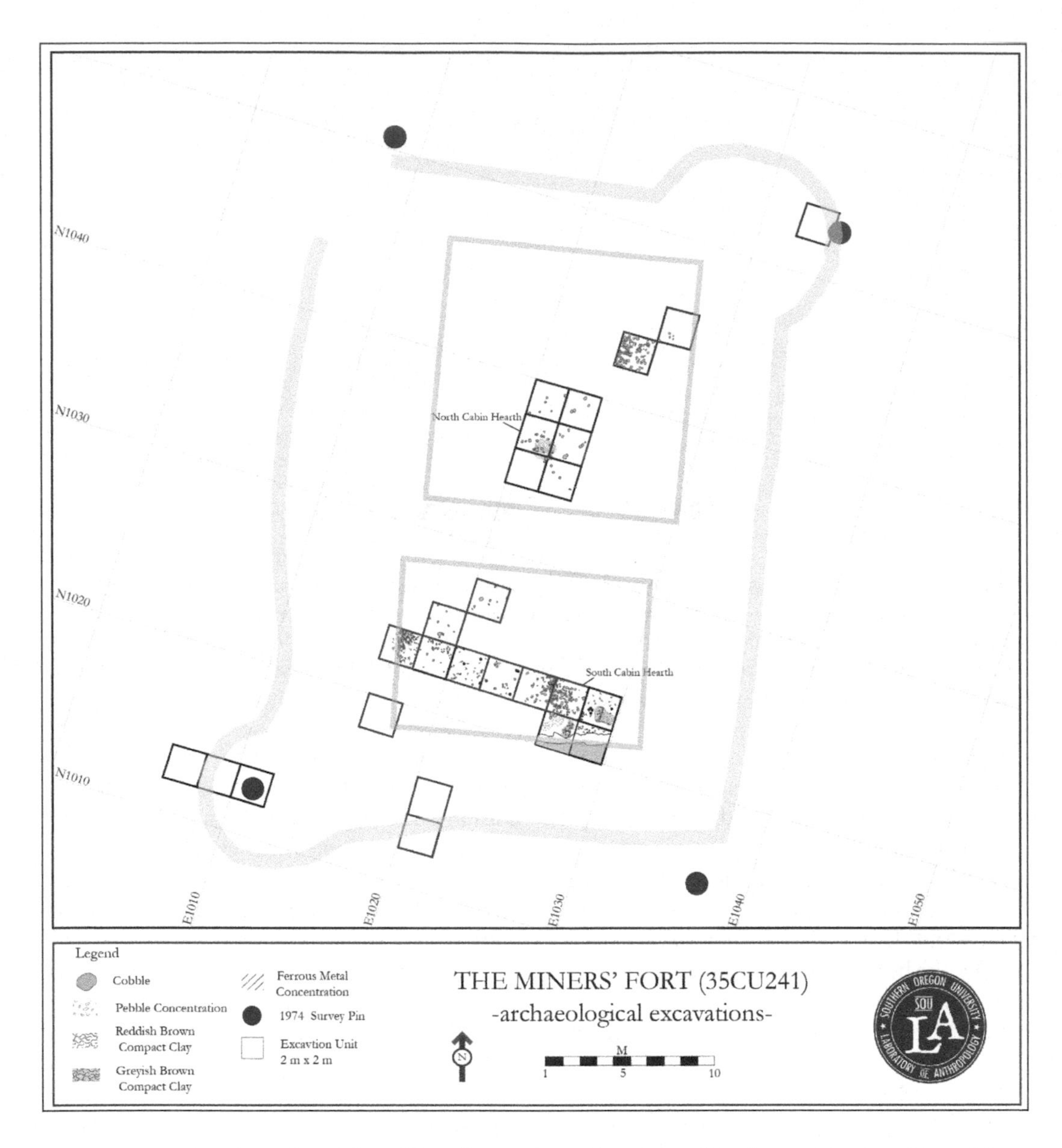

FIGURE 10.4. A plan view of the Miners' Fort. The walls and bastions of the fort and the locations of the two internal cabins were determined through electrical resistivity and magnetometer geophysical survey. Subsequent excavations uncovered a hearth feature in each cabin: a stone-ringed pit filled with burned earth in the northern cabin and a lenticular feature of beach or river cobbles in the southern cabin. The latter feature is a style consistent with earth ovens of Native American design. Courtesy of Southern Oregon University Laboratory of Anthropology.

close political, social, and ethnic ties with Betsy's Tolowa/Dee-ni' and Chetco family, and, thus, Betsy herself.

That Betsy was instrumental to the release of the Geisel women is perhaps obvious in hindsight. At least one contemporary eyewitness noted that both "Charley an' his squaw [Betsy] went right out among 'em; an' the chiefs came up an' shook hands with Charley" (Jones 1856:522–526). Rather than Charles Brown negotiating on his own outside the fort, it was Betsy who, on her own, "had to go out more'n once," to affect the release of the Geisel women (Jones 1856: 522–526). Betsy Brown agreed, like many Indigenous women of that era, to partner with a settler man and assisted in negotiations between her husband's people and her own, a political act at least as complicated, brave, and dangerous, if not more than, her husband's.

The erasure of Betsy Brown from the historical memory of the Rogue River War began from the moment that the siege of Miners' Fort was lifted by the United States Army on March 20, 1856 (Crescent City Herald 17 May 1856:2). Captain Edward O.C. Ord, who was part of this command, was struck by the hostility exhibited by Christina Geisel (whom he named) and the other white women towards the Indigenous women, despite their shared ordeal and the agency shown by Mrs. Brown to secure the release of Mrs. Geisel and her daughters (Jones 1856:522–526).[4] This antipathy went beyond a refusal to share quarters. The white women asked the soldiers to "kill all the squaws and the copper colored young ones," and one even offered, in Ord's words, "in Lady Macbeth style… to do the bloody work with her own hands" (Jones 1856:525).

Although Ord and the other officers did not allow the Indigenous women and their children to be killed, they did insist that they be removed to the Coast Reservation unless their settler partners agreed to marry them in legal, European fashion. Two of the men agreed, including Charles Brown. Again, by Ord's account,

> there, on the banks of the Rogue River, by the shore of the great Pacific, with a circle of rough-looking miners standing around, the marriage ceremony was performed. Charley promised to have her, and her only, for his lawful wedded wife, and then translated the words of the ceremony for the benefit of his dusky tattooed bride [Jones 1856:525].

Conclusion

The ordeal and redemption of Christina Geisel and Mary Harris anchor many narratives about the Rogue River War of the 1850s, and the places where these events took place remain memorialized and inscribed in southern Oregon identity and historical memory. Told through the lens of the captivity narrative, these stories, and the social experiences of the celebrated places where they took place, rationalize settler colonialism through the suffering of white women at the hands of Indigenous people. While such narratives exclude Indigenous women, a close reading of historical documents, the oral history of descent communities, and the archaeological record can liberate these women and others from the confining settler narrative and explore the complexities of landscapes of settler colonialism.

Women in Oregon and elsewhere on the western frontier were not simply shrinking violets nor Indian concubines purchased from their families against their will for trinkets. Christina Geisel might have lost her family on that tragic day, but she endured, eventually surviving three more husbands, and her eldest daughter Mary's home is now the site of a local pioneer museum. Likewise, Mary Harris and her daughter lived influential lives, and their descendants were heralded as pioneering women farmers who were instrumental in early historic preservation efforts in southern Oregon. Both families capitalized on their fame to a certain extent, although Christina was once again victimized—murdered in 1899 while being robbed of her first pension check of $25, awarded for her wartime ordeals (Anonymous 1901). Christina's body was left behind as the house was burned down over her, in a macabre repetition of her first husband's fate 45 years earlier.

If the narrative accounts of the Geisel and Harris women were meant to honor their accomplishments as women, we need to equally honor Queen Mary, Betsy Brown, and the many other Indigenous women who served their own people, acted as cross-cultural mediators, and provided critical resources for newcomers to the region. Mary, Betsy Brown, and many other Indigenous women also survived the 1850s, often to raise families that continue to share their experiences and knowledge to the present day. In the case of Betsy Brown, her descendants remember her and her family as leaders of traditional dance, language, and culture that, in part, helped the Tolowa Dee-ni' persist as a community through the era of settler colonialism to the present day (Slagle 1985:26–36; Joel Bravo, personal communication, 2017).

Epilogue

While the tragedy suffered by the Geisel and Harris families is preserved in historical narratives and highway waysides of Oregon to the present day, the victims of settler-led massacres remain largely unacknowledged. Just as Beckham used the Geisel narrative as a literary device to open his 1971 book, he likewise ended it by returning to the Geisel Monument State Wayside in the book's final pages. The last paragraph of *Requiem for People* reads:

> near the weathering granite marker inscribed with the fate of those pioneers named Geisel, still lay the scattered and unburied bones of the last of the Rogues on the way from their homeland [Beckham 1971:191].

The "scattered bones" in this passage belong to the victims of a massacre perpetrated in June, 1858 in revenge for the death of Mr. Geisel and his sons (Beckham 1971:189).[5] Beckham's source was the memoir of William Tichenor (1883), who described how he and his companions, in a dawn ambush, murdered 16 Indigenous people camped at the remains of the Geisel Homestead while prisoners of the United States government en route from southern Oregon to the Coast Reservation. The historical memory of this massacre remained, however, among local people of Indigenous descent. Lucy Smith, a Tolowa/Tututni woman who worked with anthropologist John Peabody Harrington, confirmed that this placemaking through blood vengeance occurred near the Geisel Homestead:

> At a place coastward of Geissel's[sic] cemetery was where they rounded the RR Inds [Rogue River Indians] up preparatory to taking them in [to the Coast Reservation] and they ran away from there so many times that at last the soldiers got mad and massacred the boys [Harrington 1942].

Likewise, George B. Wasson Jr., a Coos/Coquille elder who grew up in the vicinity, recalled attempts by himself and other local residents to protect this massacre site as it was encroached upon by Highway 101 before the advent of cultural resource protection laws (George B. Wasson Jr., personal communication to Mark Tveskov 1996; Ron Crook, personal communication 2016).

The massacres of Indigenous people, such as that perpetrated by William Tichenor in 1858, are muted in historical memory (see also Lewis 2014; Tveskov 2001). Such massacres remain unmemorialized at the Geisel Memorial State Wayside and elsewhere, imagined instead as a requiem, as a terminal narrative to describe the melancholy price paid by the "Last of the Rogues" for the advance of settler colonialism. Against such erasure stand Betsy Brown, Queen Mary, Lucy Smith, and other Indigenous people who took steps to ensure the survivance of indigenous communities through settler colonialism and whose stories need to be celebrated alongside those of settler ancestors.

Notes

1. Today the whereabouts of this rifle, and its exact provenience, are unknown.
2. Jetéé (2010:168–169) suggests that a French-Canadian man named Adolphe Jette, who was at Miners' Fort during the siege, may have been accompanied by his wife Julie, an Indigenous woman from the Rogue River area.
3. In the family's history recorded in the Tolowa petition for federal recognition, Charles Brown's home is said to be Petrograd, a name used for Saint Petersburg, Russia, during the First World War (Slagle 1985:35).
4. Ord wrote anonymously as "Sargent Jones" in this 1856 *Harpers* article.
5. The massacre was covered in the Jacksonville newspaper. "Indians Killed on the Coast" (Oregon Sentinel, 3 July 1858).

11

"The Battlefields Are the Only Thing We Have"

Archaeology, Race, and Thanatourism in the Trans-Mississippi South

CARL G. DREXLER

Arkansas lies in the easternmost reaches of the West and, in the minds of many people today, is a Southeastern, not a Western, state. This association has not always been the case, as the Natural State was one of the first areas to arise in the American consciousness as "the West." In the early nineteenth century, it was the American frontier, where settlers encountered Native Americans, wild animals, and what they took to be unclaimed farmland. In both fiction and nonfiction of the period, Arkansas was the Wild West, and it remained so until the 1860s. This image endures in recent Western fiction in the characters of Sheriff July Johnson in Larry McMurtry's *Lonesome Dove* and Ms. Mattie Ross of Charles Portis's *True Grit* (Blevins 2009; McMurtry 1985; Portis 1968).

This chapter explores how archaeological research in the eastern margins of the West engages with the process of placemaking in two different senses. The first sense is in historical context, as "the West" is taken to be a distinct place defined both by contemporary culture and the development of the Civil War in a distinctly "Western" fashion. Second, archaeology and place come together through the deliberate revivification of that conflict to remake those same places as sites of *thanatourism*, tourism focused on places of death and dying. Archaeologists have a crucial role to play in this second form of placemaking, although doing so poses important questions about how all involved (archaeologists, preservationists, and stakeholders) deal with issues that vex us to this day. The most obtrusive of these is race, specifically how archaeologists can aid placemaking in support of thanatourism while also navigating the legacies of racialized violence that laces through American history.

I also examine my own connections to this process. As a white Southerner (raised in Texas and capable of managing a convincing drawl), my participation frequently entails assumptions by many members of the public concerning certain understandings of heritage I embody. My relation to "our" heritage (see below) is a matter of concern when I contribute my archaeological expertise to tourist-focused preservation efforts across the region.

The place of thanatourism in American culture, particularly associated with the American Civil War, is a shifting landscape. Between January 2017, when I presented the conference paper that gave rise to this chapter, and the completion of its first draft in January 2018, the United States saw a summer of neo-Nazi rallies and counterprotests in Charlottesville, Virginia, that threw American national interest onto the Civil War to a degree not seen in recent years. The stories archaeologists and Americans tell about this conflict have never been neutral, but the attention created by the Charlottesville rallies and counterprotests underscores how powerful work on these sites can be. This chapter appears in the midst of renewed public discussion, and revisiting the questions and musings presented here in another 10 or 15 years will likely arrive at different conclusions.

Place in the First Sense: The Western Reaches of the American Civil War

As this chapter deals with the most easterly of contexts amongst the contributions to this volume, I must first explore what "The West" meant in the mid-nineteenth century and, crucially, during the American Civil War (1861–1865). Further, the role of the conflict in the western reaches of the country, known as the Trans-Mississippi Theater, differed from the war in the Cis-Mississippi, and I examine that as well. These differences focus around scale, ethnicity, and the practicalities of mobilizing for the conflict.

Though far from the storied battlefields of Gettysburg, Chancellorsville, and Antietam, the Trans-Mississippi was no sleepy backwater of the conflict. Arkansas followed only Virginia, Tennessee, Missouri, and Mississippi in the number of combat actions during the war, with 771 battles, engagements, skirmishes, and actions (Dyer 1908:582). What separated the Trans-Mississippi from the other theaters, however, was that most of those violent clashes were primarily between small units, perhaps only a few hundred soldiers on a side. The grand movements of large armies were rarely seen in the West. Instead, men fought and died in small conflicts over very localized contestations for terrain and populace. The previously referenced figure comes from Frederick Dyer's (1908) *A Compendium of the War of the Rebellion*, a tabulation of engagements and losses drawn from official reports. Beyond those actions that Dyer counted lie hundreds of clashes between national forces of both sides and gangs of irregular troops (known as bushwhackers, Jayhawkers, and partisans) that harried military and civilian alike, as all struggled to subsist in a war-torn land isolated from international and intranational change. Run-ins with irregulars were very common in the West. The war in Arkansas, and in the Trans-Mississippi more generally, was much closer to the style of warfare later used against Native American groups or in today's conflicts in Iraq and Afghanistan (Collett 2007) than the Napoleonic clashes of the eastern theaters.

The men and women who endured the war in the Trans-Mississippi understood that the war created a separation between East and West. In 1862, a group of Arkansans wrote to Confederate President Jefferson Davis complaining that they were part of "a separate war, beyond the reach and cut off from all aid by the Confederacy, whether of men, arms, or ammunition" (Johnson et al. 1902:815). The Trans-Mississippi was a different place, often referred to as "Kirby-Smithdom" in recognition of the Confederate commander, General Edmund Kirby Smith, who exercised near-total power, civil and military, in the absence of attention from Richmond (Kerby 1991).

Second, to an extent not seen elsewhere during the war, the conflict in the West brought together soldiers of much more complex ethnic heritages. In addition to the thousands of white soldiers on both sides, many regiments of African American soldiers served in the West (Cornish 1987). Black regiments from Louisiana, Arkansas, Missouri, Iowa, and Kansas all served in the Trans-Mississippi Theater, and their numbers were proportionally greater than elsewhere. Of course, black and white troops served together in all theaters, but the ethnic mix in the West transcended the simple white/black dichotomy. Both sides enjoyed a substantial Native American contribution, as Cherokee, Choctaw, Chickasaw, Creek, and Seminole troops served in both armies (Warde 2013). Several Texas units, both US and Confederate, had large numbers of Hispanic soldiers in their ranks and officer corps. The complex blend of people reflected the ethnic borderlands that cross-cut the region during the war, as Indian, Hispanic, White, and Black communities were all well represented on the frontier.

Finally, the war in the West was one fought from scratch, at least on the Confederate side. Almost no industrial facilities existed in Arkansas, Texas, or Louisiana before the war, giving the region few resources to meet the demands of the conflict. Missouri, stuck in the limbo of being a border state (it attempted to claim neutrality while its citizenry split their support between the two sides), tried to supply its pro-Confederate militia, the Missouri State Guard, with limited success (Brooksher 1995). To make the situation more dire, by 1861, the Confederate authorities in Richmond told leaders in the West to expect little help from the East, which was preoccupied with the war in Virginia and Tennessee. In fact, men were taken from the Trans-Mississippi for service in the east, forcing the region to raise new armies afresh to defend itself (DeBlack 2003; Dougan 1972; Moneyhon 2002). The fact that the conflict endured in the West as long as it did is testimony to the energy and perseverance of white Southerners and the political and military power of General Kirby Smith, who exercised great civil governmental control as well (Kerby 1991). Though better-equipped, US forces in the West still faced supply and manpower shortages throughout the conflict.

The upshot of these factors is that the Confederate territory west of the Mississippi became a place recognized at the time as being set apart from the rest of the conflict. The war there was fought by a host of smaller groups in briefer encounters, using a different mix of peoples than seen anywhere else during the war.

Place in the Second Sense: Archaeology and the Western Civil War in Arkansas

As argued above, the Trans-Mississippi became a distinct place as a reaction to outside pressures done to meet military necessity. Making the places of the Trans-Mississippi, in the second sense (in the present), has also been a local reaction to outside pressures, though primarily economic. Archaeologists have been part of this second placemaking process, as archaeological research is one of the major bridges between the past and present. Despite this involvement, archaeologists are not usually in charge of the process.

Archaeologists have a long history of engagement with thanatourism in Arkansas. Since 1965, archaeologists have helped establish war-related local, state, and national parks at Pea Ridge, Prairie Grove, Arkansas Post, Fort Smith, and Helena (Brent et al. 2011; Carlson-Drexler et al. 2008; Coleman and Scott 2003; Holder 1957; Stewart and Brandes 1994). These sites are all archaeological engagements with thanatourism and placemaking, and cover the state's war experience in terms of geographic spread, from the Ozark Mountains to the Mississippi River Delta, and the temporal sweep of the war. Another effort, dealing with the last major campaign of the war in Arkansas, known as the Camden Expedition, claims the spotlight today.

Historical Context: The Camden Expedition

In early 1864, US Major General Nathaniel Banks, stationed in New Orleans, launched a campaign up the Red River and headed for the cotton-rich lands of East Texas. The ill-fated Red River Campaign, as it came to be known, included an attempt by the US Army to divert Confederate attention and divide their defensive efforts (Johnson 1958). Part of the campaign strategy involved a diversionary movement by the 7th Army Corps, commanded by Major General Frederick Steele. Steele's force was stationed in Little Rock, and Banks ordered them to march across southwest Arkansas to meet their US comrades in Texas. This campaign was a difficult one, as the region was picked over after three years of supporting the resident Confederate forces without outside help. The 7th Corps started the march on half rations, and throughout the campaign, hunger presented as much of a concern to US soldiers as Confederate soldiers (DeBlack 2003).

The first major combat actions of the Camden Expedition occurred at Terre Noire Creek and at Okolona on April 3, followed by encounters at Elkins' Ferry, Prairie D'Ane, and Moscow Church. From there, hearing that Banks's effort had failed in Louisiana, Steele marched on and

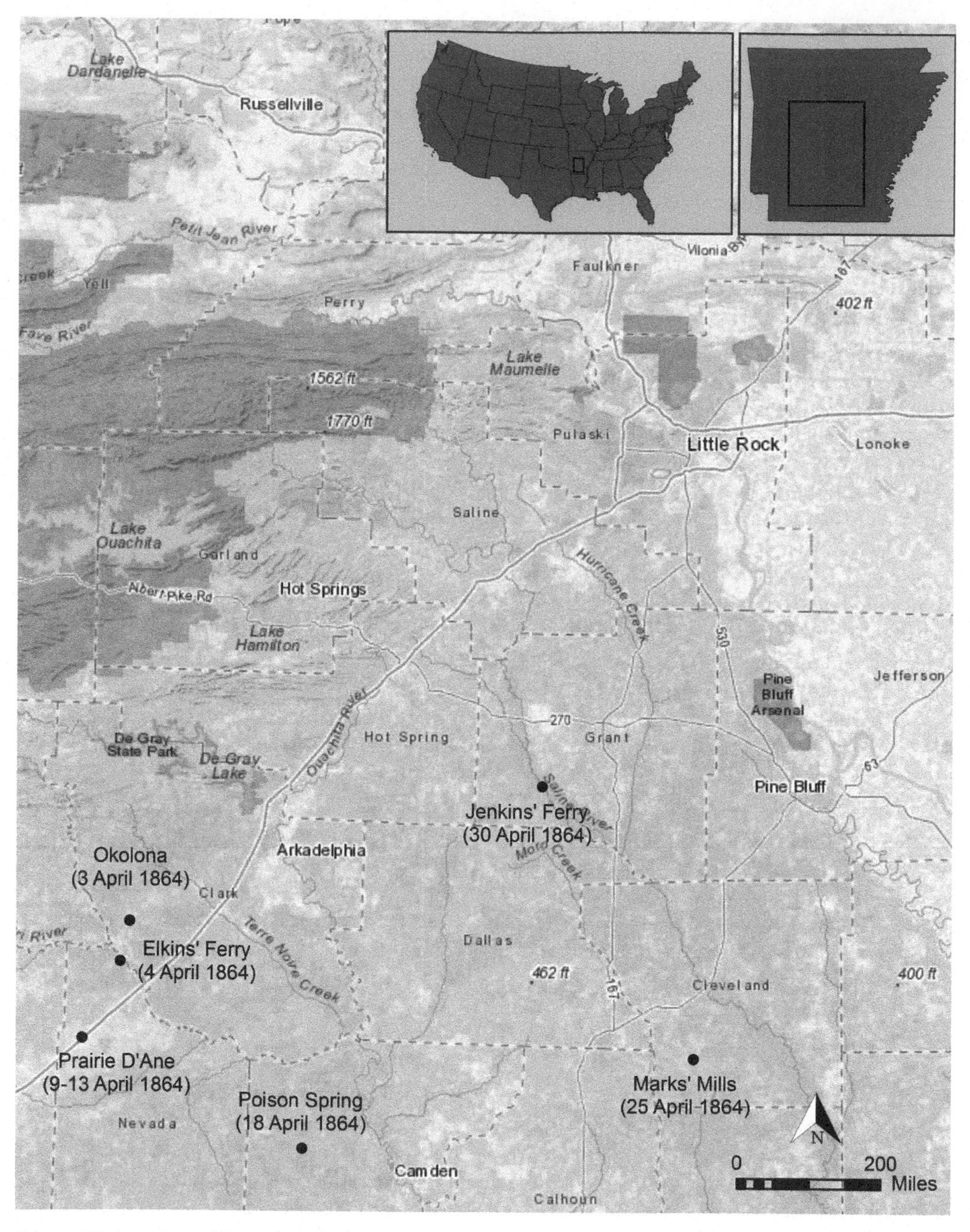

FIGURE 11.1. Location of the major Civil War engagements discussed in the text. Map by Carl G. Drexler.

took Camden, the second largest city in the state and the seat of Confederate military power, thus giving the campaign its name. The Federals held it for 11 days, during which time a column sent in search of food was ambushed and decimated at Poison Spring, and another group sent to seek refuge at Pine Bluff was surprised and routed at Marks Mills. The federal forces subsequently vacated Camden and, after fighting one last major battle at Jenkins' Ferry (depicted in the rainy opening scene of *Lincoln* [Spielberg 2012]), returned to Little Rock (DeBlack 2003). Figure 11.1 shows the location of the major engagements.

Neither force numbered more than 15,000 soldiers, and many of the engagements featured only a few thousand on either side. Despite the small scale, these engagements were the last major conflicts of the war in Arkansas.

The sites associated with the campaign offer a unique opportunity in Civil War heritage tourism. Arkansas has, for good and ill, a slower, smaller economy than other states and remains focused primarily on agriculture. Cotton, corn, soybeans, watermelons, timber, and chickens are the state's major exports. As global demands for these goods change, and as commodity chains reconfigure, cities across the region that were once locally important shipping and commercial hubs falter. The tracks still go through town, but the trains no longer stop, and the kids all move to Little Rock or Dallas for work. The city square gets eaten by Walmart, an ambivalent eventuality given the superstore's in-state headquarters. Most of the region's rural counties are losing population, and some are smaller now than they were in 1860.

Depressing as this can seem, this depopulation means that Arkansas's cities, outside of Little Rock and Fayetteville, do not grow as fast or vast as elsewhere, and do not eat up battlefield land as voraciously as in Virginia and Tennessee. The sites of the Camden Expedition have largely gone undeveloped, though not forgotten. Eight properties, mostly those battles mentioned above, were recognized as the Camden Expedition Sites National Historic Landmark (NHL) in 1994, and they collectively represent one of the best-preserved conflict landscapes anywhere in the country. Despite that preservation, many of these sites are only cursorily interpreted. We did not even have documented locations for two battlefields before the fieldwork began, meaning that new archaeological research led to an immediate form of placemaking by identifying a spot on the landscape to which we could tie the history of those battles.

Civil War Thanatourism in Southwest Arkansas

In the past few years, Arkansas governor Asa Hutchinson identified tourism, particularly heritage tourism, as a key means of diversifying the state's economy (TalkBusiness.net 2015). Among all the efforts sparked by this, the Camden Expedition sites stand out as one of the areas of greatest public activity and focus. Efforts to find, mark, and interpret them have been significant, timely, and urgent. After all, as one local respondent related to me in 2016, "[our town] is dying, the battlefields are the only thing we have."

Initial efforts occurred during the recent sesquicentennial commemorations, with archeologists and heritage specialists writing preservation plans for several sites in the Camden Expedition NHL (Brent and Brent 2014). Local efforts focused on acquiring battlefield land for creating parks and other interpretive resources. The first of these came in the form of a purchase of a large portion of the Elkins' Ferry battlefield (ACWHT 2015), an effort now being repeated for parts of Prairie D'Ane. Community advocacy groups are also working on acquiring Jenkins' Ferry, the forts around Camden, and several other sites. These entities all have a significant interest in tourism as well as outright preservation. Many of those efforts emphasize the Western nature of the war, particularly the strategic importance of western Arkansas, Texas, and connections to Mexico (Brent and Brent 2013). This focus reasserts the mid-nineteenth-century meaning of "The West" within modern heritage management.

In support of these efforts, the Arkansas Archeological Survey recently completed fieldwork at Elkins' Ferry, working within the recently purchased tract (Drexler et al. 2016). Its archaeologists mapped Camden's Fort Lookout and are working to record other related archaeological sites. A new project on Prairie D'Ane battlefield is in progress, as well as calls for research on Jenkins' Ferry, Poison Spring, and other associated sites. This work is being done within the emerging standard of battlefield archaeology (Geier et al. 2010) and has produced valuable information about these sites while also supporting tourism development efforts. The work also raises new questions about the Camden Expedition, which lie at the heart of this chapter.

Among these questions is how do archaeologists understand the wider context of the archaeological fieldwork, particularly its application to tourism development, as they give place to past events? Such concerns have been raised by others working on sites of difficult subjects located elsewhere (Hartmann 2014; Light 2017; Stone and Sharpley 2008). By constructing place through the production of new research and creation of visitor guides, monuments, and other media, tourism, particularly thanatourism, monetizes the experiences, sometimes painful and dehumanizing, of others. It forces those involved in the development of these places as tourist attractions to choose how they present these sites to visiting publics. How archaeologists do this is not neutral, and the history of the Camden Expedition and the Civil War in the West requires everyone involved in developing tourist industry around these sites to think through these issues as these efforts advance.

Race and Place: Thanatourism, Archaeology, and the Way Forward

Archaeologists recognize the importance of working with the public in the abstract to create heritage sites, and increasing numbers of archeologists are taking a scholarly interest in how they engage with heritage tourism and memory (Logan and Leone 1997; Rothman 2001; Shackel 2005). Most of the scholarship in this area focuses on giving voices to those traditionally held out of the history books. Herein lies the crux of the issue: as they contribute to the construction of place through research and public engagement, whose narratives do archaeologists embrace, and which marginalized groups are archaeologists representing?

As James Cobb (2005:289–290) wrote of the South, "blacks and whites defined their frustrations, failure, and defeats so differently that one group's tragedy quite frequently represented the other's triumph [and] contemporary black and white southerners have been and remain a people more divided than united by their common past." The most obvious example of this zero-sum situation is the American Civil War, where white southerners' tragedy of defeat spelled emancipatory triumph for black southerners.

The easiest answer to questions focused on representation in the case of the Camden Expedition is that African American heritage is the most neglected, and that African American contributions to Arkansas, Western, and Southern heritage need the most remedial work to balance the 150 years of silence that has typified attention to their role. This failure is not the result of simple historical fate: Blight (2001) and others have documented the deliberate effacement of African American stories from our collective memory of the conflict. Not only does this erasure leave a gap in our story; it marginalizes African Americans who, as Coates (2017) notes, often ignore the conflict despite its important place within African American history and the prominent role that African American soldiers played in earning and claiming freedom through force of arms. As noted above, this role was particularly significant in the West.

Archaeologists working on sites associated with thanatourism confront a problem, however, when looking at who is in the room (often literally) when working with stakeholder communities on Civil War places. Those represented demographics are commonly different from those with whom an archaeologist with a crusading social justice agenda might expect to partner. Based on my own participation in numerous public meetings, public history events, and reenactments, clearly the people who are most engaged with this area are largely white and mostly descendants of Confederate soldiers, with a keen sense of who their ancestors were and what they did during the war. Frankly, few nonwhites show up. Frequent calls to preserve "our" history and heritage read in context as truly meaning that those involved should be working to preserve white Confederate heritage, largely within the Lost Cause mythology. As a Pennsylvania-born Quaker descendant of two German-American US soldiers, my heritage is not included within "our" heritage, and under this reading, neither is the history and heritage of African American soldiers and their descendants. It comes as little surprise to me, then, that people of color are rarely in the room for any of the meetings or listening sessions focused on creating and developing these places of memory and heritage.

Certainly others have experienced difficulties in getting African American engagement with sites of the period, though much of the scholarly work attempting to garner black engagement focuses on sites of enslavement. Not surprisingly, the horrors and dehumanization of the slave system are issues on which few descendants want to focus (Small 2013; Tyler-McGraw 2006). Yet, Civil War sites in Arkansas frequently offer different narratives. Over 5,000 Arkansans of color served in the US Army during the war, most of them in-state. Thousands of others donned blue coats to fight for their rights, and battlefields all over the state included black soldiers throughout the final stages of the war. The city of Helena-West Helena, in the Arkansas Delta, has created several heritage tourism sites focused on emancipation and loyal service during the war, which has had a major impact on the local economy and worked to significantly change the focus of heritage narratives presented in public facilities in the region (Bowman 2015).

The archaeologists and historians assisting with the efforts in Helena found that the story fighting for freedom and citizenship is something that does attract significant positive returns amongst African Americans. Why, then, has the development of thanatourism around the Camden Expedition commemoration been so white? The answer can be readily identified when one looks at the properties in the Camden Expedition NHL. Major projects are in process at Elkins' Ferry, Fort Lookout, Jenkins' Ferry, and Prairie D'Ane. The Confederate capitol in Washington and Fort Sutherland, one of the forts surrounding Camden, have been fully developed already. This leaves out two places, the Poison Spring and Marks Mills battlefields. Both had small parks created to interpret the sites to the public in the 1960s, but no active efforts are working to do more with them today. What sets Poison Spring and Marks Mills apart? Without adequately identifying or addressing this difference, the current tourist initiative, to which archaeology is fundamental, cannot rectify the alienations created by traditional Civil War narratives. Those narratives have been written into the landscape by past thanatourism development initiatives and have deadened the significance of the war to many Americans, as Coates (2017) observes. Not surprisingly, race lies at the heart of the matter.

The Exceptionalism of Poison Spring and Marks Mills

On April 17, 1864, a column of US soldiers marched along the Prairie D'Ane Road to Camden, escorting a convoy of 200 wagons loaded with corn. Among the escorts marched the 1st Kansas Colored Infantry. As they marched past Poison Spring, they were surprised and overwhelmed in a brief but bitter fight by a much larger Confederate force. In the aftermath of the battle, many African American soldiers were deliberately murdered by Confederate soldiers, an incident second only to the Massacre at Fort Pillow, Tennessee in the annals of Civil War racial atrocities (Christ 2003). Unlike Fort Pillow, Poison Spring is reenacted every year, with the post-battle massacre acknowledged, but not portrayed. The Battle of Marks Mills, took place a week later and featured a similar, smaller post-battle atrocity.

In both instances, the usually positive narratives of black self-emancipation and citizenship through military service are subverted by the horrors of the post-battle atrocities. That African American soldiers were killed post-surrender is not just a cancelling-out of the narrative of armed opposition to slavery, it adds the passivity of being killed while in a subordinated, dominated position, paralleling the killing of slaves and the lynching that would come in the years following the war. The atrocity at Poison Spring, and its links to antiblack violence that continues today, is not a history that any descendant community would be eager to engage with, and the lack of interest in promoting either Poison Spring or Marks Mills in recent years is a wider recognition of the dilemma posed by this history. Any initiative to do more with these sites for tourism must confront the atrocious reality attached to these places and communicate it to the public.

What about Jenkins' Ferry?

One curious aspect of the wider tourism effort is that post-battle racial atrocities, which are at least tacitly recognized as problematic in the case of Poison Spring, are not categorically ignored by those white community members involved in preserving the Camden Expedition. One of the most once-active community groups was focused on the last engagement of the Camden Expedition: the Battle of Jenkins' Ferry. In addition to being the last major combat action in Arkansas during the war, it was also where the 2nd Kansas Colored Infantry slit the throats of wounded Confederates the night after the battle. That incident, referenced in *Lincoln* (Spielberg 2012), has been a fixture in the list of stories told about the battle.

Two subtexts underlie this eagerness. First, it is a tacit recognition, on the part of local whites, of the veracity of the massacre at Poison Spring, and that the retributive murders at Jenkins' Ferry somehow offset the preceding event, making the earlier massacre permissible. It creates a perceived tit-for-tat that they imply lessens the inhumanity of what happened at Poison Spring.

Second, it is a kind of legible expression of victimization that represents white anxiety about their waning social power and position. Though locally dominant, rural Southern whites are not in a position of power nationally by many different measures and often construe themselves as a marginalized people, eager for America to be made great again. Paul Shackel (2004b:10) described heritage as "what each one of us individually or collectively wishes to preserve and pass on to the next generation" and noted that heritage helps root "us" in our communities and becomes a force of resistance against the demands of a globalizing world. Those passionate stakeholders with whom archaeologists have worked most closely on these sites often construe "heritage" as being "their heritage," by which they mean Confederate heritage.

In fairness, they likely restrict "heritage" to the war years and do not consciously recognize the ends to which Confederate memory was placed in the years after the war. These developments stem from the fabrication of the Lost Cause myth to the opposition to desegregation in more recent years, things that spring readily into the minds of others.

The Civil War, in many minds, appears to mean a last gasp of a prosperous and honored time, one that can be remade through heritage tourism. Places thus made serve as an anecdote to an "official history" that recapitulates whites' perceived decentering within modern economic and social landscapes. They know their history and their heritage, and they want that passed on to younger generations as a way of maintaining their significance and communicating the value of communities that are rapidly losing their place in the modern world. By creating places where those stories can be told, their heritage may endure. Many communities across the country, of many different ethnic and racial backgrounds, yearn for no less.

Conclusion

Where does this leave archaeologists engaged in research that feeds into thanatourism? Archaeologists are part of a much wider, community-led initiative to make places of heritage throughout the region, but so far the communities with which archaeologists work are not representative of the population. For this statewide effort to succeed, it must do the hard work of bringing everyone to the table. If the process becomes, or continues as, a primarily white initiative, it will ultimately rehash the structural violence of the past and fail to create a tourist resource that carries any real relevance to people who are not from the immediate region. This reckoning will not happen until we (archaeologists, historians, and the general public) find a way to deal with Poison Spring.

What should be archaeologists' role in developing thanatourism resources such as battlefield sites and, specifically, massacre sites? There is no solid answer. Archaeologists can assist with the technical details of assisting with land acquisition and doing archaeological surveys, or writing up and designing signage, but the harder, subtler work of dealing with the legacies of the conflict, which have largely not been put to rest, are not easily fundable and do not often generate positive, feel-good stories. Community-oriented archaeology can eventually serve as a platform for bringing different communities together to start grappling with the war's legacies, though the places archaeologists help to make are haunted by many spirits.

12

Terminal Narratives and Indigenous Autonomy

Fragmented Historicity in the Santa Ana Mountains of Orange County, California

Nathan Acebo

Humanistic geographers have argued that the concept of place is not simply a discrete location in the Cartesian sense but formed out of spaces imbued with cultural meanings by human interaction (Tuan 2001). People may physically recognize the specificity of a place through tactile sensation and, more abstractly, by the participant's internalization of symbols or narratives at or about said location through their prior knowledge (Thomas 2012). In the Los Angeles basin, the process of placemaking is played out in a landscape prescribed by the enduring culture of Indigenous Southern Californians, the physical remains of the state's Spanish and Mexican colonial eras, and the ongoing post-annexation development of the cosmopolitan metropole.

Since the 1930s, maintaining the premodern heritage sites of the Los Angeles basin troubled historical preservationists to the extent that the earliest archaeological societies were formed to salvage Native Californian sites and restore the colonial missions, forts, and ranches as tourist destinations and historical landmarks (Frierman and Greenwood 1992). Thanks in part to these early preservationists, modern-day residents and tourists are still able to interact with an urban landscape that retains some of its pre-American heritage. By their anachronistic material remains or associated historical narratives, Los Angeles basin heritage sites possess a sense of being from the past, or *historicity*. Through human interaction, interpretation, and, at times, institutional backing they also are recognized as *places* of historical significance.

While these historic places as heritage sites may seek to educate people about a time or culture long past, the development of a factual or unbiased understanding of local history is not always guaranteed. This chapter presents an example of how the historical sense of place for one heritage site, the California Historical Landmark (#217) Black Star Canyon Indian Village, became disconnected from its Indigenous history. I highlight how the village's historicity and associated history-making processes—that is, historiography, archaeological research, and folklore traditions—influence the modern understandings of the landmark as a historic place.

Historicity and Placemaking

A universal property of place that provokes an awareness of its historical relevance is its historicity. Historicity is defined as the qualities of an entity (e.g., objects, people, events, places, or landscapes) that signify or authenticate its actuality for the human subject, whose experience with said entity then establishes a form of historical consciousness (i.e., perception of the past) (Ruin 1994). The concept of historicity originates from phenomenological philosophy concerned with the relationship between the ontology of human beings and history (Hirsch and Stewart 2005). To exist is to have a bare condition of historicity, but the qualities that define an entity's historicity can be factually substantiated or denigrated by narratives or ideologies about history held by the human subject that reference or deny the authenticity of an entity's historical existence (Bunnin 2004:159).

Interrogating "history" as the objective record of past events is a contentious but core element of historical archaeology (Lucas 2006). Alternatively, the study of historicity in archaeology has recently emerged as an analytical direction in the transdisciplinary fields of archaeological ethnography (Hamilakis 2011) and heritage ethnography (Carman and Sørensen 2009). These fields draw attention to the relationship between the archaeological record's historicity and the roles played by heritage management, academic research, and the ideologies held by present-day observers. Specifically, archaeologies of historicity account for how an archaeological collection, site, or historical landscape came into existence (i.e., its material life-history) and the forms of historical consciousness that arise from human interaction with the enduring material presence of the archaeological remains and their associated historical legacies in the present.

California's colonial missions typify places of the past whose historicity was altered to generate selective historical understandings regarding the state's colonial heritage. Since the widespread restoration efforts of the late nineteenth century, the rustic missions have become what Elizabeth Kryder-Reid (2016:179–181) classified as "heritage-scapes" or cohesive landscapes that afford a connection to the colonial past. The mission heritage-scape attracts approximately 5 million visitors a year. The ruins of the missions now act as formal museums or heritage sites that represent a time before urban claustrophobia, while simultaneously outlining the institutional logic from which the Western frontier was initially "civilized."

The mission ruins possess historicity through their physical existence within the landscape, but their historicity is enhanced by decades of preservation work, historical studies, and public outreach and education. One critique leveraged against the mission heritage experience is that it overwhelmingly reemphasizes the culture and power of the colonizers, while minimizing the agency of Indigenous people and the violent trauma suffered during the colonization process (Miranda 2013). The historical obfuscation of the Indigenous colonial experience at these places of heritage exemplifies Michael Wilcox's (2009) concept of Indigenous terminal narratives, known as histories, stories, folklore, or scientific theories that argue for the disappearance and alienation of Indigenous peoples from their own past. In the last few decades, historians and archaeologists (e.g., Lightfoot 1995; Panich and Schneider 2014; Silliman 2000) have shed light on the topics of Indigenous agency in southern California, while many of the missions have increased their visibility of Indigenous culture. Still, the legacy of the Spanish colonial project looms large in public discourse on the missions (Panich 2016).

It is reasonable to assume that human interaction with the historicity of colonial heritage sites, like Spanish missions, would facilitate a historical awareness centered on European colonization. I would like to complicate this line of thinking by providing a case study on how a place of Indigenous heritage that existed beyond reach of the Spanish and Mexican settlements was reconstituted by its base features of historicity into a colonial heritage site. Specifically, this chapter examines the forms of historical understandings generated from the historicity of the Black Star Canyon Village site, a registered California Historical Landmark (#217, ORA-132; Figure 12.1).

The village is one of the most publicly visited archaeological sites in the Santa Ana Mountains of Orange County and is recognized as an "official" historical entity by the California Office of Historic Preservation. The historicity of the site, inclusive of written accounts, oral history, and the archaeological record of the village itself, was studied by archaeologists, historians, and local nonacademic folklorists (Acebo 2017).

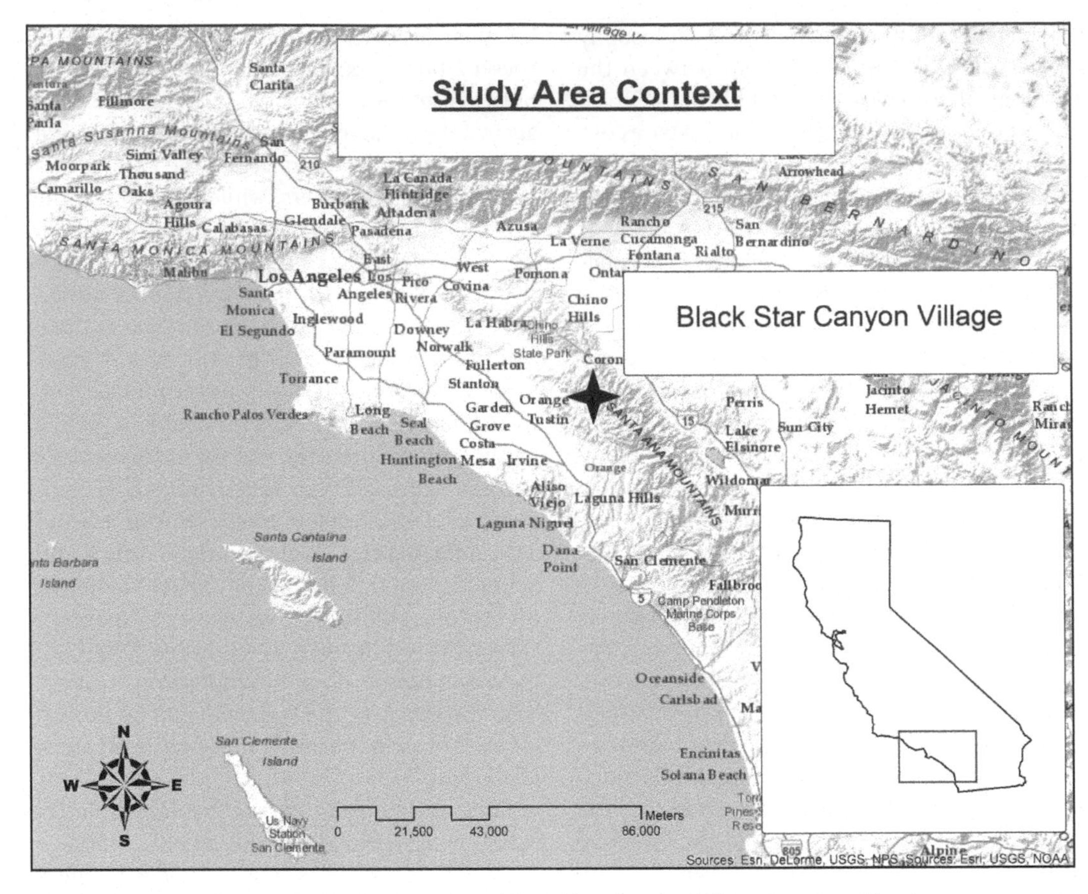

FIGURE 12.1. Map of Los Angeles Basin and the Black Star Canyon Village location. Map by Nathan Acebo.

The resultant interaction with the historicity of the site has only produced conflicting and partially disconnected interpretations of the village for academics and the Orange County public. I argue here that the disjointed interpretations of the extant archaeological and historical record and the dissemination of said interpretations into the public contribute a sense of place characterized by a colonial terminal narrative focused on the disappearance of Indigenous people and their autonomy.

Orange County Precolonial and Colonial Contexts

During the terminal-Late Prehistoric and Protohistoric eras (1300–1770), Tongva, Acjachemen, and Payómkawichum Indigenous hunter-gatherers maintained a system of large, semi-sedentary villages that were supplied by a system of interconnected procurement camps in different ecosystems, including oceans, beaches, and mountains (Koerper et al. 2002). The collection of subsistence resources and their redistribution in extraregional trade in exotic stones, shell beads, and baskets established villages as the centers of economic, ceremonial, and political production under the control of chiefs or larger clan lineages (McCawley 1996; O'Neil 2014).

After 1770, Spanish colonization restructured the coastal plains and valleys of the Los Angeles Basin. The new missions, presidios (forts), and pueblos (towns) served as home for a diverse collection of transplanted Spanish and Indigenous military settlers from northern Mexico and the American southwest (Hackel 2005). Under the Spanish administrative policy of the *reducción* (forced relocation), Indigenous communities were transported to colonial institutions, which resulted in religious assimilation, agrarian labor, and population decline for Indigenous peoples (Phillips 2014; Sandos 2004).

After 1821, the transition into Mexican-*Californio* society redistributed native populations around the privately owned *ranchos* (ranches) outside of the mission. Disenfranchised native populations were instruments of labor for the lucrative international tallow and leather trade (Haas 1995). Increasing numbers of American travelers and traders also made their home in Southern California at this time, many of whom were later memorialized post-annexation as pioneering figures, including Jedediah Smith and Kit Carson (Sanchez 1997).

The cultural change created by colonization led historians and anthropologists to believe that pre-Hispanic traditions and settlement systems collapsed (Cook 1976; Kroeber 1976). Contrary to this belief, Indigenous Californians survived the colonization process while adopting new cultural practices and creatively maintaining precontact traditions (Lightfoot 2005). Known by colonial settlers as the uncontrolled hinterlands, the uncontrolled interior valleys, mountains, and desert territories linked Indigenous communities through legal and illicit activities, including mission-sanctioned excursions, *cimmarones* (native runaways), and interregional Indigenous traders, horse thieves, and bandits (Blackhawk 2006; Zappia 2012).

The Deconstruction of a Village

Prior to the "Black Star" title (named after a local coal mine established in 1879), the canyon was known as *La Cañón de los Indios* (Canyon of the Indians) during the initial colonial eras and was legally incorporated into the Mexican land grant system as part of *Rancho Lomas de Santiago* in 1846 for cattle grazing. Apart from ranching activities, the canyon and mountains have largely avoided urban development. The village was registered as a state historical landmark in 1935 (Office of Historic Preservation 2012). As of 2018, the site's archaeological features include a series of 17 sandstone bedrock mortar complexes and a mounded midden (4500 m^2). The canyon landscape is managed by the US Forest Service, Orange County Parks, and the Wildlands Conservancy as a nature preserve.

The landmark status ascribed to the village memorializes the famous 1832 "Battle of *La Cañón de los Indios*," the only massacre of Native Americans by American colonists in Orange County. First published in Terry Stephenson's (1931:109–111) historical chronicle, *Shadows of Old Saddleback*, the massacre account details the activities of a band of fur trappers led by William Wolfskill. The trappers were hired by *Californio* ranchers to retrieve stolen horses and punish the group of "Shoshonean Indians" residing at the village. The characterization of the event as a massacre is substantiated by the climax of the narrative, which culminated in the lopsided ambush, death, and retreat of the Indigenous village occupants into the wilderness. The events of the massacre were relayed to Stephenson by Wolfskill's ranch foreman, J. E. Pleasants, in 1929. Pleasants' account was originally acquired from Wolfskill during a hunting expedition in Black Star Canyon.

The written record of the massacre and the remaining archaeological materials of the village constitute the two central features of the village's historical authenticity. Their existence and endurance attest to the presence of a "past" at the village. Yet the site's features of historicity were/are mobilized in different historiographic epistemologies that produced different historical understandings about the village's "past" and its use in the present.

Material Historicity in Archaeology

The looting of archaeological sites was a common practice in Southern California during the early twentieth century (Koerper and Chace 1995), and the Black Star Village was not exempt. Looting activities at the village before the 1930s included pot hunting by Herman Strandt, who eventually led the first formal "archaeological" excavation under the Works Progress Administration Anthropological Projects wing from 1936 to 1937 (Winterbourne 1937). The 1930s project

FIGURE 12.2. Sample of Late Prehistoric projectile points collected by the Works Progress Administration from the Black Star Canyon Village in 1937. Photograph by Nathan Acebo.

was followed by an Archaeological Survey Association project between 1952 and 1954 and a Pacific Coast Archaeological Society Landmark Survey project in 1971 (Chace 1971). As with the preservationists mentioned in the introduction, the goal of the post-1930s projects was to salvage known historical sites (Figure 12.2).

For archaeologists, the archaeological record possesses historicity and produces insights about the past through interpretation. Therefore, the archaeological practices and the resultant interpretations constitute an epistemological domain that alters the capacity to understand the material historicity of the village. To varying degrees, each project at the village surveyed, mapped, and excavated portions of the large habitation midden, which collectively resulted in the recovery of over 136 kg of cultural artifacts and documents.

Collections and documents from each project were never fully cataloged or analyzed, but the unfinished state of each project did not inhibit the dissemination of the different investigators' interpretations, which occurred in the form of formal publications or rumors about the site. The preliminary findings from the various projects were remarkably homogeneous. All characterized the site as a Late Prehistoric acorn procurement camp that did not display evidence of complex social behavior present at permanent residential basecamp villages, such as long-distance trade or high-volume domestic production. These interpretations were largely based upon the presence of the surface level milling features, without incorporating the actual excavated artifacts. Further, none of the projects engaged with the 1832 events as an Indigenous period of occupation.

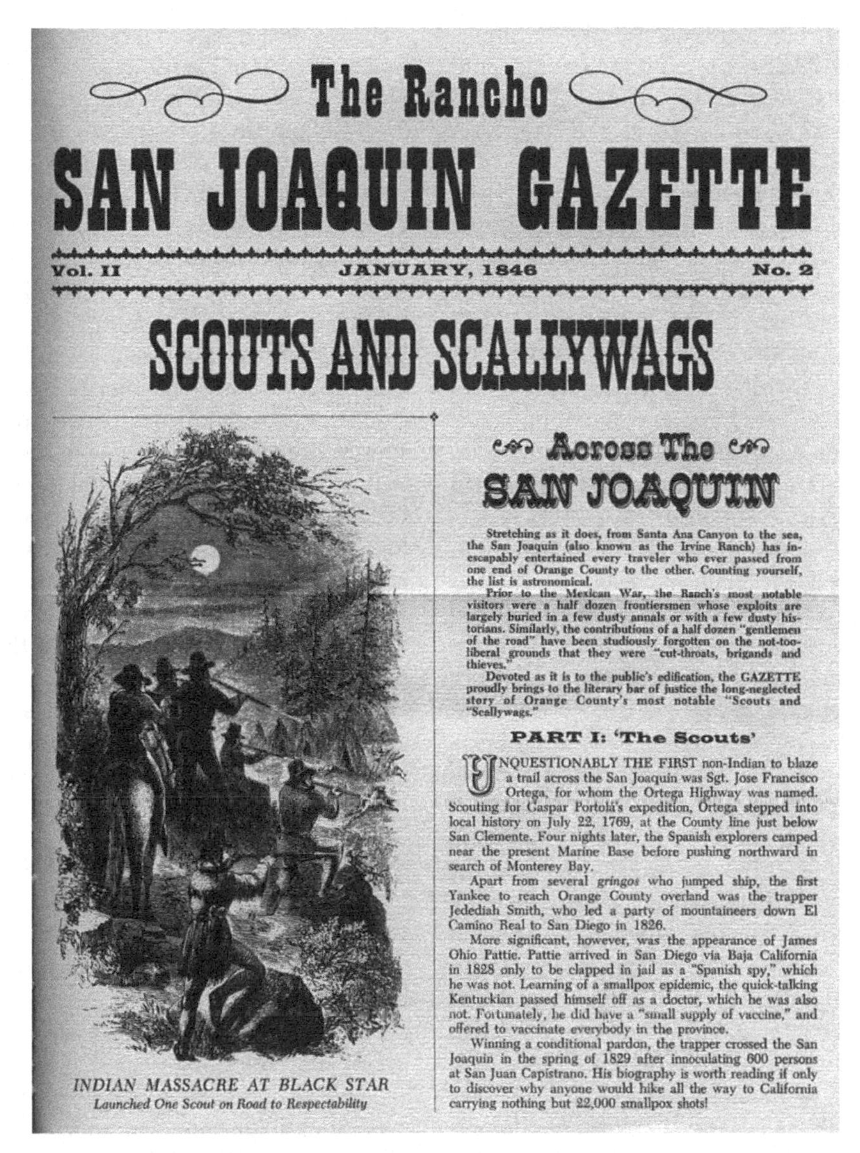

The Rancho
SAN JOAQUIN GAZETTE

Vol. II JANUARY, 1846 No. 2

SCOUTS AND SCALLYWAGS

INDIAN MASSACRE AT BLACK STAR
Launched One Scout on Road to Respectability

Across The
SAN JOAQUIN

Stretching as it does, from Santa Ana Canyon to the sea, the San Joaquin (also known as the Irvine Ranch) has inescapably entertained every traveler who ever passed from one end of Orange County to the other. Counting yourself, the list is astronomical.

Prior to the Mexican War, the Ranch's most notable visitors were a half dozen frontiersmen whose exploits are largely buried in a few dusty annals or with a few dusty historians. Similarly, the contributions of a half dozen "gentlemen of the road" have been studiously forgotten on the not-too-liberal grounds that they were "cut-throats, brigands and thieves."

Devoted as it is to the public's edification, the GAZETTE proudly brings to the literary bar of justice the long-neglected story of Orange County's most notable "Scouts and "Scallywags."

PART I: 'The Scouts'

UNQUESTIONABLY THE FIRST non-Indian to blaze a trail across the San Joaquin was Sgt. Jose Francisco Ortega, for whom the Ortega Highway was named. Scouting for Gaspar Portolá's expedition, Ortega stepped into local history on July 22, 1769, at the County line just below San Clemente. Four nights later, the Spanish explorers camped near the present Marine Base before pushing northward in search of Monterey Bay.

Apart from several *gringos* who jumped ship, the first Yankee to reach Orange County overland was the trapper Jedediah Smith, who led a party of mountaineers down El Camino Real to San Diego in 1826.

More significant, however, was the appearance of James Ohio Pattie. Pattie arrived in San Diego via Baja California in 1828 only to be clapped in jail as a "Spanish spy," which he was not. Learning of a smallpox epidemic, the quick-talking Kentuckian passed himself off as a doctor, which he was also not. Fortunately, he did have a "small supply of vaccine," and offered to vaccinate everybody in the province.

Winning a conditional pardon, the trapper crossed the San Joaquin in the spring of 1829 after innoculating 600 persons at San Juan Capistrano. His biography is worth reading if only to discover why anyone would hike all the way to California carrying nothing but 22,000 smallpox shots!

FIGURE 12.3. Reimagined publication of the Black Star Canyon Massacre, from Sleeper's (1968) "historical" newsletter for the Irvine Company.

In describing the site in this manner, the titular "village" in the Black Star Village site became a misnomer within the documented archaeological record of Orange County, and placed the site on the periphery of the Late Prehistoric settlement hierarchy (e.g., Cameron 2000). The archaeological collections and project records were stored across different museum institutions in the Los Angeles Basin. In combination with the uncatalogued state of individual project collections, the decentralized curation of the village has prevented any synthesis of primary evidence of life at the village.

Historicity in Colonial History with a Capital "H"

Stephenson's publication of the "Battle of *La Cañón de los Indios*" is the first written record of life at the village. As the editor of the *Santa Ana Register* and president of the Orange County

Historical Society, Stephenson established much of the local academic production and dissemination of orthodox history. The publication of the battle narrative clearly was part of a larger political project.

In Stephenson's account, Wolfskill arrived in California and secured his place in the upper echelon of Mexican-Californio society by leveraging his hunting skills to the "bumbling Mexican dons" who were at the mercy of "wild Indian" populations (Stephenson 1931:109). In doing this, Wolfskill annihilated the native population and was awarded ranching lands. Wolfskill later converted his new lands into prosperous farmland after annexation through his dual Mexican-American citizenship.

As documented by Arellano's (2013) archival investigation, Stephenson also worked as an Orange County booster, where his historical projects focused on bolstering the achievements of local foundational figures. Stephenson's work was sympathetic to the goals of borderland scholars like Herbert Bolton and Charles Lummis, who sought to glamorize the achievements of the European colonists and Anglo pioneers of California (Keen 1985). In the Black Star battle account, Wolfskill is the protagonist, and his motivations and actions affect change within the narrative. An Indigenous population is present, but they are pawns in the larger power play for social mobility in Mexican-*Californio* society.

Evaluating Stephenson's account against biographic works on Wolfskill reveals historical inaccuracies in the massacre account (Barrows 1902; Wilson 1969). First, the skills, physiological prowess, and lucrative status of Wolfskill's trapping party were greatly overstated. Mission records and Wolfskill's personal ledger for the expedition reveal that when the group arrived at Mission San Gabriel they did so in poor health and immense debt due to route miscalculations, and they failed to procure sufficient furs. Further, the 1832 battle is omitted from Wolfskill's personal records and biography (Wilson 1969).

This is not to say that Wolfskill was nonviolent or the massacre was a myth. Much of his life in the Los Angeles Basin outside of his agricultural pursuits was dedicated to vigilante justice against Indigenous horse thieves or local murderers for political gain (Cleland 2003). However, clearly if the massacre was fact, then Wolfskill's motivations may be more complex than the assertion of American exceptionalism in the "Wild West." Most local historians acknowledge the factual conflicts within the battle account, yet the publication is still held as the exclusive line of evidence for life and death at the village.

Terry Stephenson's account was later republished in a variety of different books on Orange County history and local newspapers across several decades. Exemplified perfectly by the annual reappearance of the massacre story in the special editions of *The Rancho San Joaquin Gazette* by Orange County folklorist and journalist Jim Sleeper (Figure 12.3), the new versions of the account would further sensationalize the achievements of Wolfskill and the state of desperate "savagery" exhibited by Indigenous thieves. The increasingly fictitious reappearance of the massacre story in history books or in news outlets cemented the massacre story in the public domain.

A Land without Natives: Historicity in Folklore

When visitors arrive at the Black Star Village today, they encounter no informative displays referencing the historic landmark status or its deep archaeological past. The lack of academic information does not mean that the Black Star Village is unknown to the public. Rather, the paucity of a substantiated archaeological and historical record allowed local folklore beliefs to structure the public discourse on the Black Star Village. Similar to the epistemological domains of archaeology and history, the public folklore of Black Star draws upon the materiality of the canyon and the survival of the massacre event within the historical consciousness of Orange County.

As a part of different private, county, and federal nature preserves, Black Star Canyon is officially presented and recognized as a local wilderness destination. The status of the canyon as a nature preserve attests to the endurance of

FIGURE 12.4. *OC Weekly* title page from Arellano's (2013) textual examination of the massacre at the Black Star Canyon Village. Courtesy of OC Weekly.

nineteenth-century environmental romanticism within land management agencies and the public, where wild or natural landscapes represent the antithesis of industrial society (Nash 2014). Case in point, real estate tycoon and Irvine Ranch Natural Landmarks founder, Donald Bren, concluded, "The magnificent open space, parks and recreational opportunities on The Irvine Ranch provide natural beauty, relief from development and secure our unique Southern California outdoor lifestyle" (Irvine Ranch Conservancy 2017a).

Segments of the public also regard the canyon as a portal into the paranormal, derived from the variety of urban legends concerned with the presence of Native American ghosts, witches, and satanic cult groups, with the "bloody" massacre event as the progenitorial act. The extreme belief in the supernatural qualities of Black Star has been documented by Orange County's leading newspapers (Staggs 2013; Figure 12.4), whose journalists have accompanied supernatural tourists, ghost hunters, and cult groups into the canyon. Activities in Black Star are frequently advertised with local folk histories or legends in mind. The Orange County Parks Department offers monthly trips into the canyon to discuss the massacre and debunk popular ghost stories.

Internet forums on various backpacking and hiking blogs emphasize the supernatural qualities of the canyon, including hauntedplaces.org, a digital repository of paranormal locations across the United States (Haunted Places 2017; Irvine Ranch Conservancy 2017b).

Discussions with visitors at the site during the field seasons of 2015 and 2017 further illuminate public perceptions specific to the village. Hikers and mountain bikers frequently used the village as a rest stop or end point for canyon excursions and, during my fieldwork, they would take time to examine our excavation units and share their knowledge of the site. Most visitors saw the site as the location of "a" massacre or believed the village to be occupied thousands of years ago. Few understood the date, plot, or characters within the massacre account. Within these perspectives, many of the visitors exclusively saw the site as a graveyard or burial ground because of the massacre event.

For the public, the implications of the massacre promote a dehumanized understanding of Black Star. This interpretation relies upon the materiality of the site without the archaeological knowledge of its Indigenous inhabitants. Nothing immediately available indicates the presence of burials at the village, but the presence of the village without its inhabitants is enough to suggest that "Indians were here." The additional abstract knowledge of a massacre marks the village as a place of death, which then allows for the accommodation of pop-cultural tropes of Indian burial grounds and their implied supernatural qualities (Boyd and Coll-Peter 2011). Following Judith Richardson's (2003) articulation of Indigenous burial grounds in the northeast United States, the focus on Native ghosts or the paranormal displaces the ability to understand the lives of the Indigenous people who produced the space, thereby embodying Wilcox's concept of terminal narrative, which haunts so many other domains of colonial historiography like the aforementioned mission landmarks.

Understanding Historicity as Guide for Archaeology

Where folklore knows the village through the fantasy of unoccupied lands and the living dead, archaeologists and historians also flattened the historical realities of Indigenous life. The act of excavation sans interpretation limited the archaeological record's capacity to address the structure of daily life at the village or its seemingly paradoxical persistence into the colonial period. Alternatively, the discipline of history cannot articulate an Indigenous past because the historiography of the village is built upon its obliteration. The endurance and persistence of the village's historicity (archaeological and historical) allows it to be "known" in the present. Even so, resultant historical consciousness seemingly is built upon ignorance, as we are still left asking: who were the people of Black Star?

Since 2013, I have led the Black Star Canyon Indigenous Archaeology project in collaboration with the Tongva, Acjachemen (Blas Aguilar Adobe Museum), and Payómkawichum (Pechanga Band of Luiseño Indians) community members. The primary goal has been mobilizing archaeology and Indigenous histories to understand the contexts of village life before and after the massacre through the perspectives of the Indigenous descendants. Together, we have analyzed and synthesized the once fragmented legacy collections with tribal village histories and can now articulate the rich political and economic autonomy exercised by the Indigenous occupants well before and after colonialization. Our examination of the village's history provides one pathway to restore an Indigenous voice at the landmark, but this intervention is made possible by understanding how the landmark's historicity creates a place of Indigenous silence.

13

From the Land

An Indigenous Perspective of Landscape and Place on the Northern Plains

Aaron B. Brien *and* Kelly J. Dixon

The mountains are as important to us as our language...many Apsáalooke leaders, both past and present have fasted in Bighorn, Wolf Teeth, and Pryor Mountains... they also fought, bled, and died protecting our people and our lands.

—Dana Wilson, Former Vice Chair,
Crow Tribe of Indians

Introduction: Creation, Spirituality, and Apsáalooke Concepts of Land and Water

Archaeologists and cultural heritage managers working in the twenty-first-century North American West should have an in-depth understanding of Indigenous Archaeology and perceptions of landscapes to avoid misunderstandings, disrespect, and damage to important cultural places. Many Indigenous people from this region perceive landscapes and the environment as part of an inherent spiritual connection to the natural world. Here we explore this relationship between people and place by sharing Apsáalooke narratives from the Great Plains of North America and endorsing methods influenced by advances in Indigenous Archaeology.

Today, the Apsáalooke people are concentrated on the Crow Reservation in south central Montana (Figure 13.1). The Apsáalooke relationship to the land is interwoven in spiritual culture and finds its roots in their creation story. The Apsáalooke creation story shows how, from the beginning, the land has played a central role in the development of Apsáalooke culture and identity:

> The Crow people say the Creator, Iichikbaalia, created the humans by instructing four ducks to go down into a body of deep water and retrieve mud from the bottom. The first three ducks failed, but after a long time, the fourth duck brought some mud from the bottom of the water. From this the Crow were formed. The Creator then breathed into his creation and for this reason Crow people say that speech or the word is sacred. Then he brought the Crow to a very clear spring and inside this spring they were shown a man with his bow drawn taught. The Creator said, "This is Crow people, I have made them to be small in number, but they will never be overcome by any

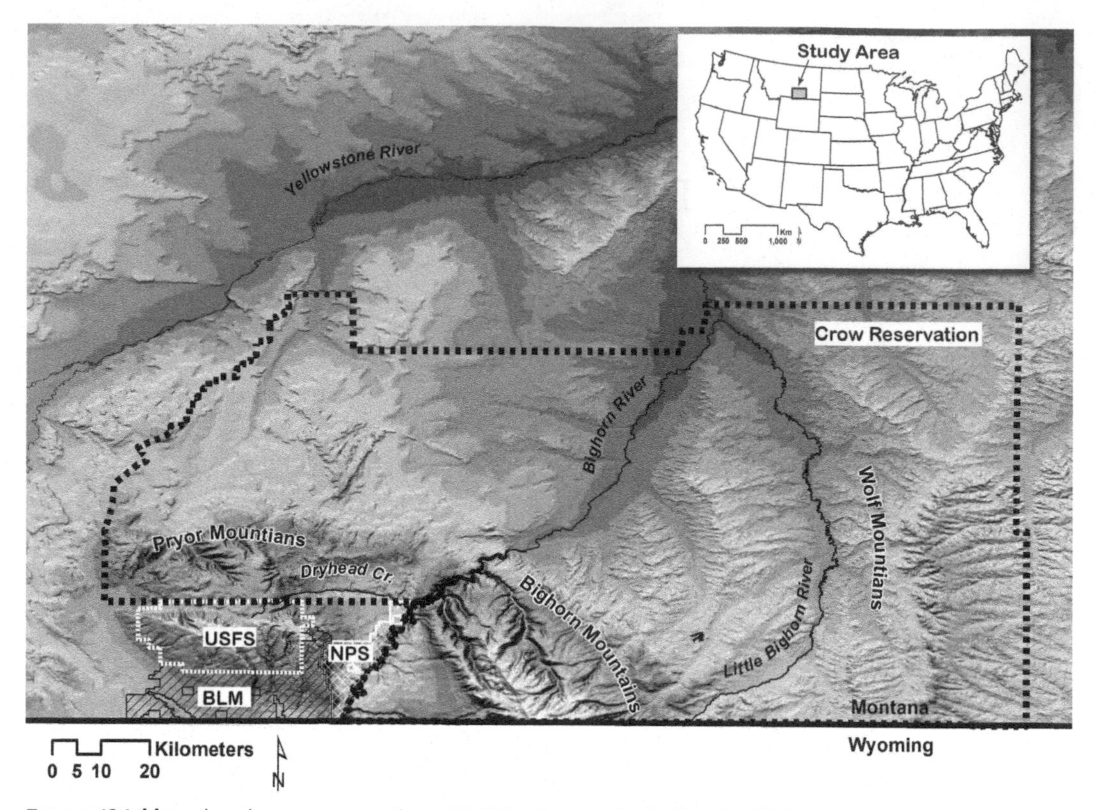

FIGURE 13.1. Map showing areas mentioned in this chapter, including the Bighorn and Pryor Mountains, as well as the Crow Reservation, all of which are situated in what is now south-central Montana. Courtesy of Diane Whited.

> outside force." The Crow people say that neither man nor woman was made first, it is simply said that the Crow were created [Old Horn and McCleary 1995:1].

When the Apsáalooke speak of the Creator, they see his power manifested on Earth through Baaxpee/Power of God. In turn, "Sacred Landscape," as defined by the Apsáalooke, can mean land or *ground* that has the direct presence of God. The Apsáalooke were originally called Awaakiiwiluupáapke, which translates to People on Top of the Ground and references the Creation of the Apsáalooke people noted above. Therefore, the ground itself is respected and held sacred not only because of past events that happened on the landscape, but also for the simple fact that the Apsáalooke come from the ground and are made from it. Apsáalooke are part of the ground, made from the same elements and given the same powers. In this traditional society, land is held in the highest regard. The quote below summarizes this view:

> We [Apsáalooke] only have one word for holy and those things, it's "baaxpee" it means "to be with God" or "Powerful source of energy"...that's why they say if you harm anything in nature it harms everything [Grant Bull Tail, personal communication 2017].

Such an understanding of Apsáalooke perceptions of landscapes would be impossible if important stories about the creation, spirituality, land, and water were not passed down from generation to generation. As elderly historians and cultural experts pass away, stories, language, lessons, and other recollections vanish if such information is not documented. Culture loss and related connections with landscape and place have subsequently become epidemic. In this chapter, we seek to inspire others to consider these issues by applying Indigenous Archaeological approaches, using methods that include (but are not limited to) field ethnography.

Indigenous Archaeology and Landscapes: Collaboration and Field Ethnography

While archaeologists have increasingly emphasized the benefits of inclusion and collaboration with descendant communities in the American West, by the early twenty-first century, Indigenous people had, for the most part, been treated like "second-class citizens in the cultural resources world of North America...in a system supposedly designed to protect their heritage" (Watkins 2003:283). In addition, they were rendered invisible during the recent past due to the paucity of formal archaeological investigations of what happened when Indigenous communities were moved to "Indian Territories" and reservations (Watkins 2017:121). Fortunately, since the turn of the twenty-first century, a growing array of scholarship has emphasized proactive participation of Indigenous peoples in archaeology in the West (e.g., Brien 2015, 2016, 2017, 2019; Colwell 2016; Colwell-Chanthaphonh et al. 2010; Darling et al. 2015; Kehoe and Schmidt 2017; Lyons et al. 2010; Makley and Makley 2010; McCleary 2015; Nicholas 2006, 2008, 2014, 2017; Schaepe et al. 2017; Silliman 2008; Teeman 2008; Watkins 2000, 2003, 2005, 2011, 2017; Wilcox 2009, 2010a, 2010b; Zedeño et al. 2014). This expanding field of inquiry, referred to as Indigenous Archaeology, "represents a methodological and theoretical commitment to the reintegration of archaeological materials and contemporary Indigenous peoples" (Wilcox 2009:236; see also Wilcox 2009:11).

Nicholas (2008:1660) defined Indigenous Archaeology as an "expression of archaeological theory and practice in which the discipline intersects with Indigenous values, knowledge, practices, ethics, and sensibilities, and through collaborative and community-originated or -directed projects [in which] archaeology is responsible to, and relevant for Indigenous communities." In more and more cases, Indigenous communities are taking the documentation of their cultural heritage into their own hands: "when archaeologists accept that an Indigenous group has the right to exercise control and make decisions regarding the group's own heritage, we get closer to...an Indigenous archaeology, archaeology for, with, and by Indigenous peoples" (Silliman 2008:18).

We find that Indigenous Archaeology is more than a philosophical notion or a theoretical base; "it is an applied method of preservation, protection, and perpetuation" (Brien 2019). Furthermore, "the application of oral histories to archaeology is at the forefront of the research... at no point is the narrative of tribal people secondary. This methodology is the foundation of our work...[and]...our job is part of a much larger movement. That movement is the restoration of identity and the preservation of heritage" (Brien 2019, #indigenousarchaeology on Instagram). Indigenous Archaeology has the potential for a diverse range of definitions encompassing innumerable Indigenous perspectives from throughout the world. Thus, it is challenging to generate one single definition that appropriately fits all.

Bearing this challenge in mind, below we present our working definition of Indigenous Archaeology to offer a framework that other researchers might adapt and apply to fit other areas of inquiry. We define Indigenous Archaeology as:

- an applied method for investigating the past and present that is grounded in a preservation ethic and that *ensures that information gathered goes back to the relevant descendant community(ies)* and engages, serves, and shares/archives information with those communities;
- a practical way of explaining and supporting ongoing efforts *to ensure continuity of culture, cultural identity, and human beings*;
- a field that *requires oral histories* and field ethnographies, as these are essential components of an Indigenous Archaeological approach (see methods under discussion in Brien 2015), along with modern investigations of archived ethnographic material from past anthropologists;
- a field that relies on diverse forms of media, such as *videography, visual anthropology,*

and documentary film to preserve ethnographic interviews and oral histories and to perpetuate far-reaching public information/education/engagement;
- a field that has the ability to privilege Indigenous place names and language when possible, with associated style guidelines that treat those place names as proper nouns, using uppercase letters for each word in the place name and avoiding the use of hyphens between words (e.g., Baahpuuo Isawaxaawuua/Hitting Rock Mountains) and
- a mechanism that can carry out cultural resource laws, but can also stand alone via *commitment to preservation, protection, and perpetuation of culture.*

Despite the advances in Indigenous Archaeology noted here, Indigenous peoples' cultural heritage interests, particularly landscapes, continue to be overlooked. While this erasure is the result of many factors, here we observe that one of those factors is the fact that legislation, such as the National Environmental Policy Act (NEPA), relies on the dominant, Western scientific worldview that "fails to consider and incorporate Native American perspectives of, values about, and relationships with the environment," with the latter getting "short shrift" (Dongoske et al. 2015:36). To complicate matters, in March 2020, organizations like the Coalition for American Heritage called for action as a result of the federal government's proposed changes to NEPA regulations and other laws that will give federal agencies the power to block National Register of Historic Places (NRHP) listings and eligibility determinations of federally owned properties. Such changes mean

> large landowners would have the ability to block historic district and property listings. These changes appear designed to allow mining and energy developers to block National Register listings that encompass large-scale landscapes, such as those in Alaska and the western United States that are culturally significant to Native Americans [Coalition for American Heritage 2020].

Community-oriented cultural heritage practices are the key to addressing such issues and also provide an increasing number of case studies that present vital Indigenous perspectives on cultural objects, sites, and landscapes (e.g., Atalay 2012; Bench 2014; Brien 2015; Carlson 2006, 2017; Carter et al. 2005; Conaty 2015; Dongoske et al. 2015; Goes Ahead et al. 2008; Kehoe and Schmidt 2017; Makley and Makley 2010; McCleary 2015; Nash et al. 2011; Schaepe et al. 2017; Scheiber and Zedeño 2015; Sears Ore 2017; Sleeper-Smith 2009; Teeman 2008; Watkins 2005, 2011, 2017; Wilcox 2009, 2010a). Such inclusive, participatory community engagement can help ensure long-term, sustainable preservation of cultural landscapes, securing the rights of future generations to learn lessons about history, culture, and respect from those places (cf. Harms 2012; Lightfoot 2005, 2006; Moldanova 2014). Here, we build on these developments in Indigenous archaeology and collaborative, community-oriented approaches with Apsáalooke examples from the North American Plains.

We are influenced by theoretical advances in collaborative and Indigenous Archaeological inquiry and consequently advocate for analyses of Indigenous cultural landscapes that engage and serve the needs of Indigenous communities living today. We, therefore, recommend methods grounded in collaboration with tribal historians and argue that field ethnography should be the first step in an Indigenous Archaeological approach (see methods outlined in Brien 2015). Basso's (1996) renowned *Wisdom Sits in Places*, involving the Western Apache, is one example of the insights and benefits of such approaches, emphasizing the value of taking historians (including elders) to important cultural sites and then documenting their stories. Underscoring the inherent connections between nature, culture, language, and place, Basso's collaborative research with the Western Apache presented the power of place names and "spatial conceptions of history," particularly the ways in which these names provide place-based, mnemonic devices that evoke an image of a cultural place in peoples' minds, making a "picture of it with words" (Basso 1996:12, 14; for related discussions on In-

FIGURE 13.2. Much was learned about this *Bilisshíissaannuua Alaxape* (fasting bed) in the Pryor Mountains as a result of closely working with Apsáalooke historians, demonstrating how such collaborations are changing how cultural heritage professionals in the region perceive, document, and protect features and related cultural landscapes (Brien 2015). Courtesy of Aaron Brien.

digenous spatial historical connections, see also Deloria 1992). As such, Basso's Western Apache colleagues demonstrate how place names are not only "natural" to Indigenous people in the American Southwest, but also how place names trigger histories, cultural and spiritual knowledge, and traditional ecological wisdom. Since places are visually unique, they represent "durable receptacles" of place-based wisdom, serving as "excellent vehicles for recalling useful knowledge" (Basso 1996:134; see also McCleary 2015). Indeed, the land provides a way to look after the people.

For many Indigenous North Americans, "the sense of place is paramount" (Momaday 1994:1), with the ancient and recent past "embedded in features of the earth—in canyons and lakes, mountains...arroyos...rocks...which together endow their lands with multiple forms of significance that reach into" peoples' lives, shaping the way they think (Basso 1996:34). In this sense, place names have the ability to make archaeologies of Indigenous cultural landscape more understandable to non-Indigenous people. Accessing such deep, cognitive connections with the landscape—and the power of place names—is for the most part impossible without field ethnography. Such place-based ethnographic undertakings accentuate the importance of going beyond "consultation" to ensure cultural landscapes are appropriately documented and preserved. It is essential for those seeking to document and preserve these places to establish meaningful, sustainable relationships with Tribal cultural heritage leaders and historians.

In an example apropos to the Apsáalooke people, Brien (2015) employed field ethnography to identify areas associated with Apsáalooke fasting in the Pryor Mountains of Montana, a case discussed in further detail below. The project demonstrated the benefits of including Tribal historians and heritage leaders in archaeological fieldwork and is changing the way archaeologists and others in the region perceive, document, and interpret fasting beds (Figure 13.2), place names, and related cultural landscapes.

Brien's (2015) and other cooperative undertakings (e.g., Goes Ahead et al. 2008; McCleary 2015; Old Horn and McCleary 1995) resulted in valuable insights about Apsáalooke cultural identity and landscapes that might otherwise have been overlooked without the inclusion of Indigenous descendant communities.

Unfortunately, in the past year alone, several elderly historians who provided crucial information for Brien's work either passed or are in poor health. Thus, connecting with people who have in-depth knowledge of cultural landscapes has become a time-critical undertaking for anyone interested in documenting and protecting Indigenous cultural landscapes. While such landscapes are under constant threat due to extractive industrial undertakings and associated air, noise, sound, and water pollution, the loss of people, specifically, people with information that can help identify, understand, and preserve these places, is just as problematic. Considering cultural identity, health, and spirituality, the information carried by these historians, and supported by associated places on the land, is important for people living today. This reality enhances the necessity of collaborating with descendant communities who have connections to landscapes in the West: "If one takes care of the land you will in turn take care of the Apsáalooke" (Brien 2016:1).

Apsáalooke Landscapes

In the case of the Apsáalooke, there are many events that took place on Western landscapes, from migration events to the signing of the Fort Laramie Treaty, but it is the idea of Spiritual Landscape that has intrigued both non-Indigenous and Indigenous scholars and researchers. The best way to understand the concept is to hear the narratives of the Apsáalooke and understand that these narratives help create a template to document, study, and protect other cultural landscapes in the American West and beyond. The story of the Pryor Mountains is one that helps to do just that.

Known for breathtaking views of vast stretches of the Northern Plains, alpine vistas, and the Pryor Mountains Wild Horse Range, the Pryors (Figure 13.3) are situated in modern south-central Montana in the heart of the Aboriginal territory of the Apsáalooke. The Apsáalooke term for the Pryor Mountains is Baahpuuo Isawaxaawuua/Hitting Rock Mountains, a place name linked with the Little People, dwarf-like people with spiritual powers who have long been associated with the region. East Pryor Mountain, the tallest peak in the Pryors [elevation 2,689 m], is an area that highlights the importance of spiritual-cultural landscapes. While many studies were conducted on the region, the work of Nabokov and Loendorf (1994) specifically used ethnographic information from elders to conduct some of their research (see also Nabokov and Loendorf 2002 and Ballenger et al. 2015). The site known to the Apsáalooke as Bishiáxpe Alíkuua/Where They Saw the Rope was identified as one of those spiritual landscapes:

> On the eastern rim of east Pryor Mountains is another important vision quest location associated with a specific individual. The place, identified by Euro Americans as the Dry Head Overlook, is known to the Crow as "Where they saw the rope." The Crow name was bestowed after some Crow Indians below the mountain saw a man fasting there. In his ordeal, he was dragging a bison skull which was attached to the end of the ropes that were fastened to his chest. The incisions in his body to attach to ropes were bleeding and it was this blood running down the ropes, glistening in the sun, that allowed the people below to witness as "Where they saw the ropes" [Nabokov and Loendorf 1994:49-52].

Understanding the Apsáalooke fasting culture and related practices is necessary to comprehend the concept of spiritual landscape(s). In many cases, place names are prescribed to the landscape in reference to the fasting; by doing this, the Apsáalooke acknowledge the importance of fasting to the individual and the tribe. These places of fasting become important land markers in the development of the fasters, and

FIGURE 13.3. Image showing the Pryor Mountain landscape. Courtesy of Aaron Brien.

the places, in turn, become important to the faster's family and community. In many cases throughout time, a place's importance grew in respect to the tribe; sometimes the characters change but the narratives stay the same. For example:

> Many years ago before the horse had come to the Apsáalooke, at this time the Apsáalooke was camped in the Bighorn Canyon area on the flat between the Bighorn Canyon and what is now known as Dry Head Mountain. A young man named Shows the Lance decided he was going to go fast and pray on top of Dry Head Mountain. So he informed the camp of this although it is unknown why he was fasting but, as we know most fasting was done for personal reasons. So Shows the Lance went and was gone for four days but while he was up there, the people could see him and noticed a powerful event. Shows The Lance was fasting and decided to pierce himself, which was common practice among the Great Plains tribes. He tied two buffalo ropes to himself then tied the other end to a tree that was close to him. He began to dance in place and pull on the ropes as it begins to rip his skin. He was in deep prayer and it ripped but he was not fazed and continued to dance. And like I said, the people from the bottom could see him from the bottom and noticed that the ropes started to dance along with him. And it's from this event that the Apsáalooke refer to Dry Head overlook as Bishiáxpe Alíkuua/Where They Saw the Rope.... Kakee Xxiisash/Shows The

FIGURE 13.4. *Bilisshíissaannuua Alaxape* (fasting bed) in the Pryor Mountains, providing a view from the Dry Head Overlook area (Brien 2015). Courtesy of Aaron Brien.

> Lance.... Shows The Lance, that was his name [Elias Goes Ahead, personal communication 2013].

The Apsáalooke place name Where They Saw the Rope is now associated with the top of Dry Head Mountain, illustrating the ways in which people, places, and events in the region are connected and in constant states of interaction. The Dry Head Overlook, situated at over 2600 m in elevation, is a place that provides exceptional "top of the world" views of the iconic Bighorn River Canyon (Figure 13.4). Even though mainstream associations of high mountains and vast viewsheds are commonly associated with fasting sites and cultural landscapes, smaller, more modest mountains have just as much importance:

> There was a time that my grandfather Little Nest was fasting near Parkman, there was a row of hills there and he was on the smallest at the end. He was facing the Bighorns. After a few days he noticed the mountain was talking to the man saying, "why are you there...that small hill has no power but we do." Then the small hill flung mud at the big mountain using a stick, the small hill did this a few more times and the big mountain began to cry. This small hill then said, "us small hills have powers too." You see this small hill near Parkman has power and it's not always the high peaks, even the small hill can have power [adapted from Marvin Stewart, personal communication 2015, 2018].

After telling this story about a little mountain and a big mountain's relationship with each other, as well as those mountains' perspectives of human fasting, Apsáalooke historian Marvin Stewart demonstrates how even the most humble and discreet places and landscapes have the power and capacity to benefit people from the past, present, and future: "A lot of people look at the mountain and that's a good place to fast but even down here, that little hill might have the power, you might have more power here [on the little hill] than the highest mountain" (Marvin Stewart, personal communication 2015). Moreover, Stewart draws attention to an important concept: these landscapes are viewed, understood, and treated as living beings.

Treating land, plants, animals, and water as living beings is an ancient practice that has ensured the sustainability of resources that are necessary for life on this planet. As cultural heritage managers navigate a world where decision makers are prioritizing mining and energy development interests, treating such "resources" as living beings is more important than ever. During March of 2017, the New Zealand government passed legislation that recognized the Whanganui River as a legal person, which means that river has rights and responsibilities that are equivalent to a person, something the Māori people have been fighting for under centuries of colonial rule because of their ancestral connection with the Whanganui River. "The decision is significant not only for granting legal rights to a natural entity; it models a practice to evolve the common law to better respect and reflect Indigenous legal principles" (Cheater 2020). We expect that important places for Apáaalooke people will someday be given the same rights as people to ensure their long-term protection.

Discussion and Concluding Thoughts

The small sample of narratives presented here are intended to cultivate a deeper awareness of Apáaalooke perceptions of cultural landscapes. This chapter is not intended to make readers "experts" in Apsaalooké cultural landscapes. Rather, the intent is to share stories of land and provide readers with examples of methods and strategies to effectively document, interpret, and preserve culture and landscapes well into the future. The narratives demonstrate how Indigenous people in the American West, in this case the Apsaalooké, maintain profound relationships with the land, so much so that land is perceived as living. For example, while broad, anthropological explanations present humans as migrating to different places on the landscape, Apsaalooké knowledge systems present migrations as the land *calling* the people.

Such connectedness is often at odds with western scientific perceptions of the world, the latter having driven both academic programs and cultural resource laws in the U.S. Thus, protecting spiritual landscapes will not be easy (e.g., Bench 2014; Borck and Sanger 2017; Kimmerer 2013; McNiven and Russell 2005; Nash et al. 2011; Nicholas and Hollowell 2007; Sleeper-Smith 2009; Tatum and Shaw 2014; Teeman 2008; Watkins 2005), especially in light of the current attempts to dismantle NEPA legislation that requires consultation (Coalition for American Heritage 2020). Nevertheless, it is critical to engage Indigenous students, hire employees and consultants, and educate cultural heritage professionals to ensure that these in-depth relationships, along with the land and water resources themselves, are integrated with cultural heritage documentation, management, and research, connecting ancient and recent pasts.

Considering how the Apsáalooke and other Indigenous communities have been impacted by the relatively sudden and drastic cultural and environmental changes taking place over the past several centuries, great efforts will have to be made to preserve and protect places and people. Given the constant suite of threats associated with extractive industries, population growth, and related air, light, sound, and water pollution, those who work or interface with Indigenous cultural landscapes have an ethical obligation to respect and uphold the spirit of Grant Bull Tail's (personal communication 2017) wise words noted above; harming *anything* in nature harms *everything*. Informed decision-making will not only protect the health and well-being of Indigenous communities, but will also protect the health of "the country" in general: "whatever benefits Tribal communities also benefits everyone" in terms of clean air, water, and other important resources associated with these landscapes (Brien 2017:1).

Collaborative, inclusive approaches to documenting culture and landscapes that engage descendant communities are essential and time-critical in today's world of rapid environmental change. As Indigenous people adapt and evolve to the transformations consistently impacting their communities and homelands, human relationships with cultural landscapes are continually evolving, too. Having said that, returning to Watkins' (2017:121) observation noting a paucity of Indigenous Archaeological studies from the relocation and reservation eras, studies of cultural landscapes will provide useful contextual backdrops for investigations of these transformative times, as well as other, more ancient eras.

Due to their continued, ongoing use by Indigenous people living today, cultural landscapes and place names blur the arbitrary line between "precontact" and "postcontact" archaeology, providing examples of a "continuous architectural landscape" and reminding people today of the ways in which these places are in a constant state of flux and use (Ballenger et al. 2015:1). This conclusion is most apparent considering how such places, as Traditional Cultural Properties (TCPs), are potentially eligible for the U.S. NRHP. Such places are considered eligible for the NRHP due to their connections to cultural practices or beliefs of a living community and because they are rooted in that community's history and are important to maintaining the *continuing* cultural identity of the community (Barker and King 1998; Tatum and Shaw 2014:268).

It is no coincidence that the powerful, spiritual narratives shared here are associated with the oldest mountain ranges in the region—the Pryor Mountains and Bighorn Mountains. Over time, these places, including rock from the mountains themselves, benefitted the Apsáalooke, who were themselves created from the land. "Land is everything to us, it binds us to our beliefs and culture. If it wasn't for the land we Apsáalooke would not exist. Therefore it is our duty to protect and preserve the land; it is our link to the past and is our path to the future" (Brien 2016:1).

Acknowledgments

We are blessed that Beverly Big Man, Grant Bull Tail, Dale Old Horn, Marvin Stewart, and Dana Wilson shared information about Apsáalooke perspectives on landscapes. We present and draw from their expertise in this chapter and recognize that the knowledge shared here would not have been possible without them. We are grateful for the stories and wisdom of the late Elias Goes Ahead; his leadership and insights provide enduring educational opportunities and outlooks for the future. And Tim McCleary continues to inspire us with his lifetime of achievements related to Apsáalooke cultural heritage. Collectively, these individuals passed on invaluable gifts of knowledge and guidance for protecting people and places for generations to come.

We also acknowledge the many ways this work has been supported by our colleagues and students at Salish Kootenai College and the University of Montana. We are especially grateful for support from the WILLOW Alliance for Graduate Education and the Professoriate (AGEP): A Model to Advance Native American Faculty in Science, Technology, Engineering, and Math (NAF-STEM), sponsored by the National Science Foundation (NSF; grant numbers: 1723248—University of Montana (UM), Missoula; 1723006—Salish Kootenai College (SKC), Pablo, Montana; and 1723196—Sitting Bull College (SBC), Fort Yates, North Dakota). The WILLOW AGEP is a collaboration aimed at developing, implementing, and studying a model for the professional success of faculty and instructional staff in science, technology, engineering, and mathematics (STEM) who are enrolled in, and/or descendants of, Native American tribes.

We appreciate the anonymous reviewers for their constructive feedback on earlier drafts of this chapter. And finally, we acknowledge special editors Emily Dale and Carolyn White for inviting us to submit a manuscript for publication in this volume and for their efforts over the past few years to ensure that our chapter could be included here. Ahóoh (Thank you)!

14

Epilogue

Widening the Western Lens

MARK WARNER

A couple of years ago, Margie Purser and I edited a volume on historical archaeology in the West (Warner and Purser 2017). As we were finishing up that book, I was contacted by one of the editors of this volume telling me that they were working on an edited volume on the West as well. My initial thought (that I kept to myself) was—why? We just did that. Sorry, that's the arrogance of academics/me. In a nutshell, I was really, really wrong for thinking that, and kudos to Emily Dale, Carolyn White, and Reba Rauch (acquisitions editor, University of Utah Press) for having more foresight than I did. When we did *Historical Archaeology through a Western Lens*, we were trying to expand the discussion on what historical archaeology in the West is. We did that to some degree, but as I read this volume I realize how much further there is to go.

As I turn to this work, what I find so compelling about *The Archaeology of Place and Space in the West* is how the authors have continued to stretch our thinking about many aspects of the west. A common theme in Western narratives is settlement/urbanism and the centrality of natural resource extraction as driving Western growth. Hardesty made this point clear in his introduction to the 1991 issue of *Historical Archaeology* that published the proceedings from the 1990 conference plenary session: "The most important processes of landscape transformation include urbanism and the technologies of extractive industries" (Hardesty 1991b:4). I certainly don't want to imply that these are not important issues, but what Dale and White have done is bring together a series of articles that explore many other themes that resonate in Western historical archaeology and which continue to broaden the lenses through which we understand the West.

In their introduction, White and Dale frame Western landscapes as the relationship between space and place. It certainly is not a reach to draw parallels with the common western theme of nature::culture, but I find the space::place framework to be more useful. This perspective distances us a bit more from the unidirectional narrative of taming the "wild West," a trope that is very hard to avoid in Western narratives.

What is always so fun about tightly edited volumes are the ancillary themes that appear in the collected works. As noted, this book is framed around Western landscape and place, but, as I read through the chapters, I saw other issues that I want to highlight. What I would like to comment on are themes of using the past, historical memory, and the peoples of the West. I will discuss these themes in a moment, but I want to begin by addressing some of the chapters that explore a topic that is overlooked in Western historical archaeology.

I would like to begin by highlighting the three chapters by Walkling, Acebo, and Brien and Dixon. I note these for a simple reason—namely that all three focus on some aspect of Native American lifeways. Archaeologists have spent well over a century exploring the lives of Indigenous peoples prior to contact; such work is in many ways the core of American archaeology, and, as we well know, relationships between archaeologists and Indigenous peoples are being renegotiated. My point, however, is not to join that important discussion but to highlight the simple fact that there are multiple chapters in this book that focus on Indigenous histories. Historical archaeology has frequently claimed exploring the lives of disenfranchised communities as one of the field's significant contributions. Yet, historical archaeology has largely overlooked the postcontact worlds of American Indians (a notable exception being the works of Sara Gonzalez; see Gonzalez et al. 2018). In this light, having three chapters that focus on Native Americans and the complexities of their histories in *present-day* America is a significant contribution—and an area of study that historical archaeologists need to continue to expand upon.

Place and placemaking is a key theme to all of the chapters, but the centrality of that theme is particularly evident in chapters by Feit, Shier, and LaValley. I particularly want to highlight a term used in Feit's chapter—"placeness," or the tension between the intended use of a place and the lived experience of that place. This idea is at least an implicit part of all of the book's chapters. Feit uses a railroad community in New Mexico to demonstrate the tension between planned ideals and lived realities, a work that documents the Foucauldian ideals of the Eddy brothers in planning several camps in the Tularosa Basin and how the lives of the Mexican residents reflected the complexity of responses to the planned vision of the railroad community both inside and outside the fence. Feit's discussion of "make-do tactics" as shaping worker life highlights a compelling theme that can be exported to many other aspects of the West. Indeed, the issue between intention and lived reality in the West and how people respond to that disconnect crops up repeatedly in Euro-American settlement narratives in the West and is ripe for historical archaeologists to explore further.

Placeness is similarly explored in unexpected ways by Shier and LaValley. Both chapters use isolated types of material culture to highlight oft-overlooked complexities—Shier exploring fencing and LaValley analyzing dendroglyphs. Fencing in the West is one of the most evocative symbols of Euro-American settlement. Fences are everywhere and their locations are regularly noted on maps, etc., but the variability of fence types and technologies is generally overlooked (with the notable exception of barbed wire; see Bennett and Abbott 2017). Shier provides us with a nuanced typology of Western fencing materials and technologies. More importantly she doesn't stop her research with a fence typology but also demonstrates how fencing choices potentially illustrate more complex relations with the space that is being controlled through fencing. Thinking creatively about the application of this work, I note that fences are everywhere and can be the bane of cultural resources surveys. Providing a tool to link fencing to broader questions (fence materials as status indicators) should compel us at least to think twice about the research potential of fences—and maybe facilitate some of those National Register nominations.

Looking more broadly at the volume, a secondary theme is malleability of the past. Malleability is perhaps not the ideal term to use, but what I want to convey is that, in addition to exploring place, several chapters also investigate how the past, or perceptions of the past, are used in contemporary contexts. The chapters by Tveskov and Rose, Drexler, and Govaerts explore how the past was employed for other purposes. Govaerts uses one of the iconic American archaeological projects, the Missouri River Basin Survey, to investigate how semimythological perceptions of the American West shaped archaeological decisions about what historical sites were recorded during the survey. The result was that the historical sites that were recorded and tested skewed toward military forts (and the perception of defending the frontier) at the expense of other, nonmilitary historical sites. As a secondary note, kudos to Govaerts for using the collections from these sites that were excavated over 50 years ago as the foundation for their dissertation work. Many historical archaeologists are doing collections driven work, but we need to be doing more of it.

A somewhat different approach is taken by Tveskov and Rose. While Govaerts looked at broad brush implications of Western mythology on an enormous archaeological project, Tveskov and Rose invert the narrative. They examine events associated with the Rogue River War to deconstruct settler colonialism, noting the discrepancy between valorizing white women, such as Christina Geisel, and the invisibility of Indigenous women, such as Betsy Brown, in memorials of the war.

Perhaps the most explicit illustration of malleability is Drexler's chapter, a work that is particularly interesting for a couple of reasons. First, the chapter is based on data from Arkansas, a state that is not typically seen as part of the Western U.S. Drexler, however, notes that Arkansas was "the West" in the early nineteenth century—just as Michigan, Ohio, Indiana, etc., were viewed as part of the "Old Northwest." The issue of what constitutes "the West" is one that scholars have been squabbling over for some time, and Drexler reminds us that for long periods of our history "the West" started east of the Mississippi River and places such as Arkansas were "The Frontier." The second issue of relevance (and core of his work) in some ways echoes Tveskov and Rose by looking at present-day heritage construction and how the past is employed, investigating how places such as Civil War battlefields are now symbolically contested venues in contemporary culture.

Finally, I want to note a series of chapters that explore specific groups and that raise interesting questions for historical archaeology. Today, archaeologists can easily generate a voluminous bibliography on historical archaeology of the Asian diaspora in North America, as well as somewhat shorter but still substantial bibliographies on archaeologies of Spanish missions, fur trading, and contact-era Indigenous lives. But what about archaeological bibliographies on nineteenth- and twentieth-century Indigenous lives, Latinx communities, or indeed many other groups that came to populate the West? What I am driving at is that historical archaeology has so much more to explore, and the chapters by Dale, Hegberg, LaValley, and Markert demonstrate that point.

Unlike the other three chapters, Dale's work adds to what is probably the most widely recognized contribution of Western historical archaeology, namely the Asian diaspora in the Americas. Her work is part of a growing body of scholarship responding to Barb Voss's (2005) call to rethink how Asian communities in the Americas are studied. In this case, Dale's focus on agency in Chinese woodcutting camps and rural/urban contrasts folds nicely into an Asian diaspora archaeology that highlights the heterogeneity of Chinese lives in the Americas and continues to move us beyond discussions of the material evidence of community boundaries.

When I read Hegberg and LaValley's chapters, I immediately thought about a conversation I had with a fellow archaeologist. Earlier this year, a close friend of mine contacted me asking for references to historical archaeology articles that explore later nineteenth- and early twentieth-century Latinx communities. I was embarrassed to tell him that I couldn't provide him with more than the one or two references that he already knew about. Hegberg, LaValley, and, to a degree, Feit, are a small step to expanding our libraries of Latinx historical archaeology, but they should also be a catalyst for historical archaeologists.

I want to put out a call to our field. Approximately 18% of the US population identifies as Hispanic. Given that fact, why are there so few archaeological projects in the West that have focused on extraordinarily interesting and complex questions of nineteenth and early twentieth-century Latinx communities outside of military or mission settings? We've done extensive theoretical work on the material complexities of race and identity but very, very little of that work based on archaeology on Latinx-occupied sites. Frankly, given the centrality of Latin American immigration as a political issue today, I think it is imperative that as archaeologists we take it upon ourselves to expand our investigations of the historical circumstances of Latinx communities.

Finally, I want to mention Markert. Simply put—who knew? At no point have I ever run across accounts of Alsatian communities in the West. In some ways this work explores the isolated migration of a fringe group; it is an account of an idiosyncratic situation. On the other hand, the nineteenth-century West was populated by myriad small groups who moved westward for a variety of reasons. So, rather than viewing this as an esoteric case study, I think it is more appropriately seen through a wider lens. Alsatian community settlements are actually illustrative of a fairly common part of Western expansion, fringe groups moving westward. The reasoning for moving westward may vary, but the processes of placemaking and settlement are fairly common, and Markert provides an interesting case study of how such groups can be explored.

I close by acknowledging again my myopia. What Dale and White have done is bring together a group of scholars that have again pushed scholarly thinking forward on what the West means. Their decision to use place as the central theme provided a framework for contributors to metaphorically roam (sorry—a book on the West needs to have some roaming in it) in several interesting directions. I still think people have a strong tendency to oversimplify the West, but I think what the editors have accomplished in this volume is to compel us (again!) to avoid such simplification. In their introduction, they ask us to consider, "What is the American West?" They may not fully answer that question (dozens of other scholars haven't either), but they have, indeed, compelled us to "embrace the push and the pull of the ideas of the West." In making this challenge, they have embraced the many complexities of the West that often get lost in the myth of the West.

The volume focuses us on place, but I want to close with people. The multicultural complexity conveyed in the chapters in the volume call to mind Robert Lewis Stevenson's account of small town California life in the late-nineteenth century:

> In my little restaurant at Monterey, we have sat down to table day after day, a Frenchman, two Portuguese, an Italian, a Mexican and a Scotchman: we had for common visitors an American from Illinois, a nearly pure-blood Indian woman and a naturalized Chinese, and from time to time a Switzer and a German came down from country ranches for the night. No wonder that the Pacific coast is a foreign land to visitors from the Eastern States [Stevenson 1944:40–41].

Bibliography

Abbott, Henry L.

1913 Reminiscences of the Oregon War of 1855. *Journal of Military Service Institution* (Nov–Dec):437–442.

Acebo, Nathan P.

2017 Report on the Reassessment of the Black Star Canyon Village Site Collections at the Bowers Museum. Manuscript on file, Bowers Museum, Santa Ana, California.

Ackley, Mary Ellen

1928 *Crossing the Plains and the Early Days of California.* San Francisco, California.

Adams, William H.

1990 Landscape Archaeology, Landscape History, and the American Farmstead. *Historical Archaeology* 24(4):92–101.

Alta California

1863 The Town of Aurora. *Alta California* 29 April. San Francisco.

Anderson, George B.

1907 *History of New Mexico: Its Resources and its People.* Pacific States Publishing Company, Los Angeles.

Andrews, William L. (editor)

1990 *Journeys in New Worlds: Early American Women's Narratives.* University of Wisconsin Press, Madison.

Andrus, Patrick W., and Rebecca H. Shrimpton (editors)

2002 National Register Bulletin. How to Apply the National Register Criteria for Evaluation. *National Register Publications.*

Anonymous

1901 Executions. *The Journal of the House of the Twenty-First Legislative Assembly, Regular Session.* W.H. Leeds, State Printer, Salem, Oregon.

Appadurai, Arjun

1996 *Modernity at Large.* Cultural Dimensions of Globalization, Vol. 1. University of Minnesota Press, Minneapolis.

Arkansas Civil War Heritage Trail

2015 Success at Elkins' Ferry! *Arkansas Battlefield Update* 23(3):1, 5.

Arellano, Gustavo

2013 Black Star Canyon's Indian Massacre. *OC Weekly* 23 November, https://www.ocweekly.com/black-star-canyons-indian-massacre-6429355/, accessed January 26, 2021.

Atalay, Sonya

2012 *Community Based Archaeology: Research with, by, and for Indigenous and Local Communities.* Left Coast Press, Walnut Creek, California.

Babcock, Matthew

2016 *Apache Adaptation to Hispanic Rule.* Studies in North American Indian History. Cambridge University Press, Cambridge.

Ballenger, Jesse, Brandi Bethke, and Maria N. Zedeño

2015 The Landscape Archaeology of the Northwestern Plains: Problems and Potential. Paper presented at the 80th Annual Meeting of the Society for American Archaeology, San Francisco, California.

Balode, Zanda

2013 Mary Rowlandson and Jessica Lynch—Two Stories of White Female Captives in American Culture. *She Knows What She Knows* (blog), December 28, 2013. https://balodiite.wordpress.com/2013/12/28/mary-rowlandson-and-jessica-lynch-two-stories-of-white-female-captives-in-american-culture/, accessed September 20, 2017.

Banks, Kimball M., and Jon S. Czaplicki

2014 Introduction: The Flood Control Act of 1944 and the Growth of American Archaeology. In *Dam Projects and the Growth of American Archaeology: The River Basin Surveys and the Interagency Archeological Salvage Program*, edited by Kimball M. Banks and Jon S. Czaplicki, pp. 11–24. Left Coast Press, Walnut Creek, California.

Barker, Patricia L., and Thomas F. King
1998 Guidelines for Evaluating and Documenting Traditional Cultural Properties. *National Register Bulletin* 38. National Park Service, United States Department of the Interior. Electronic document, https://www.nps.gov/subjects/nationalregister/upload/NRB38-Completeweb.pdf, accessed January 22, 2020.

Basso, Keith H.
1996 *Wisdom Sits in Places: Landscape and Language Among the Western Apache*. University of New Mexico Press, Albuquerque.

Barrows, Harold D.
1902 William Wolfskill, The Pioneer. *Annual Publication of the Historical Society of Southern California and of the Pioneers of Los Angeles County* 5(3):287–294.

Baxter, John O.
1987 *Las Carneradas: Sheep Trade in New Mexico 1700–1860*. University of New Mexico Press, Albuquerque.

Baxter, Paul W., Brian L. O'Neill, and Christopher L. Ruiz
2011 Subsurface Reconnaissance of the I-5 Chancellor Quarry Stockpile Project, and Metal Detector Survey within the George and Mary Harris 1854–55 DLC (35JO246), Josephine County. OSMA Report 2011-002, Museum of Natural and Cultural History University of Oregon, Eugene.

Becker, Karin L.
2016 The Paradox of Plenty: Blessings and Curses in the Oil Patch. In *The Bakken Goes Boom: Oil and the Changing Geographies of Western North Dakota*, edited by William B. Caraher and Kyle Conway, pp. 13–29. The Digital Press at the University of North Dakota, Grand Forks.

Beckham, Stephen Dow
1971 *Requiem for a People: The Rogue Indians and the Frontiersmen*. University of Oklahoma Press, Norman.

Bench, Raney (editor)
2014 *Interpreting Native American History and Culture at Museums and Historic Sites*. Rowman and Littlefield, Lanham, Maryland.

Bender, Barbara
2001 Introduction. In *Contested Landscapes: Movement, Exile and Place*, edited by Barbara Bender and Margot Winer, pp. 1–18. Bloomsbury, New York.

Bennett, Lyn Ellen, and Scott Abbott
2014 Barbed and Dangerous: Constructing the Meaning of Barbed Wire in Late Nineteenth-Century America. *Agricultural History* 88(4):566–590.
2017 *The Perfect Fence: Untangling the Meanings of Barbed Wire*. Texas A&M University Press, College Station.

Berry, William J., Alex Sutherland, and O. W. Weaver
1856 Fort Miner, Gold Beach. *Crescent City Herald* 21 May:2.

Bickers, Margaret A.
2010 Three Cultures, Four Hooves and One River: The Canadian River in Texas and New Mexico, 1848–1939. PhD dissertation, Department of History, Kansas State University, Manhattan. University Microfilms International, Ann Arbor, Michigan.

Billings County Pioneer
1953 Time is Running Out for Archeologists at Garrison. *Billings County Pioneer* 24 September:2. Medora, North Dakota.

Black, William M.
1930 Roof Covering. US Patent 1,775,085, filed July 8, 1929, and issued September 9, 1930.

Blackhawk, Ned
2006 *Violence over the Land: Indians and Empires in the Early American West*. Harvard University Press, Cambridge, Massachusetts.

Blanton, Dennis R.
2003 The Weather is Fine, Wish You Were Here, Because I'm the Last One Alive: "Learning the Environment in the English New World Colonies." In *Colonization of Unfamiliar Landscapes: The Archaeology of Adaptation*, edited by Marcy Rockman and James Steele, pp. 190–200. Routledge, New York.

Blevins, Brooks
2009 *Arkansas/Arkansaw: How Bear Hunters, Hillbillies, and Good Ol' Boys Defined a State*. University of Arkansas Press, Fayetteville.

Blight, David W.
2001 *Race and Reunion: The Civil War in American Memory*. Belknap Press, Cambridge, Massachusetts.

Boag, Peter
2014 Death and Oregon's Settler Generation. *Oregon Historical Quarterly* 115(3):344–79.

Bodie Daily News
1880 Shooting at Rough Creek. *Bodie Daily News* 9 July. Bodie, California.

Bodie Morning News
1880 Notes About Town. *Bodie Morning News* 22 April. Bodie, California.
Bodie Standard News
1880 Notes About Town. *Bodie Standard News* 10 August:3. Bodie, California.
Bodie Weekly Standard
1878 Untitled. *Bodie Weekly Standard* 4 December. Bodie, California.
1883 Enterprising Man. *Bodie Weekly Standard* 13 November. Bodie, California.
Borck, Lewis, and Matthew C. Sanger
2017 An Introduction to Anarchism in Archaeology. *SAA Archaeological Record* 17(1):9–16.
Boster, Sam
2017 Aspens and Their Carvings Hold Forgotten Colorado History. *The Gazette*, September 18, 2017. http://gazette.com/aspens-and-their-carvings-hold-forgotten-colorado-history/article/1611384, accessed November 17, 2017.
Bourcier, Paul
1984 "In Excellent Order": The Gentleman Farmer Views His Fences, 1790–1860. *Agricultural History* 58(4):546–564.
Bowman, Michael
2015 Completing an Incomplete History: The African American Narrative in Civil War Helena. *Race, Gender & Class* 22(1/2):236.
Boyd, Colleen, and Thrush Coll-Peter (editors)
2011 *Phantom Past, Indigenous Presence: Native Ghosts in North American Culture and History*. University of Nebraska Press, Lincoln.
Boyd, Elizabeth
1974 *Popular Arts of Spanish New Mexico*. Museum of New Mexico Press, Santa Fe.
Branton, Nicole
2009 Landscape Approaches in Historical Archaeology: The Archaeology of Places. In *International Handbook of Historical Archaeology*, edited by Teresita Majewski and David Gaimster, pp. 51–65. Springer Science, New York.
Braun, Sebastian
2016 Revised Frontiers: The Bakken, the Plains, Potential Futures, and Real Pasts. In *The Bakken Goes Boom: Oil and the Changing Geographies of Western North Dakota*, edited by William Caraher and Kyle Conway, pp. 91–116. The Digital Press at the University of North Dakota, Grand Forks.
Brent, Joseph E., W. Stephen McBride, and Martin Smith
2011 *Helena Civil War Earthworks Project*. Mudpuppy & Waterdog, Versailles, Kentucky.
Brent, Maria C., and Joseph E. Brent
2013 *Jenkins' Ferry Battlefield Preservation Plan. Report to Friends of Jenkins' Ferry Battlefield, Sheridan, AR*. Mudpuppy & Waterdog, Versailles, Kentucky.
2014 *An Interpretive Plan for Fort Lookout, Civil War Earthwork, Camden, Arkansas*. Mudpuppy & Waterdog, Versailles, Kentucky.
Brewer, Chris
1999 *Images of America: Southern San Joaquin Valley Scenes*. Arcadia, Charleston, South Carolina.
Brien, Aaron
2015 Bilisshíissaannuua: The Importance of Fasting to the Apsáalooke. Master's thesis, Department of Anthropology, University of Montana, Missoula.
2016 Landscape and TCP Module. Manuscript on file, Department of Anthropology, University of Montana, Missoula.
2017 From Informant to Investigator: My Approach to Archaeology. Paper presented at the First Peoples Buffalo Jump State Park, Ulm, Montana.
2019 Writing Native American History: Understanding Plenty Coups from the Crow Perspective. Presentation and workshop at the University of Montana's Mansfield Library Archives and Special Collections, 2 April 2019. See also #indigenousarchaeology on Instagram.
Brooksher, William R.
1995 *Bloody Hill: The Civil War Battle of Wilson's Creek*. Brassey's, Washington, DC.
Brown, Bill
1997 *Reading the West: An Anthology of Dime Westerns*. St. Martin's Press, New York.
Bunnin, Nicholas
2004 *The Blackwell Dictionary of Western Philosophy*. Blackwell, Malden, Massachusetts.
Bunting, Bainbridge
1976 *Early Architecture in New Mexico*. University of New Mexico Press, Albuquerque.
Burnett, Edmund
1948 The Passing of the Old Rail Fence: A Farmer's Lament. *Agricultural History* 22(1): 31–32.

Buss, James Joseph
2011 *Winning the West With Words: Language and Conquest in the Lower Great Lakes.* University of Oklahoma Press, Norman.
California Department of Transportation
2007 *A Historical Context and Archaeological Research Design for Agricultural Properties in California.* Division of Environmental Analysis, California Department of Transportation, Sacramento, California.
Cameron, Constance
2000 Animal Effigies from Coastal Southern California. *Pacific Coast Archaeological Society Quarterly* 36(2):30–52.
Campbell, Randolph B.
2003 *Gone to Texas: A History of the Lone Star State.* Oxford University Press, Oxford.
Carlson, Catherine C.
2006 Indigenous Historic Archaeology of the 19th-Century Secwepemc Village at Thompson's River Post, Kamloops, British Columbia. *Canadian Journal of Archaeology* 30(2): 193–25.
2017 Listening to the Late-Nineteenth Century Jesup North Pacific Expedition to the British Columbia Plateau. *SAA Archaeological Record* 17(4):21–23.
Carlson-Drexler, Carl G., Douglas D. Scott, and Harold Roeker
2008 *"The Battle Raged...With Terrible Fury": Battlefield Archaeology of Pea Ridge National Military Park.* Technical Report No. 112. USDI/NPS Midwest Archeological Center, Lincoln, Nebraska.
Carman, John, and Marie Louise Stig Sørensen
2009 Heritage Studies: An Outline. In *Heritage Studies Methods and Approaches*, edited by John Carman and Marie Louise Stig Sørensen, pp. 11–28. Routledge, London.
Carrillo, Richard, Abbey Christman, and Roche Lindsey
2011 *Cultural Resources Survey of the Purgatoire River Region.* Colorado Preservation, Denver.
Carter, Timothy, E. Chappell, and Timothy McCleary
2005 In the Lodge of the Chickadee: Architecture and Cultural Resistance on the Crow Indian Reservation, 1884–1920. *Perspectives in Vernacular Architecture* 10:97–111.
Casey, Edward S.
1996 How to Get from Space to Place in a Fairly Short Stretch of Time: A Phenomenological Prolegomena. In *Senses of Place*, edited by Steven Feld and Keith Basso, pp. 13–52. School of American Research Press, Santa Fe, New Mexico.
2008 Place in Landscape Archaeology: A Western Philosophical Prelude. In *Handbook of Landscape Archaeology*, edited by Bruno David and Julian Thomas, pp. 44–59. Left Coast Press, Walnut Creek, California.
Cassell, Mark S. (editor)
2005 Landscapes of Industrial Labor. Thematic issue, *Historical Archaeology* 39(3).
Cassell, Mark S., and Myron O. Stachiw
2005 Perspectives on Landscapes of Industrial Labor. In *Landscapes of Industrial Labor*, edited by Mark S. Cassell. Thematic issue, *Historical Archaeology* 39(3):1–7.
Castro Colonies Heritage Association
1994 *The History of Medina County, Texas*, Vol. 1. Curtis Media, Dallas, Texas.
Chalfant, W.A.
1933 *The Story of Inyo.* Chalfant Press: Bishop, California.
Chace, Paul G.
1971 *The Black Star Canyon Project: A Landmarks Survey.* Pacific Coast Archaeological Society, Costa Mesa, California.
Cheater, Dan
2018 I Am the River and the River Is Me: Legal Personhood and the Emerging Rights of Nature. *Environmental Law Alert* (blog), West Coast Environmental Law, March 22, 2018. https://www.wcel.org/blog/i-am-river-and-river-me-legal-personhood-and-emerging-rights-nature, accessed March 20, 2020.
Chicago Steel Post Company Co.
1919 Design only. US Patent 71109939, filed April 3, 1918, and issued May 27, 1919.
Christ, Mark K. (editor)
2003 *"All Cut to Pieces and Gone to Hell": The Civil War, Race Relations, and the Battle of Poison Spring.* August House, Little Rock, Arkansas.
Chung, Sue Fawn
2015 *Chinese in the Woods: Logging and Lumbering in the American West.* University of Illinois Press, Urbana.
Church, Minette C.
2002 The Grant and the Grid: Homestead Landscapes in the Late Nineteenth-Century Borderlands of Southern Colorado. *Journal of Social Archaeology* 2(2):220–244.
Cisneros, Josue David
2014 *The Border Crossed Us: Rhetorics of Borders,*

Citizenship, and Latina/o Identity. University of Alabama Press, Tuscaloosa.

Clarendon (pseudonym for Charles S. Drew)
1855 Letters from the South. *Weekly Oregonian* 27 October:3.

Clark, Bonnie J.
2012 *On the Edge of Purgatory: An Archaeology of Place in Hispanic Colorado*. University of Nebraska Press, Lincoln.

Cleland, Robert G.
2003 *The Irvine Ranch*. 3rd ed. The Huntington Library, San Marino, California.

Clemons, Leigh
2008 *Branding Texas: Performing Culture in the Lone Star State*. University of Texas Press, Austin.

Coalition for American Heritage
2020 Advise the Government on Heritage Preservation. Electronic document, https://heritagecoalition.org/regulations-2/, accessed March 20, 2020.

Coates, Ta-Nehisi
2017 *We Were Eight Years in Power: An American Tragedy*. One World Publishing, New York.

Cobb, James C.
2005 *Away Down South: A History of Southern Identity*. Oxford University Press, New York.

Cohen, Henry
1897 Henry Castro, Pioneer and Colonist. *Publications of the American Jewish Historical Society* 5:39–43.

Coleman, Roger E., and Douglas D. Scott
2003 *An Archaeological Overview and Assessment of Fort Smith National Historic Site*. USDI/NPS/Midwest Archeological Center, Lincoln, Nebraska.

Collett, Chris
2007 *Counteracting Irregular Activity in Civil War Arkansas—A Case Study*. United States Army War College, Carlisle Barracks, Pennsylvania.

Colwell-Chanthaphonh, Chip
2016 Collaborative Archaeologies and Descendant Communities. *Annual Review of Anthropology* 45:113–127.

Colwell-Chanthaphonh, Chip, T. J. Ferguson, Dorothy Lippert, Randall H. McGuire, George P. Nicholas, Joseph E. Watkins, and Larry J. Zimmerman
2010 The Premise and Promise of Indigenous Archaeology. *American Antiquity* 75(2): 228–238.

Conaty, Gerald T. (editor)
2015 *We Are Coming Home: Repatriation and the Restoration of Blackfoot Cultural Confidence*. Athabasca University Press, Edmonton, Alberta.

Connolly, Nicholas J.
2012 *Environmental Variables Associated with the Location of Arborglyphs in the Eastern Sierra Nevada, Alpine County, California*. Master's thesis, Department of Geography, University of Nevada, Reno. University Microfilms International, Ann Arbor, Michigan.

Cook, S. F.
1976 *The Conflict Between the California Indian and White Civilization*, Vol. 1. University of California Press, Berkeley, California.

Cordero, Robin M., Erin Hegberg, and Christian Solfisburg
2016 Homesteads, Herding, and Hunting along the Canadian Escarpment: A 9,335-Acre Survey Near Mosquero, Harding and San Miguel Counties, New Mexico. Report to the New Mexico Department of Game and Fish, Santa Fe, from the Office of Contract Archaeology, University of New Mexico, Albuquerque.

Cornish, Dudley T.
1987 *The Sable Arm: Black Troops in the Union Army, 1861–1865*. University Press of Kansas, Lawrence.

Costner, Kevin (director)
1990 *Dances with Wolves*. Orion Pictures, Los Angeles.

Cothran, Boyd
2014 *Remembering the Modoc War: Redemptive Violence and the Making of American Innocence*. University of North Carolina Press, Chapel Hill.

Crescent City Herald
1856 The Indian War on the Rogue River. 17 May:2. Crescent City, California.

Cronon, William
1983 *Changes in the Land: Indians, Colonists, and the Ecology of New England*. Hill and Wang, New York.
1991 *Nature's Metropolis: Chicago and the Great West*. W.W. Norton, New York.

Curry Historical Society (CHS)
2017 Biography: Geisel Family. Electronic document, http://www.curryhistory.com/historic-resources/biographies/11-biography-geisel-family, accessed October 27, 2017.

Daily Bodie Standard
1879a The Fourth. *Daily Bodie Standard* 5 July, (2)36:3. Bodie, California.
1879b The "Bar" Hunt. *Daily Bodie Standard* 24 October, (2)131:3. Bodie, California.
1880a Brief Mention. *Daily Bodie Standard* 27 May, (3)137:3. Bodie, California.
1880b A Piute Perforated. *Daily Bodie Standard* 15 June, (3)152:3. Bodie, California.
1880c Brief Mention. *Daily Bodie Standard* 16 June, (3)153:3. Bodie, California.

Daily Evening Bulletin
1862 Wood and the Red Skins. *Daily Evening Bulletin* 16 April. San Francisco, California.

Daily Free Press
1880a Chinese-Indian Boom. *Daily Free Press* 3 March. Bodie, California.
1880b The Superior Court. *Daily Free Press* 11 August. Bodie, California.
1880c A Whiskey Fight. *Daily Free Press* 19 November. Bodie, California.
1881a Hawthorne. *Daily Free Press* 8 May. Bodie, California.
1881b Piute War Dance: Advertisement. *Daily Free Press* 29 May:2. Bodie, California.
1881c Native Drunks. *Daily Free Press* 1 July. Bodie, California.
1881d The Third Division. *Daily Free Press* 6 July. Bodie, California.
1881e A Wood Merchant. *Daily Free Press* 16 July. Bodie, California.
1881f Gathering the Pine Nuts. *Daily Free Press* 28 August. Bodie, California.
1881g A Drunken Piute. *Daily Free* Press 30 September. Bodie, California.
1881h In and Out of Town. *Daily Free Press* 3 September. Bodie, California.
1881i In and Out of Town. *Daily Free Press* 4 October. Bodie, California.
1882a In and Out of Town. *Daily Free Press* 20 January. Bodie, California.
1882b In and Out of Town. *Daily Free Press* 10 March. Bodie, California.
1882c Gold Washing. *Daily Free Press* 15 April. Bodie, California.
1882d In and Out of Town. *Daily Free Press* 25 June. Bodie, California.
1882e In and Out of Town. *Daily Free Press* 31 August. Bodie, California.
1882f In and Out of Town. *Daily Free Press* 1 October. Bodie, California.
1883a In and Out of Town. *Daily Free Press* 6 February. Bodie, California.
1883b In and Out of Town. *Daily Free Press.* 8 February. Bodie, California.
1883c In and Out of Town. *Daily Free Press.* 21 February. Bodie, California.
1883d In and Out of Town. *Daily Free Press.* 8 March. Bodie, California.

Dale, Emily
2011 *Archaeology on Spring Street: Discrimination, Ordinance 32, and the Overseas Chinese in Aurora, Nevada.* Master's thesis, Department of Anthropology, University of Nevada, Reno.
2015 Households of the Overseas Chinese in Aurora, Nevada. In *Beyond the Walls: New Perspectives on the Archaeology of Historical Households*, edited by Kevin R. Fogle, James A. Nyman, and Mary C. Beaudry, pp. 144–160. University Press of Florida, Gainesville.
2019 Anopticism: Invisible Populations and the Power of Not Seeing. *International Journal of Historical Archaeology* 23(3): 596–608.

Danhof, Clarence
1944 The Fencing Problem of the Eighteen-Fifties. *Agricultural History* 18(4):168–186.

Darling, J. Andrew, Barnaby V. Lewis, Robert Valencia, and B. Sunday Eiselt
2015 Archaeology in the Service of the Tribe: Three Episodes in Twenty-First Century Tribal Archaeology in the US-Mexico Borderlands. *Kiva: Journal of Southwestern Anthropology and History* 81(1–2):62–79.

David, Bruno, and Julian Thomas
2008 Landscape Archaeology: Introduction. In *Handbook of Landscape Archaeology*, edited by Bruno David and Julian Thomas, pp. 27–43. Left Coast Press, Walnut Creek, California.

David, Bruno, and Julian Thomas (editors)
2008 *Handbook of Landscape Archaeology.* Left Coast Press, Walnut Creek, California.

DeBlack, Thomas A.
2003 *With Fire and Sword: Arkansas, 1861–1874.* Histories of Arkansas. University of Arkansas Press, Fayetteville.

de Certeau, Michel
1984 *The Practice of Everyday Life.* University of California Press, Berkeley.

DeCordova, Jacob
1856 *The Texas Immigrant and Traveller's Guide Book.* DeCordova and Frazier, Austin, Texas.

DeKorne, James B.
1970 *Aspen Art in the New Mexico Highlands.* Museum of New Mexico Press, Santa Fe.
Deloria, Vine
1992 *God Is Red: A Native View of Religion.* North American Press, Golden, Colorado.
De León, Arnoldo
1983 *They Called Them Greasers: Anglo Attitudes toward Mexicans in Texas, 1821–1900.* University of Texas Press, Austin.
Derounian-Stodola, Kathryn Zabelle
1998 *Women's Indian Captivity Narratives.* Penguin Books, New York.
De Yoanna, Michael
2014 Etchings in the Aspens Provide a Fading Glimpse into Colorado's Past. *Colorado Public Radio,* October 7, 2014. http://www.cpr.org/news/story/etchings-aspens-provide-fading-glimpse-colorados-past, accessed November 17, 2017.
Deutsch, Sandra
1989 *No Separate Refuge: Culture, Class, and Gender on an Anglo-Hispanic Frontier in the American Southwest, 1880–1940.* Oxford University Press, Oxford.
Dixon, J.
1918 *Campsite at 1500 Ft.* Historic Photographs, Wind Wolves Preserve Headquarters, Bakersfield, California.
Dixon, Kelly J.
2014 Historical Archaeologies of the American West. *Journal of Archaeological Research* 22: 177–228.
Dixon, Kelly J., and Carrie Smith
2017 Rock Hearths and Rural Wood Camps in Jinshan/Gam Saan: National Register of Historic Places Evaluations of 19th-Century Chinese Logging Operations at Heavenly Ski Resort in the Lake Tahoe Basin. In *Historical Archaeology Through a Western Lens,* edited by Mark Warner and Margaret Purser, pp. 138–173, Society for Historical Archaeology and University of Nebraska Press, Lincoln.
Dixon, Kelly J. Julie M. Schabiltsky, and Shannon A. Novak
2011 *An Archaeology of Desperation: Exploring the Donner Party's Alder Creek Camp.* University of Oklahoma Press, Norman.
Dodge, Orville
1898 *Pioneer History of Coos and Curry County, Oregon.* Capital Printing Company, Salem, Oregon.
Dodge, William A.
2009 *Watering Orogrande. The Story of a Pipeline and its Reservoirs in Southern New Mexico.* Van Critters Historic Preservation, LLC, Albuquerque, New Mexico.
Domenech, Abbé
1858 *Missionary Adventures in Texas and Mexico: A Personal Narrative of Six Years Sojourn in those Regions.* Longman, Brown, Green, Longmans, and Roberts, London.
Dongoske, Kurt E., Theresa Pasqual, and Thomas F. King
2015 The National Environmental Policy Act (NEPA) and the Silencing of Native American World Views. *Environmental Practice* 17(1):36–45.
Dougan, Michael B.
1972 Life in Confederate Arkansas. *The Arkansas Historical Quarterly* 31(1):15–35.
Douthit, Nathan
2002 *Uncertain Encounters: Indians and Whites at Peace and War in Southern Oregon, 1820s–1860s.* Oregon State University Press, Corvallis.
Drexler, Carl G., Katherine W. Gregory, Anthony C. Newton, Elizabeth T. Horton, Katie Leslie, Robert Scott, and Carol Colaninno
2016 *Crossing the Little Missouri: Archeological Perspectives on the Engagement at Elkins' Ferry, Nevada County, Arkansas (3NE217).* Arkansas Archeological Survey, Fayetteville.
Du Bois, Willard Edward Burghardt (W.E.B.)
1897 The Strivings of the Negro People. *The Atlantic* 80(8):194–198.
Dyer, Frederick H.
1908 *A Compendium of the War of the Rebellion.* Dyer Publishing Company, Des Moines, Iowa.
Eaton, Charles, and Gertrude Martin
2000 Two Popular Nineteeth Century Tales. In *Olaudah Equiano, Mary Rowlandson, and Others: American Captivity Narratives,* edited by Gordon M. Sayre, pp. 382–385. Wadsworth Cengage Learning, Boston.
Eddy, J. J.
1998 Twenty-Fifth Anniversary of the Founding of Alamogordo, 1923. In *Things Remembered: Alamogordo New Mexico 1898–1998,* edited by Linnie Townsend and the History Committee of the Alamogordo/Otero County Centennial Celebration, pp. 137–146. Alamogordo/Otero County Centennial Celebration, Alamogordo, New Mexico.

Edwards, Herbert Rook
1917 Diplomatic Relations between France and the Republic of Texas, III. *The Southwestern Historical Quarterly* 20(4):341–357.
Emery, W. N.
1936 *Mosquero*. Manuscript on file, Works Progress Administration New Mexico Collection, Fray Angelico History Library, New Mexico History Museum, Santa Fe.
Esmeralda Daily Union
1864 City Ordinance 32. *Esmeralda Daily Union* 15 April. Aurora, Nevada.
The Esmeralda Herald
1880 The Glorious Fourth. *Esmeralda Herald*, 3 July (4)3:2. Aurora, Nevada.
Faragher, John Mack
2012 The Myth of the Frontier: Progress or Lost Freedom. The Gilder Lehrman Institute of American History. Electronic document, https://www.gilderlehrman.org/history-by-era/art-music-and-film/essays/myth-frontier-progress-or-lost-freedom, accessed November 12, 2017.
Farmer, Jared
2013 *Trees in Paradise: A California History*. W. W. Norton, New York.
Farnsworth, Paul
1989 Native American Acculturation in the Spanish Colonial Empire: The Franciscan Missions in Alta California. In *Center and Periphery: Comparative Studies in Archaeology*, edited by T. C. Champion, pp. 186–206. Unwin Hyman, London.
Faunce, K. V.
1997 The Fort Bliss Preacquisition Project: A History of the Southern Tularosa Basin. Cultural Resources Management Program. Directorate of Environment, United States Army Air Defense Artillery Center, Fort Bliss, Texas.
2005 Railroads and Ranches: A Fort Bliss Testing Project. Fort Bliss Cultural Resources Report 95-04, Miratek Corporation, El Paso, Texas.
Feit, Rachel, and Amy Silberberg
2015 The Road to Wealth: The El Paso and Northeastern Railroad in Southeastern New Mexico. A Historical Context and Evaluation of Six Railroad Properties on Fort Bliss, Otero County, New Mexico. Stell Environmental and AmaTerra Environmental, El Paso, Texas, and Las Cruces, New Mexico.
Feld, Steven, and Keith H. Basso (editors)
1996 *Senses of Place*. School of American Research Press, Santa Fe, New Mexico.
Feld, Steven, and Keith H. Basso
1996 Introduction. In *Senses of Place*, edited by Steven Feld and Keith Basso, pp. 3–11. School of American Research Press, Santa Fe, New Mexico.
Filson, John
1784 The Discovery, Settlement and Present State of Kentucke. *Electronic Texts in American Studies* 3. University of Nebraska, Lincoln, http://digitalcommons.unl.edu/etas/3/, accessed November 12, 2017.
Finger, Jack
2012 *A Walking Tour of Beautiful Downtown D'Hanis…with Detours*. Self-published, San Antonio, Texas.
Forrest, Suzanne
1998 *The Preservation of the Village: New Mexico's Hispanics and the New Deal*. University of New Mexico Press, Albuquerque.
Fortier, Anne-Marie
1999 Re-Membering Places and the Performance of Belonging(s). In *Performativity and Belonging*, edited by Vikki Bell, pp 41–64. Sage, London.
Frierman, Jay, and Roberta S. Greenwood
1992 *Historical Archaeology of Nineteenth-Century California*. William Andrews Clark Memorial Library, University of California, Los Angeles.
Geier, Clarence R., Lawrence E. Babits, Douglas D. Scott, and David G. Orr (editors)
2010 *Historical Archaeology of Military Sites: Method and Topic*. Texas A&M University Press, College Station.
Gilchrist, Roberta
2005 Introduction: Scales and Voices in World Historical Archaeology. *World Archaeology* 37:329–336.
Glassie, Henry
1968 *Pattern in the Material Folk Culture of the Eastern United States*. University of Pennsylvania Press, Philadelphia, PA.
Glover, Vernon J.
1984 *Logging Railroads of the Lincoln National Forest, New Mexico*. Cultural Resources Report No. 4. United States Department of Agriculture Forest Service, Southwestern Region. Electronic document, https://forest

history.org/wp-content/uploads/2017/01/Logging-Railroads-of-the-Lincoln-National-Forest.pdf, accessed January 22, 2020.

Goes Ahead, Elias, David Eckroth, Howard Boggess, and Mike Penfold

2008 Ashkoota Binnaxchikua (Where the Camp Was Fortified), 1863–1864. Report prepared with funding from the American Battlefield Protection Program (ABPP, 2255-04-002) for Frontier Heritage Alliance, Billings, Montana.

Gonzales-Berry, Erlinda, and David R. Maciel

2000 Introduction. In *The Contested Homeland: A Chicano History of New Mexico*, edited by Erlinda Gonzales-Berry and David R. Maciel, pp. 3–9. University of New Mexico Press, Albuquerque.

Gonzalez, Sara L., Ian Kretzler, and Briece Edwards

2018 Imagining Indigenous and Archaeological Futures: Building Capacity with the Confederated Tribes of Grand Ronde. *Archaeologies: Journal of the World Archaeological Congress* 14(1):85–114.

González-Tennant, Edward

2011 Creating a Diasporic Archaeology of Chinese Migration: Tentative Steps Across Four Continents. *International Journal of Historical Archaeology* 15(3):509–532.

Govaerts, Lotte

2014 Resource Guide to River Basin Surveys (RBS) Publications on Historical Archaeology. *Rogers Archaeology Lab* (blog), September 10, 2014. http://nmnh.typepad.com/rogers_archaeology_lab/2014/09/resourceguiderbshistoricalarchaeology.html, accessed November 12, 2017.

2015 River Basin Surveys Historic Sites: Collections and Resources. Rogers Archaeology Lab. Electronic document, http://nmnh.typepad.com/rogers_archaeology_lab/river-basin-surveys-historic-sites.html, accessed November 12, 2017.

Groover, Mark

2008 *The Archaeology of North American Farmsteads.* University Press of Florida, Gainesville.

Guerric, Mercedes Martinez

1999 Castroville Folk Houses: A Comparative Study Between South Texas Regional Architecture and its Alsatian Counterpart. Master's thesis, Division of Architecture and Interior Design, University of Texas, San Antonio.

Haas, Lisbeth

1995 *Conquests and Historical Identities in California 1769–1936.* University of California Press, Berkeley.

Hackel, Steven

2005 *Children of Coyote.* University of North Carolina Press, Chapel Hill.

Hagemeier, Harold

2010 *Barbed Wire Identification Encyclopaedia*, 5th ed. Morris Publishing, Kearney, Nebraska.

Hamilakis, Yannis

2011 Archaeological Ethnography: A Multitemporal Meeting Ground for Archaeology and Anthropology. *Annual Review of Anthropology* 40:399–414.

Hardesty, Donald L.

1991a Toward an Historical Archaeology of the Intermountain West. *Historical Archaeology* 25(3):29–35.

1991b Historical Archaeology in the American West. *Historical Archaeology* 25(3):3–6.

2002 Power and the Industrial Mining Community in the American West. In *Social Approaches to an Industrial Past: The Archaeology and Anthropology of Mining*, edited by Eugenia W. Herbert, A. Bernard Knapp, and Vincent C. Pigott, pp. 81–96. Routledge, London.

2003 Mining Rushes and Landscape Learning in the Modern World. In *Colonization of Unfamiliar Landscapes: The Archaeology of Adaptation*, edited by Marcy Rockman and James Steele, pp. 81–95. Routledge, New York.

2010 *Mining Archaeology in the American West: A View from the Silver State.* University of Nebraska Press and the Society for Historical Archaeology, Lincoln.

Hardesty, Donald, and Barbara Little

2009 *Assessing Site Significance: A Guide for Archaeologist and Historians.* 2nd ed. AltaMira Press, New York.

Harms, Cecily

2012 NAGPRA in Colorado: A Success Story. *Colorado Law Review* 83(2):593–632.

Harrington, John Peabody

1942 *John Peabody Harrington Papers: Alaska/Northwest Coast.* National Anthropological Archives, Washington, DC.

Hartmann, Rudi
2014 Dark Tourism, Thanatourism, and Dissonance in Heritage Tourism Management: New Directions in Contemporary Tourism Research. *Journal of Heritage Tourism* 9(2):166–182.
Harvey, David
1996 *Justice, Nature, and the Geography of Difference.* Blackwell, Oxford.
Harwell, Beth
1998 Alamogordo Improvement Company, the Early Years. In *Things Remembered: Alamogordo New Mexico 1898–1998*, edited by Linnie Townsend and the History Committee of the Alamogordo/Otero County Centennial Celebration, pp. 71–84. Alamogordo/Otero County Centennial Celebration, Alamogordo, New Mexico.
Hattori, Eugene
1975 *Northern Paiutes on the Comstock: Archaeology and Ethnohistory of an American Indian Population in Virginia City, Nevada.* Nevada State Museum, Carson City.
Haunted Places
2017 Black Star Canyon. Electronic document, https://www.hauntedplaces.org/item/black-star-canyon/, accessed January 23, 2020.
Hayden, Dolores
1995 *The Power of Place: Urban Landscapes as Public History.* MIT Press, Cambridge, Massachusetts.
Hayter, Earl
1939 Barbed Wire Fencing: A Prairie Invention: Its Rise and Influence in the Western States. *Agricultural History* 13(4):189–207.
1945 The Fencing of the Western Railways. *Agricultural History* 19(3):163–167.
Healy, Meghan, Heather Edgar, Carmen Mosley, and Keith Hunley
2018 Associations Between Ethnic Identity, Regional History and Genomic Ancestry in New Mexicans of Spanish-speaking Descent. *Biodemography and Social Biology* 64(2):152–170.
Hirsch, Eric, and Charles Stewart
2005 Introduction: Ethnographies of Historicity. *History and Anthropology* 16(3):261–274.
Holder, Preston
1957 *Archeological Field Research on the Problem of the Locations of Arkansas Post, 1686–1803: A Preliminary Report on Work in Progress at the Menard Mounds Site.* United States Department of the Interior/National Park Service, Richmond, Virginia.
Hsu, Madeline
2000 *Dreaming of Gold, Dreaming of Home: Transnationalism and Migration Between the US and South China, 1882–1943.* Stanford University Press, Stanford, California.
Iñárritu, Alejandro González (director)
2015 *The Revenant.* Twentieth Century Fox, Los Angeles.
Irvine Ranch Natural Landmarks
2017a About the Land: From the Mountains to the Sea. Electronic document, https://letsgooutside.org/about/, accessed November 15, 2017.
2017b Black Star Canyon Wilderness Park—Irvine Ranch Natural Landmarks. Black Star Canyon Wilderness Park. Electronic document, https://letsgooutside.org/explore/black-star-canyon-wilderness-park/, accessed November 15, 2017.
Jefferson, Thomas
2010 *The Selected Writings of Thomas Jefferson: Authoritative Texts, Contexts, Criticism,* edited by Wayne Franklin. W.W. Norton, New York.
Jennings, Jesse D.
1985 River Basin Surveys: Origins, Operations, and Results, 1945–1969. *American Antiquity* 50(2):281–96.
Jetéé, Melinda Marie
2010 Betwixt and Between the Official Story: Tracing the History and Memory of a Family of French-Indian Ancestry in the Pacific Northwest. *Oregon Historical Quarterly* 111(2):142–183.
Jimenez, Corri Lyn
2000 Bodie, California: Understanding the Architecture and Built Environment of a Gold Mining Town. Master's thesis, Historic Preservation, Interdisciplinary Studies Program, University of Oregon, Eugene.
Johns Manville
2021 Johns Manville Historical Timeline. Electronic document, https://www.jm.com/en/our-company/HistoryandHeritage/company-history/. Accessed January 19, 2021.
Johnson, Craig M.
2007 *A Chronology of Middle Missouri Plains Village Sites.* Smithsonian Contributions to Anthropology 47. Smithsonian Institution Scholarly Press, Washington, DC.

Johnson, Ludwell
1958 *Red River Campaign: Politics and Cotton in the Civil War.* Johns Hopkins Press, Baltimore, Maryland.
Johnson, Matthew
2007 *Ideas of Landscape.* Blackwell, Malden, Massachusetts.
Johnson, Robert W., Charles B. Mitchell, Grandison D. Royston, Thomas B. Hanly, and Felix I. Batson
1902 To the President. In *The War of the Rebellion: A Compilation of the Official Records of the Union and Confederate Armies: Additions and Corrections to Series I, Volume XIII,* edited by John S. Moodey, pp. 814–816. Government Printing Office, Washington, DC.
Johnson, Susan Lee
2000 *Roaring Camp: The Social World of the California Gold Rush.* W.W. Norton, New York.
2004 "A Memory Sweet to Soldiers": The Significance of Gender in the History of the "American West." In *Women and Gender in the American West,* edited by Mary Ann Irvin and James F. Brooks, pp. 89–109. University of New Mexico Press, Albuquerque.
Jones, Sian, and Lynette Russell
2012 Archaeology, Memory, and Oral Tradition: An Introduction. *International Journal of Historical Archaeology* 16(2):267–283.
Jones, Sergeant [Captain Edward O.C. Ord]
1856 Soldiering in Oregon. *Harper's Magazine* XIII:522–26.
Jordan, Gilbert J.
1977 W. Steinert's View of Texas in 1849. *The Southwestern Historical Quarterly* 80(4): 399–416.
Jordan, Terry G.
1966 *German Seed in Texas Soil: Immigrant Farmers in Nineteenth-Century Texas.* University of Texas Press, Austin.
Karpinski, Sharon
2007 Tough Country: Portraits from New Mexico's High Plains. Master's thesis, Department of History, University of New Mexico, Albuquerque.
Keen, Benjamin
1985 Main Currents in United States Writings on Colonial Spanish America. *Hispanic American Historical Review* 65(4):657.
Kehoe, Alice B., and Peter R. Schmidt
2017 Introduction: Expanding our Knowledge by Listening. *SAA Archaeological Record* 17(4):15–19.
Keleher, William A.
2008 [1962] *The Fabulous Frontier: 1846–1912.* 2008 facsimile ed. Sunstone Press, Santa Fe, New Mexico.
Kelman, Ari
2013 *A Misplaced Massacre: Struggling over the Memory of Sand Creek.* Harvard University Press, Cambridge, Massachusetts.
Kerby, Robert L.
1991 *Kirby Smith's Confederacy: The Trans-Mississippi South, 1863–1865.* University of Alabama Press, Tuscaloosa.
Kern County Land Company
1969 San Emidio Ranch. [Map] Scale 1:2,000. Wind Wolves Preserve Headquarters, Bakersfield, California.
Kimmerer, Robin Wall
2013 *Braiding Sweetgrass: Indigenous Wisdom, Scientific Knowledge, and the Teachings of Plants.* Milkweed Editions, Minneapolis, Minnesota.
Koerper, Henry C., and Paul G. Chace
1995 Heizer, Strandt, and the Effigy Controversy. *Journal of California and Great Basin Anthropology* 17(2):280–284.
Koerper, Henry C., Roger D. Mason, and Mark L. Peterson
2002 Complexity, Demography and Change in Late Holocene Orange County. In *Catalysts to Complexity: Late Holocene Societies of the California Coast,* edited by Jon M. Erlandson and Terry Jones, pp. 63–81. Perspectives in California Archaeology, Costen Institute of Archaeology, University of California, Los Angeles.
Kökény, Andrea
2004 The Construction of Anglo-American Identity in the Republic of Texas, as Reflected in the "Telegraph and Texas Register." *Journal of the Southwest* 46(2): 283–308.
Kovacik, Joseph J., George L. Arms, Kirsten J. Campbell, and Hunter L. Simpkins
2000 *Life on the Railroad: Cultural Resources Survey from the Texas Panhandle to Strauss, New Mexico.* Parsons, Brinckerhoff Archaeology Group Report No. 153, United States Army Corps of Engineers, Albuquerque, New Mexico.
Kraus-Friedberg, Chana
2008 Transnational Identity and Mortuary Material Culture: The Chinese Plantation

Cemetery in Pahala, Hawai'i. *Historical Archaeology* 42(3):123–135.

Kroeber, A. L.
1976 *Handbook of The Indians of California.* Dover, New York.

Kroes, Rob
1999 American Empire and Cultural Imperialism: A View from the Receiving End. *Diplomatic History* 23(3):463–77.

Krumgold, Joseph (director)
1953a *...And Now Miguel* (film). United States Information Service, Washington, DC.

Krumgold, Joseph
1953b *...And Now Miguel.* Harper and Row, New York.

Kryder-Reid, Elizabeth
2016 *California Mission Landscapes: Race, Memory, and the Politics of Heritage.* University of Minnesota Press, Minneapolis, Minnesota.

Kumar, Deepa
2004 War Propaganda and the (AB)uses of Women: Media Constructions of the Jessica Lynch Story. *Feminist Media Studies* 4(3): 297–313.

Kutsche, Paul (editor)
1979 *The Survival of Spanish American Villages.* Colorado College, The Colorado College Studies 15, Colorado Springs.

Lang, Amy Shrager
1990 A True History of the Captivity and Restoration of Mrs. Mary Rowlandson. In *Journey's in New Worlds: Early American Woman's Narratives*, edited by William L. Andrews, pp. 11–83. University of Wisconsin Press, Madison.

Larsen, Esther, and Pehr Kalm
1947 Pehr Kalm's Observations on the Fences of North American. *Agricultural History* 21(2):75–78.

Latta, Frank
2006 *The Saga of El Tejon.* Bear State Books, Exeter, California.

Lawler, Ruth C.
1974 *The Story of Castroville: Its People, Founder, and Traditions.* LaCoste Ledger, LaCoste, Texas.

Lawson, Michael L.
2009 *Dammed Indians Revisited: The Continuing History of the Pick-Sloan Plan and the Missouri River Sioux.* South Dakota State Historical Society Press, Pierre.

Lees, William B.
2014 Missouri Basin Projects and the Emergence of Historical Archaeology on the Great Plains. In *Dam Projects and the Growth of American Archaeology: The River Basin Surveys and the Interagency Archeological Salvage Program*, edited by Kimball M. Banks and Jon S. Czaplicki, pp. 151–66. Left Coast Press, Walnut Creek, California.

Lesure, Richard G
2005 Linking Theory and Evidence in an Archaeology of Human Agency: Iconography, Style, and Theories of Embodiment. *Journal of Archaeological Method and Theory* 12(3):237–255.

Lewis, David G.
2014 Four Deaths: The Near Destruction of Western Oregon Tribes and Native Lifeways, Removal to the Reservation, and Erasure from History. *Oregon Historical Quarterly* 115(3):414–437.

Light, Duncan
2017 Progress in Dark Tourism and Thanatourism Research: An Uneasy Relationship with Heritage Tourism. *Tourism Management* 61:275–301.

Lightfoot, Kent G.
1995 Culture Contact Studies: Redefining the Relationship Between Prehistoric and Historical Archaeology. *American Antiquity* 60(2):199–217.
2005 *Indians, Missionaries, and Merchants: The Legacy of Colonial Encounters on the California Frontier.* University of California Press, Berkeley.
2006 Mission, Gold, Furs, and Manifest Destiny: Rethinking an Archaeology of Colonialism for Western North America. In *Historical Archaeology*, edited by Martin Hall and Stephen W. Silliman, pp. 272–292. Blackwell, Malden, Massachusetts.

Limerick, Patricia
1987 *The Legacy of Conquest: The Unbroken Past of the American West.* W. W. Norton, New York.
1991 What on Earth Is the New Western History? In *Trails: Toward a New Western History*, edited by Patricia Nelson Limerick, pp.81–88. University of Kansas Press, Lawrence.
2000 *Something in the Soil: Legacies and Reckonings in the New West.* W. W. Norton, New York.

Lindberg, Christer
2013 The Noble and Ignoble Savage. *Ethnoscripts* 15(1):16–32.

Loeffler, Jane
1992 Landscape as Legend: Carleton E Watkins in Kern County, California. *Landscape Journal* 11(1):1–21.
Logan, George C., and Mark P. Leone
1997 Tourism with Race in Mind: Annapolis, Maryland Examines its African-American Past through Collaborative Research. In *Tourism and Culture: An Applied Perspective*, edited by Erve Chambers, pp. 129–146. State University of New York Press, Albany.
Lucas, Gavin
2006 Historical Archaeology and Time. In *The Cambridge Companion to Historical Archaeology*, edited by Dan Hicks and Mary Beaudry, pp. 34–47. Cambridge University Press, Cambridge.
Lundquist, Bill
2004 Remembering Miner's Fort. *Curry Coastal Pilot*. 28 August:1–2.
Lyons, Natasha, Peter Dawson, Matthew Walls, Donald Uluadluak, Louis Angalik, Mark Kalluak, Philip Kigusiutuak, Luke Kiniksi, Joe Katetak, and Luke Suluk
2010 Person, Place, Memory, Thing: How Inuit Elders are Informing Archaeological Practice in the Canadian North. *Canadian Journal of Archaeology* 34(1):1–31.
Makley, Michael S., and Matthew J. Makley
2010 *Cave Rock: Climbers, Courts, and a Washoe Sacred Space*. University of Nevada Press, Reno.
Mallea-Olaetxe, Joxe
2008 *Speaking Through the Aspens: Basque Tree Carvings in Nevada and California*. University of Nevada Press, Reno.
2009 *Images of America: The Basques of Reno and the Northeastern Sierra*. Arcadia Publishing, San Francisco, California.
Marincic, Amanda M.
2018 The National Historic Preservation Act: An Inadequate Attempt to Protect the Cultural and Religious Sites of Native Nations. *Iowa Law Review* 103(4):1777–1809.
Martinez, Reyes N.
2012 A Shepherd at Work in Taos County, New Mexico. In *Stories from Hispano New Mexico*, edited by Ann Lacy and Anne Valley-Fox, pp. 63–69. Sunstone Press, Santa Fe, New Mexico.
Mather, Eugene, and John Hart
1954 Fences and Farms. *Geographical Review* 44(2):201–223.
Mattes, Merrill J.
1947 "Historic Sites in Missouri Valley Reservoir Areas," *Nebraska History* 28:161–175.
1960 Historic Sites Archeology on the Upper Missouri. In *Bureau of American Ethnology Bulletin 176*, edited by Frank H. H. Roberts, pp. 159–238. Smithsonian Institution, Washington, DC.
Mayne, Alan, and Tim Murray (editors)
2001 *The Archaeology of Urban Landscapes: Explorations in Slumland*. Cambridge University Press, Cambridge.
McBride, Terri
2002 *Exploration and Early Settlement in Nevada*. Nevada State Historic Preservation Office, Carson City.
McCawley, William
1996 *The First Angelinos: The Gabrielino Indians of Los Angeles*. Malki Museum Press and Ballena Press, Banning, California.
McCleary, Timothy
2015 *Crow Indian Rock Art: Indigenous Perspectives and Interpretations*. Routledge, New York.
McFadden, Joseph
1978 Monopoly in Barbed Wire: The Formation of the American Steel and Wire Company. *The Business History Review* 52(4):465–489.
McManamon, Francis P.
2018 Developments in American Archaeology: Fifty Years of the National Historic Preservation Act. *Annual Review of Anthropology* 47(1):553–74.
McMichael, George (editor)
1985 *Anthology of American Literature: Colonial Through Romantic*. Vol. 1, 3rd ed. MacMillan, New York and London.
McMurtry, Larry
1985 *Lonesome Dove*. Simon & Schuster, New York.
McNiven, Ian, and Lynette Russell
2005 *Appropriated Pasts: Indigenous Peoples and the Colonial Culture of Archaeology*. AltaMira, Walnut Creek, California.
Michno, Gregory
2007 *The Deadliest Indian War in the West: The Snake Conflict, 1864–1868*. Caxton Press: Caldwell, Idaho.
Midwest Archaeological Center
2008 Fort Union Trading Post National Historic Site— Accomplishments. https://www.nps.gov/MWAC/fous/accomplishments.htm, accessed November 12, 2017.

Miller, Myles R., N.A. Kenmotsu, and M.R. Landreth (editors)
2009 *Significance and Research Standards for Prehistoric Archaeological Sites at Fort Bliss: A Design for Evaluation, Management and Treatment of Cultural Resources.* Report submitted to the Environmental Division, Garrison Company, Fort Bliss, Texas. Geo-Marine, El Paso, Texas.
Mills, John E.
1960 Historic Sites Archeology in the Fort Randall Reservoir, South Dakota. In *Bureau of American Ethnology Bulletin 176*, edited by Frank H.H. Roberts, pp. 159–238. Smithsonian Institution, Washington, DC.
Miranda, Deborah A.
2013 *Bad Indians A Tribal Memoir.* E-Book. Heyday, Berkeley, California.
Moldanova, Alisa
2014 Two Narratives of Intergenerational Sustainability: A Framework for Sustainable Thinking. *American Review of Public Administration* 46(5):526–545.
Momaday, N. Scott
1994 Value. In *Words and Power: Voices from Indian America*, edited by Norbert S. Hill, Jr., p. 1. Fulcrum, Golden, Colorado.
Moneyhon, Carl H.
2002 *The Impact of the Civil War and Reconstruction on Arkansas: Persistence in the Midst of Ruin.* University of Arkansas Press, Fayetteville.
Montgomery, Charles
2002 *The Spanish Redemption: Heritage, Power, and Loss on New Mexico's Upper Rio Grande.* University of California Press, Oakland.
Morgan, Wallace
1914 *History of Kern County with Biographical Sketches of the Leading Men and Women of the County, Who Have Been Identified with Its Growth and Development from the Early Days to Present.* Historical Record Company, Los Angeles.
Moser, Lee
1989 Photographs for San Emigdio. Album. Lee Moser Realty, Wind Wolves Preserve Headquarters, Bakersfield, California.
Mueggler, Walter F.
1989 Age Distribution and Reproduction of Intermountain Aspen Stands. *Western Journal of Applied Forestry* 4(2):41–45.
Mullins, Paul R.
2004 Ideology, Power, and Capitalism: The Historical Archaeology of Consumption. In *Companion to Social Archaeology Reader*, edited by Lynn Meskell and Robert W. Preucel, pp. 195–211. Blackwell, Malden, Massachusetts.
Munn, Nancy D.
2013 The "Becoming-Past" of Places: Spacetime and Memory in Nineteenth-Century, Pre-Civil War New York. *HAU: Journal of Ethnographic Theory* 3(2):359–380.
Myrick, David
1970 *New Mexico's Railroads: A Historical Survey.* Revised ed. University of New Mexico Press, Albuquerque.
Nabokov, Peter, and Lawrence Loendorf
1994 Every Morning of the World: Ethnographic Resources Study, Big Horn Canyon National Recreation Area [Montana and Wyoming], Including on Adjacent Lands Managed by the Custer National Forest and the Bureau of Land Management. (Confidential) Report Prepared for the Rocky Mountain Regional Office, National Park Service, Denver, Colorado, Department of Anthropology, University of Wisconsin, Madison. On file at National Park Service, Regional Office, Denver.
2002 *American Indians and Yellowstone National Park: A Documentary Overview.* National Park Service, Yellowstone Center for Resources, Yellowstone National Park, Wyoming.
Nash, Roderick Frazier
2014 *Wilderness and the American Mind.* 5th ed. Yale University Press, New Haven, Connecticut.
Nash, Stephen E., Chip Colwell-Chanthaphonh, and Steven Holen
2011 Civic Engagements in Museum Anthropology: A Prolegomenon for the Denver Museum of Nature and Science. *Historical Archaeology* 45(1):135–151.
Neal, Dorothy Jensen
1966 *The Cloud-Climbing Railroad.* Alamogordo Printing Company, Alamogordo, New Mexico.
New Mexico State Highway Department
1938 *General Highway Map, Harding County, New Mexico.* Map and Geographic Infor-

mation Center, University of New Mexico, Albuquerque.

New Mexico, World War II Service Records, 1941–1945

1946 Digital image. Military Discharges, Box 16612, Military Discharges: Martinez–Masingale. New Mexico Commission of Public Records, State Records Center and Archives; Santa Fe, New Mexico, and Ancestry.com, accessed June 4,2017.

Nicholas, George P.

2006 Decolonizing the Archaeological Landscape: The Practice and Politics of Archaeology in British Columbia. *American Indian Quarterly* 30(3):350–380.

2008 Native Peoples and Archaeology, In *Encyclopedia of Archaeology*, Vol. 3, edited by Deborah Pearsall, pp. 1660–1669. Academic Press, New York.

2014 Indigenous Archaeology. *Oxford Bibliographies.* Electronic document, http://www.oxfordbibliographies.com/view/document/obo-9780199766567/obo-9780199766567-0073.xml, accessed August 25, 2017.

2017 Lessons Learned from Listening. *SAA Archaeological Record* 17(4):30–31.

Nicholas, George, and Julie Hollowell

2007 Ethical Challenges to a Postcolonial Legacy of Scientific Colonialism. In *Archaeology and Capitalism: From Ethics to Politics*, edited by Yannis Hamilakas and Philip Duke, pp. 59–82. Left Coast Press, Walnut Creek, California.

Nieto-Phillips, John M.

2004 *The Language of Blood: The Making of Spanish-American Identity in New Mexico, 1880s–1930s.* University of New Mexico Press, Albuquerque.

Norris, Frank

1901 *The Octopus: A Story of California.* Grosset & Dunlap, New York.

O'Brien, Jean

2010 *Firsting and Lasting: Writing Indians out of Existence in New England.* University of Minnesota Press, Minneapolis.

O'Donnell, Terence

1991 *An Arrow in the Earth: General Joel Palmer and the Indians of Oregon.* Oregon Historical Society Press, Portland.

Office of Historic Preservation

2012 Black Star Canyon Indian Village Site Historical Landmark. Office of Historic Preservation, California State Parks, Sacramento.

Old Horn, Daniel D., and Timothy McCleary

1995 *Apsáalooke Social and Family Structure.* Little Big Horn College, Crow Agency, Montana, http://lib.lbhc.edu/about-the-crow-people/history-and-culture/creation-story.php, accessed January 25, 2018.

O'Neil, Stephen

2014 *The Acjachemen (Juaneño) Indians of Coastal Southern California.* Malki Museum Brochure. Malki-Ballena Press, Banning, California.

O'Neill, Brian, Paul Baxter, and Christopher Ruiz

2014 The Harris Homestead: A Rogue Indian War Battle Site. In *Alis Volat Propriis: Tales from the Oregon Territory (1848–1859),* edited by Chelsea Rose and Mark Axel Tveskov, pp. 157–180. Occasional Papers No. 9, Association of Oregon Archaeologists, Eugene.

Oregon Sentinel

1858 Indians Killed on the Coast. 3 July 1858. Jacksonville, Oregon.

Panich, Lee M.

2013 Archaeologies of Persistence: Reconsidering the Legacies of Colonialism in Native North America. *American Antiquity* 78(1):105–122.

2016 After Saint Serra: Unearthing indigenous histories at the California missions. *Journal of Social Archaeology* 16(2):238–258.

Panich, Lee, and Tsim Schneider (editors)

2014 *Indigenous Landscapes and Spanish Missions: New Perspectives from Archaeology and Ethnohistory.* University of Arizona Press, Tucson.

Parks, Willard Z.

1965 *Willard Z. Park's Ethnographic Notes on the Northern Paiute of Western Nevada, 1933–1940.* Compiled and edited by Catherine S. Fowler. University of Utah Press, Salt Lake City.

Pauketat, Timothy

2001 Practice and History in Archaeology: An Emerging Paradigm. *Anthropological Theory* 1(1):73–98.

Phillips, George Harwood

2014 *Chiefs and Challengers.* 2nd ed. University of Oklahoma Press, Norman.

Pickard, John

2005 Post and Rail Fences: Derivation, Development, and Demise of Rural Technology in Colonial Australia. *Agricultural History* 79(1):27–49.

Portis, Charles
1968 *True Grit.* Simon & Schuster, New York.

Pratt, Boyd C.
1990 Homesteading the High Plains of New Mexico: An Architectural Perspective. *Panhandle-Plains Historical Review* 63:1–33.

Pratt, Boyd C., Jerry L. Williams, and Laurie Kalb
1986 *Gone But Not Forgotten: Strategies for the Comprehensive Survey of the Architectural and Historic Archaeological Resources of Northeastern New Mexico.* 2 Vols. New Mexico Historic Preservation Division, Santa Fe.

Primack, Martin
1969 Farm Fencing in the Nineteenth Century. *Journal of Economic History* 29(2):287–291.

Pritzker, Barry M.
2000 *A Native American Encyclopedia: History, Culture, and Peoples.* Oxford University Press, New York.

Purser, Margaret
2017 Boomtimes and Boomsurfers: Toward a Material Culture of Western Expansion. In *Historical Archaeology Through a Western Lens,* edited by Mark Warner and Margaret Purser, pp. 3–31. University of Nebraska Press and the Society for Historical Archaeology, Lincoln.

Putnam, Michael C. J.
1987 *Tibullus: A Commentary.* University of Oklahoma, Norman.

Raup, H. F.
1947 The Fence in the Cultured Landscape. *Western Folklore* 6(1):1–7, 9–12.

Reed, S. G.
1981 *A History of Texas Railroads: And of Transportation Conditions under Spain and Mexico and the Republic and the State.* St. Clair Publishing Company, Houston, Texas.

Relph, Edward
2017 Placeness, Place, Placelessness. Electronic document, http://www.placeness.com, accessed November 5, 2017.

Remley, David
1993 *Bell Ranch: Cattle Ranching in the Southwest, 1824–1947.* University of New Mexico Press, Albuquerque.

Richardson, Judith
2003 *Possessions: The History and Uses of Haunting in the Hudson Valley.* Harvard University Press, Cambridge, Massachusetts.

Robbins, William
1994 *Colony and Empire: The Capitalist Transformation of the American West.* University Press of Kansas, Lawrence.

Rockman, Marcy, and James Steele (editors)
2003 *Colonization of Unfamiliar Landscapes: The Archaeology of Adaptation.* Routledge, New York.

Rodaway, Paul
1994 *Sensuous Geographies: Body, Sense, and Place.* London: Routledge.

Roesch, Karen A.
2012 *Language Maintenance and Language Death: The Decline of Texas Alsatian.* John Benjamins Publishing, Philadelphia.

Rogers, J. Daniel
1990 *Objects of Change: The Archaeology and History of Arikara Contact with Europeans.* Smithsonian Institution, Washington, DC.

Rose, Chelsea
2013 Lonely Men and Loose Ladies: Rethinking the Demographics of a Multi-Ethnic Mining Camp, Kanaka Flat, Oregon. *Historical Archaeology* 47(3):23–35.

Rose, Chelsea, and Mark Axel Tveskov
2017 The Carolina Company: Identity and Isolation in a Southwestern Oregon Mountain Refuge. *Oregon Historical Quarterly* 118(1):74–107.

Rose, Chelsea, Mark Axel Tveskov, and Katie Johnson
2018 Archaeological Findings at the Harris Cabin Site (35JO246). SOULA Research Report 2017-06. Southern Oregon University Laboratory of Anthropology, Ashland.

Ross, Douglas E.
2012 Transnational Artifacts: Grappling with Fluid Material Origins and Identities in Archaeological Interpretations of Culture Change. *Journal of Anthropological Archaeology* 31:38–48.
2013 *An Archaeology of Asian Transnationalism.* University Press of Florida, Gainesville.

Rothman, Hal
2001 Shedding Skin and Shifting Shape: Tourism in the Modern West. In *Seeing and Being Seen: Tourism in the American West,* edited by David M. Wrobel and Patrick T. Long, pp. 100–120. University Press of Kansas, Lawrence.

Rowe, Matthew J., Judson Byrd Finley, and Elizabeth Baldwin.
2018 Accountability or Merely Good Words: An

Analysis of Tribal Consultation under the National Environmental Policy Act and the National Historic Preservation Act. *Arizona Journal of Environmental Law and Policy* 8:1–47.

Rubertone, Patricia
2008 Engaging Monuments, Memories, and Archaeology. In *Archaeologies of Placemaking: Monuments, Memories, and Engagement in Native North America*, edited by Patricia E. Rubertone, pp. 13–33. Left Coast Press, Walnut Creek, California.

Rubertone, Patricia (editor)
2008 *Archaeologies of Placemaking: Monuments, Memories, and Engagement in Native North America.* Left Coast Press, Walnut Creek, California.

Ruin, Hans
1994 Yorck von Wartenburg and the Problem of Historical Existence. *The Journal of the British Society for Phenomenology* 25(2):111–130.

Sacramento Daily Union
1856 Further from Northern California. *Sacramento Daily Union.* 21 March:1. Sacramento, California.
1861 Eastern Boundary Sketches. *Sacramento Daily Union* 7 August:1. Sacramento, California.
1868 Advices from Aurora, Nevada. *Sacramento Daily Union* 24 February. Sacramento, California.
1873 Aurora, Nev., and Vicinity. *Sacramento Daily Union* 3 July:2. Sacramento, California.

Salgado, Casandra D.
2018 Mexican American Identity; Regional Differentiation in New Mexico. *Sociology of Race and Ethnicity*. DOI: 10.1177/2332649218795193, accessed January 23, 2021.

Sanchez, Joseph
1997 *Explorers, Traders, and Slavers: Forging the Old Spanish Trail, 1678–1850*. University of Utah Press, Salt Lake City.

Sandos, James A.
2004 *Converting California*. Yale University Press, New York and London.

Santos, Robert
1997 *The Eucalyptus of California: Seeds of Good or Seeds of Evil.* Alley-Cass Publication, Denair, California.

Sayre, Gordon M.
2000 *Olaudah Equiano, Mary Rowlandson, and Others: American Captivity Narratives.* Wadsworth Cengage Learning, Boston.
2010 Renegades from Barbary: The Transnational Turn in Captivity Studies. *American Literary History* 22(2):347–359.

Schablitsky, Julie M. (editor)
2007 *Box Office Archaeology: Refining Hollywood's Portrayals of the Past.* Left Coast Press, Walnut Creek, California.

Schaepe, David M., Bill Angelback, David Snook, and John R. Welch
2017 Archaeology as Therapy: Connecting Belongings, Knowledge, Time, Place, and Well-Being. *Current Anthropology* 58(4): 502–533.

Scheiber, Laura L., and Maria N. Zedeño (editors)
2015 *Engineering Mountain Landscapes: An Archaeology of Social Investment.* University of Utah Press, Salt Lake City.

Schneiders, Robert Kelley
1997 Flooding the Missouri Valley: The Politics of Dam Site Selection and Design. *Great Plains Quarterly* 17:237–249.

Schrader, Joohi, Dennis G. A. B. Oonincx, and Maria Pontes Ferreira.
2016 North American Entomophagy. *Journal of Insects as Food and Feed* 2(2):111–120.

Schwartz, E. A.
1997 *The Rogue River Indian War and Its Aftermath: 1850–1980*. University of Oklahoma Press, Norman.

Scott, Douglas D.
1998 Euro-American Archaeology. In *Archaeology on the Great Plains*, edited by W. Raymond Wood, pp. 481–519. University of Kansas Press, Lawrence.

Sears Ore, Kathryn
2017 Form and Substance: The National Historic Preservation Act, Badger-Two Medicine, and Meaningful Consultation. *Public Land and Resources Law Review* 38: 205–244.

Sears Roebuck & Co
1897 *Sears Roebuck & Co Catalog*. Issue: 105; Fall. Sears, Roebuck and Co., Chicago. Historic Catalogs of Sears, Roebuck and Co., 1896–1993, http://ancestry.com, accessed April 10, 2016.
1909 *Sears Roebuck & Co Catalog*. Issue: 119R; Fall. Sears, Roebuck and Co., Chicago. Historic Catalogs of Sears, Roebuck and Co., 1896–1993, http://ancestry.com, accessed April 10, 2016.
1924 *Sears Roebuck & Co Catalog*. Issue: 149T; Fall. Sears, Roebuck and Co., Chicago.

Historic Catalogs of Sears, Roebuck and Co., 1896–1993, http://ancestry.com, accessed April 10, 2016.
1935 *Sears Roebuck & Co Catalog.* Issue: 171K; Fall. Sears, Roebuck and Co., Chicago. Historic Catalogs of Sears, Roebuck and Co., 1896–1993, http://ancestry.com, accessed April 10, 2016.
1941 *Sears Roebuck & Co Catalog.* Issue: 183K; Fall. Sears, Roebuck and Co., Chicago. Historic Catalogs of Sears, Roebuck and Co., 1896–1993, http://ancestry.com, accessed April 10, 2016.
1942 *Sears Roebuck & Co Catalog.* Issue: 184L; Spring. Sears, Roebuck and Co., Chicago. Historic Catalogs of Sears, Roebuck and Co., 1896–1993, http://ancestry.com, accessed April 10, 2016.
1948 *Sears Roebuck & Co Catalog.* Issue: 197D;. Fall. Sears, Roebuck and Co., Chicago. Historic Catalogs of Sears, Roebuck and Co., 1896–1993, http://ancestry.com, accessed April 10, 2016.
1955 *Sears Roebuck & Co Catalog.* Issue: 211D; Fall. Sears, Roebuck and Co., Chicago. Historic Catalogs of Sears, Roebuck and Co., 1896–1993, http://ancestry.com, accessed April 10, 2016.
1965 *Sears Roebuck & Co Catalog.* Issue: 231G; Fall. Sears, Roebuck and Co., Chicago. Historic Catalogs of Sears, Roebuck and Co., 1896–1993, http://ancestry.com, accessed April 10, 2016.

Seligman, Gustav L.
1958 The El Paso and Northeastern System and its Economic Influence in New Mexico. Master's thesis, Department of History, New Mexico College of Agriculture and Arts, Las Cruces.

Shackel, Paul A.
2004a Labor's Heritage: Remembering the American Industrial Landscape. *Historical Archaeology* 38(4):44–58.
2004b Working with Communities: Heritage Development and Applied Archaeology. In *Places in Mind: Public Archaeology as Applied Anthropology*, edited by Paul A. Shackel and Erve Chambers, pp. 1–16. Taylor & Francis, New York.
2005 Local Identity, National Memory, and Heritage Tourism: Creating a Sense of Place with Archaeology. *African Diaspora Archaeology Newsletter* 8(5):2.

Shaw, Clifford Alpheus
2009 *An 1864 Directory and Guide to Nevada's Aurora: Embracing a General Directory of Businesses, Residents, Mines, Stamp Mills, Toll Roads, Etc., Including an Account of the Grand Celebration of July 4, 1864, and a Brief History of the Wide West Mine.* Clifford Alpheus Shaw, CreateSpace.
2016 *Aurora, Nevada 1860–1960: Mining Camp, Frontier City, Ghost Town.* Clifford Alpheus Shaw, CreateSpace.

Shier, Melonie
2016 Towards an Archaeology of Belonging: Corporate Agriculture in the San Emigdio Hills, California and the Transformation of the Modern American West. PhD dissertation, Department of Archaeology, University of Central Lancashire, Preston.

Silliman, Stephen
2000 Colonial Worlds, Indigenous Practices: The Archaeology of Labor on a 19th Century California Rancho. PhD dissertation, Department of Anthropology, University of California, Berkeley.
2001 Agency, Practical Politics, and the Archaeology of Culture Contact. *Journal of Social Archaeology* 1(2):190–209.
2004 Social and Physical Landscapes of Contact. In *North American Archaeology*, edited by Timothy R. Pauketat and Diana DiPaolo Loren, pp. 273–296. Blackwell, Malden, Massachusetts.
2006 Struggling with Labor, Working with Identities. In *Historical Archaeology*, edited by Martin Hall and Stephen W. Silliman, pp. 147–166. Blackwell, Malden, Massachusetts.
2008 Collaborative Indigenous Archaeology: Troweling at the Edges, Eyeing the Center. In *Collaborating at The Trowel's Edge: Teaching and Learning in Indigenous Archaeology*, edited by Stephen Silliman, pp. 1–21. University of Arizona Press, Tucson.
2009 Change and Continuity, Practice and Memory: Native Persistence in Colonial New England. *American Antiquity* 74(2): 211–230.

Slagle, Al Logan
1985 *Huss: The Tolowa People. A Petition for Status Clarification/Federal Recognition for Submission to the United States Department of Interior.* Center for Community Development, Humboldt State University, Arcata, California.

Sleeper-Smith, Susan (editor)
2009 *Contesting Knowledge: Museums and Indigenous Perspectives*. University of Nebraska, Lincoln.
Slotkin, Richard
1973 *Regeneration through Violence: The Mythology of the American Frontier, 1600–1860*. Wesleyan University Press, Middletown, Connecticut.
Small, Stephen
2013 Still Back of the Big House: Slave Cabins and Slavery in Southern Heritage Tourism. *Tourism Geographies* 15(3):405–423.
Smith, G. Hubert
1939 Archaeological Report, Fort Laramie National Historic Site, Fort Laramie, Wyoming. Report to National Park Service from Midwest Archaeological Center. G. Hubert Smith Papers, Minnesota Historical Society, P816, Box 4.
1960 Archaeological Investigations at the Site of Fort Stevenson (32ML1), Garrison Reservoir, North Dakota. In *Bureau of American Ethnology Bulletin 176*, edited by Frank H. H. Roberts, pp. 159–238. Smithsonian Institution, Washington, DC.
1968 *Big Bend Historic Sites*. Publications in Salvage Archeology 9. Smithsonian Institution, Washington, DC.
Staggs, Brooke Edwards
2013 Confronting the Shadows of Black Star Canyon. *The Orange County Register* 29 October, http://www.ocregister.com/2013/10/29/confronting-the-shadows-of-black-star-canyon/, accessed January 23, 2021.
Stephenson, Terry E.
1931 *Shadows of Old Saddleback*. Press of the Santa Ana High School and Junior College, Santa Ana, California. Southern Pacific Rio Grande Division Archives (SPRGDA), C. L. Sonnichsen Special Collections Department, University of Texas El Paso Library, El Paso.
Sowell, Andrew Jackson
1986 *Texas Indian Fighters*. State House Press, McMurry University, Abilene, Texas.
Spencer-Wood, Suzanne M.
2010 A Feminist Framework for Analyzing Powered Cultural Landscapes in Historical Archaeology. *International Journal of Historical Archaeology* 14: 498–526.
Spielberg, Steven (director)
2012 *Lincoln*. DreamWorks, Twentieth Century Fox, and Reliance Entertainment, Los Angeles.
Starzmann, Maria T. and John R. Roby (editors)
2016 *Excavating Memory: Sites of Remembering and Forgetting*. University Press of Florida, Gainesville.
Steinbach Haus and Castroville Visitor Center
2018 About the Steinbach Haus. *Steinbach Haus & Castroville Visitor Center: Where Texas Meets France*, http://www.steinbachhaus.com/home/, accessed November 7, 2018.
Stevenson, Robert Lewis
1944 *Robert Lewis Stevenson's Story of Monterey: The Old Pacific Capital*. Colt Press: San Francisco, California.
Steward, Julian H.
1942 The Direct Historical Approach to Archaeology. *American Antiquity* 7(4):337–43.
Stewart, Jack H., and Howard Brandes
1994 Recent Archaeological Investigations at the Prairie Grove Battlefield State Park. Paper presented at the 1994 Conference of the Arkansas Archeological Society, Fayetteville.
Stewart, Robert E.
2004 *Aurora: Nevada's Ghost City of the Dawn*. Nevada Publications: Las Vegas.
Stone, Philip, and Richard Sharpley
2008 Consuming Dark Tourism: A Thanatological Perspective. *Annals of Tourism Research* 35(2):574–595.
Swan, Susan, and Elmer J. Martinez
1994 *Survey of Historical and Architectural Resources of Northeastern New Mexico*. Prepared for the New Mexico Historic Preservation Division, Santa Fe.
Sutton, Dorothy, and Jack Sutton
1969 *Indian Wars of the Rogue River*. Josephine County Historical Society, Grants Pass, Oregon.
TalkBusiness.net
2015 Stacy Hurst: Heritage Tourism Benefitting State's Economy. *Talk Business & Politics* (blog) March 2, 2015. http://www.talkbusiness.net/2015/03/stacy-hurst-heritage-tourism-benefitting-states-economy/, accessed November 3, 2016.
Tate, Michael L.
2006 *Indians and Emigrants: Encounters on the Overland Trail*. University of Oklahoma Press, Norman.
Tatum, Melissa, and Jill Kappus Shaw
2014 *Law, Culture & Environment*. Carolina Academic Press, Durham, North Carolina.

Teeman, Diane
2008 Cultural Resource Management and the Protection of Valued Tribal Spaces: A View from the Western United States. In *Handbook of Landscape Archaeology*, edited by Bruno David and Julian Thomas, pp. 626–637. Left Coast Press, Walnut Creek, California.

Thiessen, Thomas D., Deborah Hull-Walski, and Lynn M. Snyder
2014 The National Park Service and the Smithsonian Institution: Partners in Salvage Archaeology. In *Dam Projects and the Growth of American Archaeology: The River Basin Surveys and the Interagency Archeological Salvage Program*, edited by Kimball M. Banks and Jon S. Czaplicki, pp. 25–40. Left Coast Press, Walnut Creek, California.

Thiessen, Thomas D., and Karin M. Roberts
2009 The River Basin Survey Collections: A Legacy for American Archaeology. *Plains Anthropologist* 54(210):121–36.

Thomas, Julian
2008 Archaeology, Landscape, and Dwelling. In *Handbook of Landscape Archaeology*, edited by Bruno David and Julian Thomas, pp. 300–306. Left Coast Press, Walnut Creek, California.
2012 Archaeologies of Place and Landscape. In *Archaeological Theory Today*, edited by Ian Hodder, pp. 167–187. 2nd ed. Polity Press, Cambridge.

Thurston, M. Seymour
1929 Tomb Recall Indians' Massacre of Miners. *Sunday Oregonian* 15 December:33. Portland.

Tichenor, William
1883 Among the Oregon Indians. Manuscript on file, Ms. PA-84, Bancroft Library, University of California, Berkeley.

Tuan, Yi-Fu
2001 *Space and Place: The Perspective of Experience*. University of Minnesota Press, Minneapolis.

Turner, Frederick Jackson
1999 [1893] The Significance of the Frontier in Western History. In *Rereading Frederick Jackson Turner: The Significance of the Frontier in American History and Other Essays*, edited by J. M. Faragher, pp. 31–60. Yale University Press, New Haven, Connecticut.
1921 *The Frontier in American History*. Henry Holt, New York.

Tushingham, Shannon, and Richard Brooks
2017 Inland Sanctuary: A Synergistic Study of Indigenous Persistence and Colonial Entanglements at Hiouchi (Xaa-yuu-chit). *Oregon Historical Quarterly* 118(1):108–139.

Tveskov, Mark Axel
2001 "A Most Horrid Massacre": The American Settlement of Coos County, Oregon. In *Changing Landscapes, "Telling our Stories," Proceedings of the Fourth Annual Coquille Cultural Preservation Conference, 2000*, edited by Jason Younker, Mark Axel Tveskov, and David G. Lewis, pp. 55–68. Coquille Indian Tribe, North Bend, Oregon.
2007 Social Identity and Culture Change on the Southern Northwest Coast. *American Anthropologist* 109(3):431–441.
2017 A "Most Disastrous" Affair: The Battle of Hungry Hill, Historical Memory, and the Rogue River War. *Oregon Historical Quarterly* 118(1):42–73.

Tveskov, Mark A., and Amy Cohen
2014 Frontier Forts, Ambiguity, and Manifest Destiny: The Changing Role of Fort Lane in the Cultural Landscape of the Oregon Territory, 1853–2007. In *Rethinking Colonial Pasts through Archaeology*, edited by Neal Ferris, Rodney Harrison, and Michael V. Wilcox, pp. 191–211. Oxford University Press.

Tveskov, Mark Axel, and Katie Johnson
2014 The Spatial Layout and Development of Fort Lane, Oregon Territory 1853–1856. In *Alis Volat Propriis: Tales from the Oregon Territory, 1848–1859*, edited by Chelsea Rose and Mark Tveskov, pp. 127–146. Occasional Papers No. 9, Association of Oregon Archaeologists, Eugene.

Tveskov, Mark Axel, and Chelsea Rose
2019 Southern Oregon University Laboratory of Anthropology Disrupted Identities and Frontier Forts: Enlisted Men and Officers at Fort Lane, Oregon Territory, 1853–1856. *Historical Archaeology* 19(1):41–55.

Tveskov, Mark Axel, Chelsea Rose, Katie Johnson, and Ben Truwe
2017 Archaeological Investigations within Geisel Monument State Heritage Site, Curry County, Oregon. SOULA Research Report 2016–17. Southern Oregon University Laboratory of Anthropology, Ashland.

Tyler-McGraw, Marie
2006 Southern Comfort Levels: Race, Heritage

Tourism, and the Civil War in Richmond. In *Slavery and Public Memory: The Tough Stuff of American Memory*, edited by James O. Horton and Lois E. Horton, pp. 151–167. New Press, New York.

United States Census Bureau

1870 Aurora, Esmeralda County, Nevada, Population Schedule. Microfilm Reel 35A. Matthewson-IGT Knowledge Center, University of Nevada, Reno.

1880a Bodie, Mono County, California, Population Schedule. Transcript provided by Corri Jimenez.

1880b Table Mountain, Esmeralda County, Nevada, Population Schedule. Microfilm Reel 56. Matthewson-IGT Knowledge Center, University of Nevada, Reno.

1900a Bodie, Mono County, California, Population Schedule. Microfilm Reel 113. Matthewson-IGT Knowledge Center, University of Nevada, Reno.

1900b Union County, New Mexico, Population Schedule. Digital images, http://ancestry heritagequest.com, accessed May 31, 2016.

1910a Orogrande, Otero County, New Mexico, Population Schedule. Digital images, http://www.ancestry.com, accessed June 1, 2015.

1910b Aurora, Esmeralda County, Nevada, Population Schedule. Microfilm Reel 190. Matthewson-IGT Knowledge Center, University of Nevada, Reno.

1910c Bodie, Mono County, California, Population Schedule. Microfilm Reel 156. Matthewson-IGT Knowledge Center, University of Nevada, Reno.

1910d Union County, New Mexico, Population Schedule. Digital images, http://ancestry heritagequest.com, accessed May 31, 2016.

1920a Orogrande, Otero County, New Mexico, Population Schedule. Digital images, http://www.ancestry.com, accessed June 1, 2015.

1920b Union County, New Mexico, Population Schedule. Digital images, http://ancestry heritagequest.com, accessed May 31, 2016.

1930a Orogrande, Otero County, New Mexico, Population Schedule. Digital images, http://www.ancestry.com, accessed June 1, 2015.

1930b Harding County, New Mexico, Population Schedule. Digital images, http://ancestry heritagequest.com, accessed May 31, 2016.

1930c Arroyo Seco, Taos County, New Mexico, Population Schedule. Digital images, http://www.ancestry.com, accessed February 28, 2015.

1940a Orogrande, Otero County, New Mexico, Population Schedule. Digital images, http://www.ancestry.com, accessed June 1, 2015.

1940b Harding County, New Mexico, Population Schedule. Digital images, http://ancestry heritagequest.com, accessed May 31, 2016.

1940c Arroyo Seco, Taos County, New Mexico, Population Schedule. Digital images, http://www.ancestry.com, accessed February 28, 2015.

1940d Valdez, Taos County, New Mexico, Population Schedule. Digital images, http://www.ancestry.com, accessed February 28, 2015.

2012 Historical Census of Housing Tables, Median Home Values: Unadjusted. Electronic document, https://www.census.gov/housing/census/data/values.html, accessed November 17, 2017.

United States Bureau of Land Management

1913 Homestead Case File 411941: Eutemia Blea (Sisneros). Land Office, Tucumcari, New Mexico. Records of the Bureau of Land Management, Record Group 49, National Archives, Washington, DC.

1914 Homestead Allotment Case File 355389: Rafael Cisneros. Land Office, Clayton, New Mexico. Records of the Bureau of Land Management, Record Group 49, National Archives, Washington, DC.

1936 Homestead Allotment Case File 1086972: Gavina A. Garcia. Land Office, Santa Fe, New Mexico. Records of the Bureau of Land Management, Record Group 49, National Archives, Washington, DC.

1937 Homestead Allotment Case File 1089960: Moises Vialpando. Serial Patent Files 1908–51, Land Office, Santa Fe, New Mexico. Records of the Bureau of Land Management, Record Group 49, National Archives, Washington, DC.

United States Department of Labor

2009 *History of Federal Minimum Wage Rates Under the Fair Labor Standards Act, 1938–2009*. Wage and Hour Division, United States Department of Labor, Washington, DC. Electronic document, https://www.dol.gov/whd/minwage/chart.htm, accessed January 13, 2019.

United States Geological Survey

1942 Untitled New Mexico aerial photograph, https://earthexplorer.usgs.gov, accessed March 8, 2021.

1948 Desert, New Mexico, 7.5-minute topographical quadrangle map, https://store.usgs.gov, accessed March 8, 2021.

United States World War II Draft Registration Cards, 1940–1947

1941 Patrocinio Valencia. Digital image. Records of the Selective Service System 147, Box 127. The National Personnel Records Center, Military Personnel Records (NPRC-MP), National Archives at St. Louis, Missouri, http://ancestry.com, accessed June 4, 2017.

2011b Juan Francisco Martinez. Digital image. Records of the Selective Service System 147, Box 77. The National Personnel Records Center, Military Personnel Records (NPRC-MP), National Archives at St. Louis, Missouri, http://ancestry.com, accessed June 4, 2017.

Van Bueren, Thad M. (editor)

2002 Communities Defined by Work: Life in Western Work Camps. Thematic issue. *Historical Archaeology* 36(3).

Van Dyke, Ruth M.

2017 Durable Stones, Mutable Pasts: Bundled Memory in the Alsatian Community of Castroville, Texas. *Journal of Archaeological Method and Theory* 24(1):1–18.

Van Ness, John R.

1976 Spanish American vs. Anglo American Land Tenure and the Study of Economic Change in New Mexico. *The Social Science Journal* 13(3)45–52.

Vaughan, Alden T. and Edward W. Clark (editors)

1981 *Puritans Among the Indians: Accounts of Captivity and Redemption, 1676–1724*. The Belknap Press of Harvard University Press, Cambridge, Massachusetts.

Voss, Barbara L.

2005 The Archaeology of Overseas Chinese Communities. *World Archaeology* 37(3):424–439.

2008 *The Archaeology of Ethnogenesis: Race and Sexuality in Colonial San Francisco.* University of California Press, Berkeley.

2016 Towards a Transpacific Archaeology of the Modern World. *International Journal of Historical Archaeology* 20(1):146–174.

Warde, Mary Jane

2013 *When the Wolf Came: The Civil War and the Indian Territory.* University of Arkansas Press, Fayetteville.

Wallerstein, Immanuel

1974 *The Modern World System I.* Academic Press, New York.

1980 *The Modern World System II.* Academic Press, New York.

Walton, John

1992 *Western Times and Water Wars.* University of California, Berkeley.

Warner, Mark and Margaret Purser (editors)

2017 *Historical Archaeology Through a Western Lens.* University of Nebraska Press, Lincoln.

Waugh, Julia N.

1934 *Castroville and Henry Castro, Empresario.* Standard Printing Co., San Antonio, Texas.

Wasson, George B.

2001 Growing Up Indian: An Emic Perspective. PhD dissertation, Department of Anthropology, University of Oregon, Eugene.

Watkins, Joe

2000 *Indigenous Archaeology: American Indian Values and Scientific Practice*, AltaMira Press, Walnut Creek, California.

2003 Beyond the Margin: American Indians, First Nationals, and Archaeology in North America. *American Antiquity* 68:273–285.

2005 Through Wary Eyes: Indigenous Perspectives on Archaeology. *Annual Review of Anthropology* 34:429–449.

2011 Indigenous Archaeology as Complement to, Not Separate from, Scientific Archaeology. *Jangwa Pana* 10(1):46–62.

2017 Can We Separate the "Indian" from the "American" in the Historical Archaeology of the American Indian? In *Historical Archaeology through a Western Lens*, edited by Mark Warner and Margaret Purser, pp. 113–137. Society for Historical Archaeology and University of Nebraska Press, Lincoln.

Weaver, Bobby D.

2005 *Castro's Colony: Empresario Development in Texas, 1842–1865*. Texas A&M University Press, College Station.

Webster, G.

1884 The Rogue River Indian War of 1855–56. *Overland Monthly*:235–240.

Wedel, Waldo R.

1967 Salvage Archaeology in the Missouri River Basin. *Science* 156(3775):589–97.

Whaley, Gray H.

2010 *Oregon and the Collapse of Illahee: US Empire and the Transformation of an Indigenous World, 1792–1859*. University of North Carolina Press, Chapel Hill.

White, Richard

1991 *"It's Your Misfortune and None of My Own":*

A New History of the American West. University of Oklahoma Press, Norman.

2011 *Railroaded: The Transcontinentals and the Making of Modern America.* W.W. Norton, New York.

Wilcox, Michael

2009 *The Pueblo Revolt and the Mythology of Conquest: An Indigenous Archaeology of Contact.* University of California Press, Berkeley.

2010a Saving Indigenous People from Ourselves: Separate but Equal Archaeology is not Scientific Archaeology. *American Antiquity* 75(2):221–227.

2010b Marketing Conquest and the Vanishing Indian: An Indigenous Response to Jared Diamond's "Guns, Germs, and Steel and Collapse." *Journal of Social Archaeology* 10:92–117.

Wilkinson, Charles

2010 *The People are Dancing Again: The History of the Siletz Tribe of Western Oregon.* University of Washington Press, Seattle.

Williams, Bryn

2008 Chinese Masculinities and Material Cultures. *Historical Archaeology* 42(3): 53–67.

Wilson, Chris

1997 When a Room Is the Hall: The Houses of West Las Vegas, New Mexico. In *Images of An American Land: Vernacular Architecture in the Western United States*, edited by Thomas Carter, pp. 113–128. University of New Mexico Press, Albuquerque.

Wilson, Iris H.

1969 *William Wolfskill 1798–1866: Frontier Trapper to California Ranchero.* Western Frontiersmen Series XII. The Arthur H. Clark Company, Glendale, California.

Wilson, John

1990 We've Got Thousands of These! What Makes an Historic Farmstead Significant? *Historical Archaeology* 24(2):23–33.

Winterbourne, J. W.

1937 *Preliminary Survey of Indian Camp Sites on Irvine Property 1935 Black Star Canyon 1937.* The Bowers Museum, Santa Ana, California.

Wood, W. Raymond, and Michael M. Casler

2015 A Revised History of Fort Floyd, North Dakota. *North Dakota History* 80(4):3–13.

Wood, W. Raymond, W. F. Hunt, and Randy H. Williams

2011 *Fort Clark and Its Indian Neighbors: A Trading Post on the Upper Missouri.* University of Oklahoma Press, Norman.

Woods, J. G.

1855 Rogue River Correspondence of the Statesman. *Oregon Statesman.* 20 October 1855:2. Salem, Oregon.

Worster, Donald

1985 *Rivers of Empire: Water, Aridity, and the Growth of the American West.* Pantheon Books, New York.

Wrobel, David M.

2002 *Promised Lands: Promotion, Memory, and the Creation of the American West.* University Press of Kansas, Lawrence.

Wylie, Alison

1992 Rethinking the Quincentennial: Consequences for the Past and Present. *American Antiquity* 57(4):591–594.

Yamin, Rebecca, and Karen Bescherer Metheny (editors)

1996 *Landscape Archaeology: Reading and Interpreting the American Historical Landscape.* University of Tennessee Press, Knoxville.

Yentsch, Anne Elizabeth

1996 Introduction: Close Attention to Place—Landscape Studies by Historical Archaeologists. In *Landscape Archaeology: Reading and Interpreting the American Historical Landscape*, edited by Rebecca Yamin and Karen Bescherer Metheny, pp. xxiii–xlii. University of Tennessee Press, Knoxville.

Zappia, N. A.

2012 Indigenous Borderlands: Livestock, Captivity, and Power in the Far West. *Pacific Historical Review* 81(2):193–220.

Zedeño, Maria Nieves, Jesse A. M. Ballenger, and John R. Murray

2014 Landscape Engineering and Organizational Complexity among Late Prehistoric Bison Hunters of the Northwestern Plains. *Current Anthropology* 55(1):23–58.

Index

Numbers in **bold** refer to tables. Numbers in *italics* refer to figures.

African Americans: as Civil War soldiers, 102; double consciousness and, 47; neglected representation of, 106–8
agency, Chinese, 39–40, 45
agricultural property as archaeological research site, 28
Alamogordo and Sacramento Mountain Railway, 20
Alsace, 79–89
Alsatian migrants, 79, 85–88
Alsatian Texas, 79–90
American Civil War: archaeology of, 103–7; engagements of, *104*; ethnic soldiers in, 102; placemaking and, 108; postbattle racial atrocities during, 107–8; thanatourism and, 105–6; western reaches of, 102–3
American West: Alsace and, 87–89; Arkansas as, 101; Civil War and, 101–8; as community, 5–6, 37–90; definition of, 15, 131; dendroglyphs in, 67–69; displacement and, 89–90; fences in, 29; mainstream culture and, 10–13, *14*, 21, 77, 91–94, 100; making and unmaking of, 6–7; mythology of, 10–11, 15, 29, 93–95; as space, 1–36, 5; study of, 1; today, 6, 91–128; tools for defining, 1–2; women in, 94–95
...*And Now Miguel* (Krumgold), 77
Anglo-Americans, 84, 84–87, 90
Apsáalooke: "sacred landscape" of, 120; collaboration with, 123, *123*; creation story of, 119–20; fasting beds of, 123, *123*, *126*; fasting culture of, 124–26; landscapes and, 124–27; place and, 119–28. *See also* Crow
archaeological regulations, 15–16
archaeologies of historicity, 111, 113–15
architecture: in Castroville, Texas, *83*, *88*; in Chinese camps, 40–42, *41*; in D'Hanis, Texas, *81*; in Mosquero, New Mexico, 62–65, *63*, *64*
Arkansas: Civil War and, 102–6; thanatourism and, 103, 105–6; as Wild West, 101
Arroyo Seco, New Mexico, 67–78
Asian diaspora, 131
aspen grove: dendroglyphs on, 67–78; example of, *68*; importance of, 78; revisiting, 75
Aurora, Nevada: Chinese woodcutters in, 37–45; map of, *38*; Northern Paiute in, 45–54, *49*
Australian fences, 29, 34

barbwire, 30
Basque sheepherders, 68–69, 76–77
battlefield archaeology, 94–96, *96*
Beckham, Stephen Dow, 91, 92, 100
Black Star Canyon Village, California, 110–18, *112*, *114*, *115*, *117*
Bodie, California, 37–45, *38*
booms, 15
Brown, Betsy, 97–100
Brown, Charles, 92, 97–99

California archaeological thematic studies, 30
Californian colonial missions and historicity, 111
Camden Expedition, 103–5, *104*, 107
canned goods, 25
Canyon of the Indians, 113
captivity archaeology, 95–99
captivity narrative, 93–94, 99
Casey, Edward S., 5, 79–90
Castro, Henry, 85–86, 90
Castroville, Texas, 79–90, *80*, *83*
cesspit, 23
Chase storm anchor, 23, *23*
Chinese woodcutters: agency of, 39–40, 44; camp construction by, 40–42, *41*; camp location by, *38*, 41; camp security for, 41–42; camp statistics of, 38–39; consumption habits of, 44–45; discrimination against, 37, 42, 45; food storage by, 44–45, *44*; gender of, 42–43; goods repurposing by, 45; leisure activity of, 43, *43*; location and number of, **42**; urban and rural place and, 45; wood harvest by, 39
Civil War, American: archaeology of, 103–7; engagements of, *104*; ethnic soldiers in, 102;

placemaking and, 108; postbattle racial atrocities during, 107–8; thanatourism and, 105–6; western reaches of, 102–3
collaborative cultural heritage practices, 122–24
colonialism: Black Star Canyon and, 113; Californian colonial missions and, 111–12; cultural landscape and, 46–47; displacement and, 89–90; historical memory and, 92–93; historicity in, 115–16; Indigenous people and, 89–90, 113; in New Mexico, 55–56; Paiute and, 50–53; placemaking and, 92–93; settler women and, 93–95, 99
community: American West as, 5–6, 37–90; colonialism and, 55; place and, 79; through affiliation, 65, 66; through architecture, 62–65; through dendroglyphs, 73–77; through topography, 56
context and persistence, 47, 53
Crow. *See* Apsáalooke
Crow reservation, 119, *120*
cultural heritage, 122, 124
cultural heritage managers, 119, 123, 127, 128
cultural landscape: colonialism and, 46–47; EP & NE railroad system and, 21; Indigenous people and, 122–28
cultural persistence, 46–47

dam projects, 8, *8*
dendroglyph: art motifs in, 76, *76*; Basque, 68, 76; by C. Martinez, *74*; definition of, 67; Hispano, 69; importance of, 77–78; near Arroyo Seco, New Mexico, 69–70, **70**; placemaking through, 73–77; by P. Valencia, *74*; by R. Martinez, *75*
Desert Siding, New Mexico, *18*, 22, **22**
D'Hanis, Texas, 79–90, *80*, *81*
direct historical approach, 9
discrimination: against African Americans, 107–8; against Chinese, 37, 45; against Indigenous people, 47–48, 93
displacement, 89–90
Dixon, Kelly, 2–3
double consciousness: African Americans and, 47; definition of, 46, 47; Paiute and, 50–53; survival skills and, 53–54; white spectatorship and, 52
"down below" strategy, 56, 57
Dry Head, 124–26, *126*

Eddy, Charles, 19–21
Eddy, John, 19–21
El Paso and Northeastern (EP & NE) railroad system: archaeology of, 21, **22**; cultural landscape and, 21; demographics of, 24; fences and, 22, *22*; history of, 17, 18–20, *18*; housing along, 23; landscape of, 21; making-do along, 25–27, *26*; placemaking and, 21
empresario, 85–87, 90
Escondida Siding, New Mexico: archaeological findings at, 22, **22**, 25; layout of, 24, *24*; location of, *18*
ethnic Civil War soldiers, 102
ethnology studies, 4–5
Eutemia Blea Sisneros homestead, 59–65, **60**, *64*

fasting bed, 123, *123*, *126*
feminist literature, 93
fence: as boundary, 28; dating strategies using, 29–31; hedge, 34, *35*; inside/outside dynamic of, 19, 22–25; map of, *22*; planning inside, 22–23; post and rail, 33–34; in San Emigdio, 29–36; space and, 130; stone, 34; types in United States, 30–31, *32*, **33**; wire, 35–36
fence post, 30–31, *32*
field ethnography, 122–24
folklore and Black Star Canyon, 116–18
forced relocation (Spanish), 112–13
Fort Bliss railroads, *18*, 19, 22
frontier: interpretations of, 13; mythology of, 10–11, 15, 29, 94–95; Texas gathering places on, 84–87; Turner's, 2, 10; women on, 94–95, 97–100

Gallegos, New Mexico: land use practices in, 56–57; lower Mosquero and, 65
Gavina A. Garcia homestead, 59–66, **60**, *61*
gathering: Alsace and, 87–89; in Castroville, Texas, 87; in D'Hanis, Texas, 88–89; E. Casey and, 79, 83–84; future work in, 89–90; on Texas Frontier, 84–87
Geisel family, 91–100, *95*
grant and grid, 56

Hardesty, Donald, 2
Harris family, 92–100, *96*
Hawkins, William, 19–20
hedge fences, 34, *35*
heritage: definition of, 108; tourism, 105–8, 110–11
Hispanic: expansion in New Mexico, 56, *57*; homesteaders in New Mexico, 66; as label, 55–56
Hispano: definition of, 68–69; sheepherders, 67–78
historic, arbitrary use of term, 54
historical archaeology: Latinx, 131–32; of RBS, 10–13; settler mythology and, 94–95
historical memory, 93–94, 95–100

historicity: archaeologies of, 111; in archaeology, 113–15; in colonial "History," 115–16; definition of, 110; in folklore, 116–18; as guide for archaeology, 118; placemaking and, 110–12
historic site and River Basin Surveys (RBS): definition of, 9; investigation of, before RBS, 9; investigation of, under RBS, 10–11, 14; RBS selection criteria for, 11
Historic Sites Act of 1935, 10
homestead: as archaeological research site, 28; sites and features, **60**; sites near Mosquero, 57–62, *58*, 65
homesteading acts, 66
homesteading periods, 65–66

IASP (Interagency Archaeological Salvage Program), 8
identity and persistence, 47, 50–52
Indigenous archaeology: definition of, 121–22; importance of, 119; landscapes and, 121–24
Indigenous people: archaeologists and, 130; archaeology and, 121; colonialism and, 89–90; cultural landscape and, 122–28; discrimination against, 47–48; displacement and, 89–90; in Los Angeles basin, 110–12; obliteration of past of, 118; in Oregon, 91–100; place and, 123–26; place names and, 122–24, 128; postcolonialization, 113; precolonial Californian, 112–13; white spectatorship and, 51–52, *51*
Indigenous terminal narrative, 111–12
Indigenous women, 94–95, 97–99, *98*
industry studies, 4
inside-the-fence/outside-the-fence dynamic, 19, 22–25
Interagency Archaeological Salvage Program (IASP), 8

Jenkins' Ferry, *104*, 107

Kern County Land Company, 29, 33–36
Khao Yai Cowboy Festival, *12*
Kirby Smith, Edmund, 102, 103
Kutzadika'a: discrimination against, 48, 53; historical background of, 47–48; labor practices of, 52; site survey summaries of, 48–50, *49*, **50**. *See also* Paiute

labor studies, 4
La Cañón de los Indios, 113, 115–16
land grants, 85–86
landscape: Apsáalooke, 124–27; centrality of, 3; continuous architectural, 128; dendroglyphs in, 67–78; importance of, 119; Indigenous archaeology and, 121–24; place gathering and, 79–80, 82–84, 87–88; sacred, of Apsáalooke, 120; spiritual, of Apsáalooke, 124, 127; of war, 94–95
landscape archaeology: placemaking and, 3–5; women and, 94–95
landscape studies, 4, 6
Latinx historical archaeology, 131–32
Lincoln, 105, 108
"Little Alsace of Texas," 82
Los Angeles basin: colonization and, 112–13; map of, *112*; placemaking in, 110

mainstream culture: American West and, 10–13, *14*, 21, 91–94; Civil War and, 105, 108; Kansas in, 101
"making-do," 25–27, *26*, 130
malleability of past, 130–31
Marks Mills, Arkansas, *104*, 107–8
Martinez family: dendroglyphs by, 69–70, **70**, 73–77, *74*, *75*; details of, 72–73, **73**
materiality without archaeological knowledge, 118
mayordomo, 69
migration, place and, 79
Miners' Fort: archaeological findings at, 95–96, *97*; C. Brown's actions at, 92; plan view of, *98*
missions of California, historicity and, 111
Missouri Basin, 8, 11
Missouri Civil War experience, 102–3
Missouri river dam projects, 8, *9*
Mosquero, New Mexico, 55–66

Native American: earth ovens of, 97; reservations, 15. *See also* Indigenous people, Indigenous women
Nature as living beings, 126–27
Newman Camp, New Mexico, *18*, 22, **22**
New Mexican vernacular building traditions, 62–64, *63*
new social history movement, 10
New Western History, 2, 10

Paiute: colonialism and, 50–53; discrimination against, 48, 53; historical background of, 47–48; labor practices of, 52; site survey summaries of, 48–50, *49*, **50**. *See also* Kutzadika'a'
Panich, Lee M., 46–47
performativity, 29, 34, 35–36
persistence: place and, 53–54; theoretical background of, 46–47; through identity, 50–52

Pick-Sloan Plan, 8, *8*, 15
place: for Alsatian immigrants, 86–87; of Apsáalooke fasting, 123–26, *123*; Casey's concept of, 5, 79; in Castroville, Texas, 80–83; for Chinese residents, 45; communities and, 79; definition of, 3, 19, 110; in D'Hanis, Texas, 80–83, *81*; gathering as, 89; history and, 83–84; Indigenous people and, 123; as organizational tool, 1; persistence and, 53–54; place names and, 122–24, 128; potential, 84–89; qualities of, 87; as rite of passage, 77; sense of, 17, 19; through architecture, 62–65; through context, 53; through identity, 50–52; through topography, 56
placemaking: across time and space, 82–83; beginnings of, 83–84; Civil War sites and, 106–8; colonialism and, 92–93; continual, 82; definition of, 3, 82, 130; dendroglyphs and, 73–77; EP & NE railroad system and, 17, 21; eucalyptus trees and, 34; fencelines and, 22–25, 28–29, 36; gathering as, 79–90; historical memory and, 92–93; historicity and, 110–12; imagined vs. reality, 86–87; landscape archaeology and, 3–5; in Los Angeles basin, 110; post and rail fences and, 33–34; race and, 106–8; represented demographics of, 106–9; stone fences and, 34; thanatourism as, 101; through blood vengeance, 100; through contracts, 85–86; through tourism, 106; in Trans-Mississippi, 103; wire fences and, 35–36
place names, 122–24, 128
placeness, 17, 19, 25, 26–27
place-unmaking, 89–90
Poison Spring, Arkansas, *104*, 107–9
post and rail fences, 33–34
practice and persistence, 47, 52
private identity, 52
Pryor Mountains, 124–26, *125*, *126*
public identity, 50–52
Purser, Margaret, 3

Queen Mary, 95, 99, 100

Rafael Cisneros homestead, 59–65, **60**
RBS (River Basin Surveys), 8–14
redemption archaeology, 95–99
Red River Campaign, 103
reducción, Spanish, 112–13
River Basin Surveys (RBS), 8–14
Rogue River War, 91, 94, 99
Rubertone, Patricia, 4–5

San Emigdio Hills, 29–36
settler narrative, 93
sheepherders: Basque, 68–69, 76–77; census data for Hispano, 70–72; Hispano, 67–78
sheepherding: dendroglyphs and, 67–69; economic measures for, 71–72; typical year of, 69
space: American West as, 1–36; for Chinese residents, 45; cultural practices in, 52; definition of, 3, 12; persistence and, 53–54; Texas Frontier as, 85
space::place framework usefulness, 129
spiritual landscape, 124–25, 127
stacked-rock, 59, 62, *63*
Steinbach House, 82–83, *83*
Stephenson, Terry, 113, 115–16
stone fences, 34
storm anchor, 23, *23*
supernatural, Black Star Canyon and, 117–18

Texas Anglicization, 84–85
Texas Frontier: gathering places on, 84–87; as space, 85
Thailand Cowboy Festival, *12*
thanatourism: archaeology and, 106–7; in Arkansas, 103, 105–6; definition of, 6, 101; placemaking and, 107–9
topography, place and community and, 56
trade posts, 15
Transect Recording Methodology (TRU), **22**
Trans-Mississippi Theater, 102–3
Tularosa Basin, New Mexico, 17–27, *18*, **22**
Turner, Frederick Jackson, 2, 10
Turner Thesis, 2, 10
Turquoise Station, New Mexico, *18*, 22, **22**

up top strategy, 56, 57

Valencia, Patrocinio, **70**, 72–73, *74*, 76, *76*

war, landscapes of, 94–95
Warner, Mark, 3
waste disposal, 25
Western expansion, 132
Western imagery exportation, 13
white spectatorship, 51–52, *51*
Wind Wolves Preserve, 29, 34–36
wire fences, 35–36
Wolfskill, William, 113, 116
World Systems Theory, 39–40